CLOCK
THIS

CLOCK
THIS

My Life as an Inventor

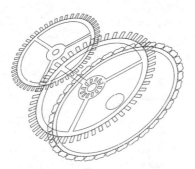

Trevor Baylis

HEADLINE

First published in 1999
by HEADLINE BOOK PUBLISHING

10 9 8 7 6 5 4 3 2 1

British Library Cataloguing in Publication Data

Baylis, Trevor
    Clock this
    1.Baylis, Trevor 2.Inventors – Great Britain – Biography
    I.Title
    609'.092

    Hardback ISBN 0 7472 7381 2
    Trade paperback ISBN 0 7472 7756 7

Typeset by Palimpsest Book Production Limited
Polmont, Stirlingshire
Printed and bound in Great Britain by
Clays Ltd St Ives plc.

HEADLINE BOOK PUBLISHING
A division of Hodder Headline PLC
338 Euston Road
London NW1 3BH

www.headline.co.uk
www.hodderheadline.com

This book is for Anthea, Bella, Deborah, Eleanor, Estelle, Geri, Jackie, Jan, Jane, Jean, Judy, Karen, Lesley, Lissa, Pauline, Polly, Rosalind, Ruth, Sheila, Valerie and Wendy.
True friends of my heart.

CONTENTS

ACKNOWLEDGEMENTS

Firstly I would like to give thanks to my loving parents. I would also like to thank those splendid fellows Christopher Staines and Rory Stear, and my friends at Edwin Coe, who have had to endure my persistent phone calls for so long and who, through their efforts, have made all my dreams come true.

'You've got to ac–cent–tchu–ate the positive
Elim–my–nate the negative
Latch on to the affirmative
Don't mess with Mister In–Between.'

Johnny Mercer

PROLOGUE

NECESSITY, ANY SCHOOLBOY WILL TELL YOU, IS THE MOTHER OF INVENTION. Your trousers keep falling down, so you think up elasticated braces. Then you realise you need something to attach the new-fangled braces to your trousers, so you come up with the button. Or a bluebottle keeps bothering you, and you sketch out the prototype for the fly swat. In short, to get the creative juices flowing, you need something to kick start your ingenuity.

I created what I regard as my first real invention as the result of a silly bet.

I was spending a Sunday at home with friends. I was supposed to take them for a cruise on the Thames in my speed boat, so that we could all act the cat's pyjamas for the benefit of the small fry on the river bank. But a sultry overcast morning turned into a drenching afternoon, and we ate our picnic indoors entertaining ourselves with gossip, liquid replenishment, and childish games.

I have never married, and now at sixty-two, only a short haul from my bus-pass years, I doubt if I ever will. But though I'm firmly on the shelf, I like to think I am up here surrounded by comfortable book-ends, among whom I count my good friend Pauline Bricker.

Neither of us remembers how the talk got round to it, but we began to discuss what it might be like to be crippled, to have only one hand, be blind, or somehow incapacitated. As the party's host and resident show off, it needed minimal encouragement for Pauline to persuade me to take centre stage. I volunteered to have my right arm strapped to my side with a belt and spend the rest of the afternoon pretending it had been amputated at the elbow.

Opening a packet of crisps one-handed is difficult, until you work out it's child's play once you decide to use your teeth. Washing and wiping a glass one-handed can be done, but it proved so time consuming as to be hardly worth it. After all, what is a dirty glass among friends? But the most difficult task of all was attempting to open a bottle of wine with one hand. A corkscrew only works effectively if you've got the use of two good strong hands. Trying to screw the thread into the cork using one hand, with the bottle jammed between my knees, ended in humiliation. I was doubled up like a contortionist having a seizure, trying not to laugh or fall over, and failing in both. It would have been easier to prise open an oyster with a bus ticket.

Someone else opened the wine eventually. I gave up the charade and had a glass with everybody to celebrate my failure.

'It would be simple if you had the right gadget,' I protested, and threw in a bit of Churchillian bluster for good measure. 'Just give us the tools and we will finish the job.' If chimpanzees can use sticks to dig out termites from their nests, I argued, and finches in the Galapagos can trim long thorns to use as pins to extract grubs from holes in trees, then it shouldn't be beyond the imagination of Homo sapiens to make a whole range of one-handed tools.

That was when the wager was struck. The late Vivian Smith, who lived round the corner from me at Thames Eyot, and had known me from National Service, bet twenty quid that I couldn't invent something in under half an hour.

'That's the easiest money I've been offered all week.'

I left them drinking my wine, using two hands to open more bottles because it was quicker that way, while I wandered through to my workshop. I was thinking of a one-handed corkscrew, but sorting through the bits and pieces of scrap littering my workbench I settled on a can opener. To make a prototype, inventors are always at the mercy of whatever odds and ends are lying around. I'm sure that Mr Marconi's first radio had Mrs Marconi's washing line in it somewhere.

I eventually emerged with my can opener. With a proud flourish I opened a tin of beans for an appreciative audience, ostentatiously using only my left hand. Then I held out the other hand to claim my money from Vivian.

He tapped the face of his watch. 'You're five minutes over the limit,' he said. 'I win.'

I paid up with the weak smile of a man who is mentally checking the state of his overdraft. No one likes losing a bet. But I had thoroughly enjoyed the challenge, and carved out the idea of a new way of trying to earn a living in the process. It was 1982, and I was about to become a full-time inventor.

CHAPTER ONE

DR CARROT,
POTATO PETE AND ME

WHEN I RECALL MY WARTIME CHILDHOOD I OFTEN WONDER HOW I MADE IT TO SIXTY-SOMETHING IN FAIR NICK, AS HEALTHY AS A CREAKY HORSE, AND WITH A SET OF BRAINS MARGINALLY LESS RELIABLE THAN MY BOWELS. I was then a young collector of shrapnel, nightly treating the blitz as a grand free fireworks display, and sleeping in an Anderson shelter that smelled of damp earth, unwashed bodies, and cat's pee.

Looking back, my most nagging and persistent memory of World War Two is an urgent and unsatisfied yearning for food.

Like many of my contemporaries I grew up to become a long-term bacon sandwich abuser, simply because when I was a lad there weren't many about. Dreams of unobtainable food used to nag my imagination. My mind was full of images of how wonderful it would be when rationing ended and I would be able to put into practice my ideal of the perfectly balanced diet – a bacon sandwich in each hand.

People of my class – honest working – are bombarded with the nutritionists' claim that, thanks to fair shares and a sensible, scientific diet, rationing meant that the lower orders were better fed than before the war. They might have been, though not nearly so agreeably. In our house we equated good red meat and a nice fry-up with proper food, as did Winston Churchill. Rationing changed that, and I suspect there was more rare roast beef on Winston's table than there ever was on ours at number 202 Lady Margaret Road, Southall Garden Village.

My mother, the poet of the gas rings, used all her ingenuity to find inspiration in our pathetic quota of provisions. In the process she discovered a new use for stale old food – we ate it. Whenever mum dished up something grey, mysterious and experimental (hot peapod soup maybe, lentil roast, or vegetable mould), dad would pull her leg. 'Very tasty Mother,' he'd say. 'Quails in aspic again.'

She had the ability to conjure small miracles out of next to nothing, devising marvellous recipes like her eggless, fatless, walnutless walnut cake. We used to refuel on nourishing stodge, eaten to keep colds and the dreaded impetigo at bay. Was there ever a more nourishing stodge than Lord Woolton's famous veg and potato pie? Too true there was, and my mother invented it – a species of Spotted Dick made from dried egg, a scrawny bit of bacon, and a few cadged scraps of suet.

I was brought up in a household where, against present-day advice, lard was revered as a prime ingredient in nourishing food, with its wholesome second cousin suet only marginally behind it in the popularity charts.

'If you don't eat that nice fatty bit Trev, you'll grow up to look like Boris Karloff.'

Cholesterol, high-fibre diets, calorie counts and healthy eating didn't come into it for the likes of us. We just ate what we could get, whenever we could get it, as often as possible. Sadly that wasn't very often. The result was that by the time we had helped defeat Hitler, me and my classmates had a lean and hungry look about us. There was less flesh on us than a pyramid full of Egyptian mummies. In 1945 I was so thin that, had I been a greyhound instead of a snotty-nosed nipper, my parents would have been reported to the RSPCA.

I've often thought it unfair that young non-combatants like me – left on the kitchen front dodging bombs and listening to the calm and cultivated tones of Alvar Liddell announcing nightly news of disaster on the Home Service – weren't given some sort of cheap tin medal to mark those years in which we were all scared out of our minds in case our careless talk cost lives. Along with our faithful allies Dr Carrot and Potato Pete, our heroic band actively fought against the evil that infected Europe by going hungry.

It all began in Buchanan Gardens, Kensal Rise, or so my dear mother almost told me. Years later when I was going out with a girl who lived in Bathurst Road, I happened to mention Kensal Rise to my mother. Her eyes lit up and she said: 'Oh that's where your Dad and I first got together.' She was far too genteel to stoop to a commercial traveller's nudge, nudge, wink, wink, but she smiled coyly and I could detect the hint of a blush through her Tokalon face powder.

So that is where I assume I was conceived. I can imagine my parents having an early night some time in September 1936. Blessedly un-acquainted with Chesterton's poem, or Chesterton himself for that matter, they took their pleasure, rolling up to Paradise by way of Kensal Rise. Nine months later, on 13 May 1937, I was the happy outcome. Born the day after the coronation of George VI, in the same year that my hero, the aeronautical engineer Frank Whittle, tested his first jet engine.

My poor mother had strained every sinew in a vain attempt to deliver me the day before. A local shop had offered a de luxe pram to every mother whose baby was born on Coronation Day, a Tansad I think the make was called. But I refused to co-operate, so the only present my parents had to mark George VI's ceremonial anointing was me.

Mum, Gladys Brown, had been raised at 35 Marylands Road, Paddington. She met my dad, who came from Kilburn, at a church social at St Peter's, Paddington. Dad had a trio of sonorous first names – Cecil Archibald Walter – the sort of Woosterish silly-ass names proud parents attached to their offspring in the days of Empire when every-thing on the maps was coloured an optimistic red. For some reason, and I never managed to work out why, everyone except mum called him Bill.

My parents' eyes met across a dimly lit church hall in the middle of a sixpenny hop. It was love at first sight. Yet another couple captivated by the tinny enchantments of strict tempo dance music on a wind-up gramophone. The first time they held each other was to dance to a record of Jack Payne and His Orchestra playing 'It's a Lovely Day Tomorrow'. For ever afterwards Jack Payne and his musicians held an honoured place in our family chronicles. Mum always spoke of 'dear old Jack' as though he was a bosom pal.

There was a spark between my parents then and there, and they instantly made a lifelong decision in a light so poor neither of them would have chosen wallpaper by it. But it was a lifelong decision nevertheless. They loved each other as tenderly as their favourite fifteen-foot-high screen sweethearts at the local Odeon. They never looked at anyone else. They never strayed.

They were perfectly contented and fulfilled in the simplicity of their lives together. They managed to sustain the fun and excitement in their marriage on a diet of beetle drives, weekly visits to the pictures, amateur theatricals with the 'church crowd', and shrinking every Sunday before the pulpit and the greater glory of the local vicar. Theirs was a love buoyed up by the songs of Al Bowlly, the aphrodisiac qualities of Spam, the excitement of the New Look, temperance holidays on the south coast, and exotic mystery tours in countless charabancs.

My half-forgotten smudges of memory are always wreathed in cigarette smoke, because my parents always were too. For some reason my father preferred to smoke De Reszke Major cigarettes. They only cost sixpence for ten, but he thought they had a particular cachet because they were widely regarded as the smokes of the stars. He once showed me an advertisement which said: 'If Stanley Holloway offered you a cigarette it would be a De Reszke – of course.' He was tickled pink at the possibility. But, of course, he never met Stanley Holloway, so there was never any question of a great star offering him – of course – a De Reszke Major, let alone a De Reszke Minor.

My parents forged a quiet bond of joy together that I have never been able to match in any relationship as an adult. I suppose I have always lacked their ability to be unstintingly committed to any one person. Or maybe I am unable to relish, as they did, the curiously agreeable monotony of tidy lives. I don't think I was cut out for the kind of contentment my parents enjoyed. It would have left me slack with boredom.

I was born in Hendon, a stop on the Northern line. That's all it remains to me – a dot on the London Underground map. When I was two, the three of us moved to a brand new downstairs maisonette in Southall. It's difficult to imagine looking at the place now – a sprawl of curry joints, halal butchers and exotic take-aways – but in those days it was regarded as 'the country'. But ribbon development has chewed up the leafy suburbs, although there wasn't much hunting, shooting and fishing in Southall Garden Village, even in those days.

Neither my mother nor my father ever got round to explaining to me why they had called a halt to procreation as soon as I arrived on the scene. Was I so perfect they thought a second child would never be able to flourish in the giant shadow cast by their first born? Or was I such a disappointment they curtailed plans to expand the Baylis clan in case the next arrival blighted their hopes even further? Maybe the outbreak of war had something to do with it. I suppose the spice does rather go out of your love life if you're both wearing gas masks.

The reality was they could only afford one child, but I still like to think they looked on me as the crowning expression of their love. Their treatment of me certainly bore that out. As they loved each other, so they loved me. Heart and soul.

I was baptised Trevor Graham, named after my father's brother, getting a marginally better deal than my cousin who was lumbered with Cecil, after my dad. Ever since, the name Trevor, along with my estuary accent, has lodged me firmly in a place that's solidly below stairs, treading water among the respectable other ranks just holding our heads above the vulgar herd. Apart from a trendy bishop – Trevor Huddleston – and the occasional sporting Trevor, in the entire history of the world I can think of few people of note who've been called Trevor.

I felt the pang of a touched nerve when, twenty-one years ago, I watched Alan Bennett's television play *Me, I'm Afraid of Virginia Woolf*. I knew exactly how his character Trevor Hopkins felt. 'In the outside line before the pistol goes. It's not Trevor Proust is it? Trevor Strachey. Trevor Sibelius. Lenin. Stalin. Where would they be if they had been called Trevor?' In my teens when I complained about my name to my mother she just said: 'It doesn't seem to have done Trevor Howard much harm does it?'

Much later, dad told me that he and mum had sat together listening to their radio set as the Prime Minister declared war on Sunday, 3 September 1939. He was speaking to us from the Cabinet Room of 10 Downing Street and we were listening to him in the scullery at 202 Lady Margaret Road. Dad used to do an impression of Chamberlain, with his butterfly collar and straggly moustache, and always referred to him as 'The man from the Pru'. I was two-and-a-half, and apparently playing on the lino with a toy made out of old cotton reels. But that scene has been acted out so many times in films and documentaries, I'm almost persuaded that somehow down there on the lino I was part of history, taking in the full gravity of that moment. 'This morning the British Ambassador in Berlin handed the German Government a final note . . . I have to tell you now that no such undertaking has been received, and that consequently this country is at war with Germany.'

My data bank of recollections from those early years is a kaleidoscope of rosy flashbacks, sometimes so vivid, tangible, and real, that I feel like a bystander, an eyewitness to history. But are those stored-up impressions not much more than a rich salmagundi of everything I've read, seen, and since been told about the war? Mere footfalls echoing in the memory down the passage which I did not take?

I may never have actually said: 'Got any gum chum?' to a candy-bearing, nylons-toting GI. But those events have such a hold on my subconscious that in my mind's eye I'm convinced I might have done, several times. My view of American soldiers is still much the same as the one I formed as a child; that they were rich, boastful, generous, over-decorated, and, in spite of Errol Flynn, not a patch on our blokes when it came to fighting. The jokes we told about them still buzz around my brain. 'Heard the one about the Yanks who went to a war film? One fainted and the other got a medal for carrying him out.'

My dad was in a reserved occupation as a quality inspector at the Britannia Rubber and Kamptulicon Company in Alperton, near Wembley. Although I didn't know what it meant, I loved that mysterious word 'Kamptulicon'. It was only much later that I learned that it was a Victorian trade name, patented by Elijah Galloway in 1843, for a floor cloth made of indiarubber, gutta-percha and cork. Rubber was vital to the war effort, used for everything from gas masks to anti-aircraft balloons, so dad was exempted from military service. He used to cycle over to the factory every day to do his bit to ensure that our rubber standards didn't let us down in the struggle against the Axis powers.

Then when he'd cycled all the way home again, he'd have his tea, put on a tin hat, and go out on his bike to patrol Southall as an air-raid warden. A bit like Hodges in *Dad's Army*, only kinder, quieter, and much less prickly. But he shared Hodges' enthusiasm as a staunch apostle of the off-switch and ardent member of the blackout police. The whole country was so fixated on not letting any stray chinks of light escape to guide *Luftwaffe* bombers onto their targets, that the whole of Britain was plunged into unaccustomed darkness. Kerbs were painted white, headlights hooded, torches regarded as the tools of saboteurs. Men were even urged to wear the tails of their shirts outside their trousers so they could be picked out as they floundered about in the gloom. The result was that in the first three months of the war deaths from air-raids were nil, while those from the blackout and air-raid precautions totalled 3,000. The invention of efficient luminous clothing, the type policemen, joggers and railway maintenance men wear today, would have saved most of them. And that tragic 3,000, not honoured on any memorial, are a reminder of the zeal for inky blackness that possessed men like my dad.

During the phoney war my mum and I were evacuated to rural Northamptonshire. My dad had read a lot of H.G. Wells, and feared that when the fighting started it would be as catastrophic as the science fiction horrors of *The War of the Worlds*. He decreed that mother and I ought to take cover in the countryside and packed us off by slow train to a billet in Brixworth. For six melancholy months we endured the smells and sounds of country life, and I saw my first haystack and first cow. Mum wasn't the type who wanted to go back to the land, she was more the type who wanted to go back to the comforts of home. As soon as she could persuade dad it was safe, she did just that, bringing me and our gas masks back with her. In the countryside, theoretically, we might have been further away from Hitler's bombs, but, actually, she was twelve miles away from the nearest picture house, and she couldn't stand that.

When we got back to Lady Margaret Road several barrage balloons loomed over the district, sagging like pregnant sows. I used to watch them, fascinated, from my pram. They lurched about on the ends of heavy cables, glowing golden in the sun, then shadowing to deep blue as the skies darkened down to rain. In high winds they engaged in a violent tug of war, straining in the turbulence against the tethers that anchored them, uttering bestial moans as the gale shrieked through the wires.

Later my dad would petrify me with the true story of a man who had been carried aloft on a windy day by a rogue barrage balloon. It had happened in Bushey Park. He'd failed to let go of his rope when the balloon broke free, and disappeared into the clouds. His body was found somewhere the other side of Wembley. It was a terrible, ridiculous way to go. I wondered whether he'd ever qualify for a medal, and if his family would eventually get to laugh about it as much as we did.

Parts of those days stick in my mind like globs of immovable gum. Smells especially trigger something in deep recesses and bring it rushing back. I can never inhale the bitter whiff of rubber without associating it with gas masks. Some days I used to parade around our maisonette wearing my blue and red Mickey Mouse gas mask. Dad used to say I was better looking with it on. I wore it for hours, treating it more like a toy than a life-saver. I soon discovered that gas masks made good farting noises, and I'd keep playing trumpet voluntaries of flatulence until mum threatened to clip me round my Mickey Mouse ears.

The spicy smell of chicken mash also weaves the same spell. Every family in our street kept chickens in their back gardens as their contribution to the war effort. Cluck for victory, or something like that. One man, Johnnie Giles, even kept a couple of goats. Though his day job was driving a bus, for the duration he was known to his neighbours as Farmer Giles.

As the sun went down the aroma of boiled chicken mash used to waft over hedges and garden fences, a smell guaranteed to make your nostrils quiver like the hint of gravy on those urchins in the Bisto ads. Dad used to boil up potato peelings, mixing them with any leftovers my mother didn't have her eye on to work her magic with next day. Then he'd bind them together with fish meal, a handful of crushed eggshells, and some linseed oil. That unforgettable spuddy, fishy, tinny smell of over-boiled scraps for the chickens brings back the war and having to make do.

I've always been fascinated by that old nut-eating teetotaller Sir Stafford Cripps, the Labour grandee who advocated a policy of misery first on the Home Front. Reading a book about those days, later, when I was doing my own military service, I learned that in 1942 he told the House of Commons: 'Personal extravagance must be eliminated.' For the likes of us personal extravagance had been eliminated long before the war. Ever since, Sir Stafford has struck me as a humourless fanatic. I'm sure he would have loved to bung a tax on our home produced hens' eggs. But to us they were as valuable as crown jewels, and the laying hens themselves, priceless – just as long as they kept laying. Every year as poor King George VI tripped and stammered through his Christmas message, we'd listen to him over the remains of some unfortunate member of dad's flock who'd chosen the wrong tactical moment to stop doing so.

CHAPTER TWO
THE SHRAPNEL MOGUL

I 'VE TRIED TO WORK OUT WHEN I SAW MY FIRST BOMBING RAID. I think it must have been a cold night in February 1943, when I was coming up to my sixth birthday. I was in bed, tucked under my pink satiny eiderdown. We hadn't heard any air-raid sirens and I was snug behind the blackout curtains reading a comic. I felt safe. All through the war I found the air-raid sirens more terrifying than the air-raids themselves. Dad had gone out the back to get a shovel of coke when he noticed the sky to the east was filled with light. Thousands of incendiaries had been dropped over London and the city glowed a brilliant shade of orange over Southall's rooftops.

He called mum and me outside and we all stood on the back step with our upstairs neighbours, Bill and Jean Evans. I was wearing a cloth coat over my pyjamas and drinking a cup of watery cocoa, as the horizon throbbed and pulsed with volcanic colour. I had no sense of danger, no appreciation that some poor sods were dying only a few postal districts away as I enjoyed the pyrotechnics. It was simply the most beautiful sight I had ever seen. The distant darkness was pierced by dazzling fountains of colour as searchlights and anti-aircraft fire tried to pinpoint the enemy. We stood there for nearly an hour, feasting our eyes on the luminous skyline, until the cold drove us back indoors.

All my childhood games revolved around the war. Our row of

dwellings had been put up by Byford the builders. When hostilities broke out several maisonettes at the end of our row were only half-finished. They stayed like that for years, with walls and footings left just as the brickies had abandoned them when they went off to war. Behind our block was a big open storage area – Byford's Yard. Enclosed behind a wire fence were all the materials intended to complete the buildings some day, great mounds of sand and bricks, hulking stacks of timber, and untidy piles of dumped scaffolding poles.

The yard and those unfinished houses served as an adventure playground for all us pint-sized desperados. As the war went on most of the building supplies gradually disappeared, knocked off by the local population. But for a long time we kids were able to enjoy everything the yard had to offer. The sandhills were perfect for digging trenches, with the rubble of 'No Man's Land' beyond the salient of stacked drain pipes. Half bricks came in handy for lobbing into enemy gun emplacements. And the scaffolding poles served as our artillery. (Or, if we tired of modern warfare and went back in history to the Crusades, the shorter lengths became our lances.)

Before the war there had been a narrow-gauge railway for transporting materials around the builder's yard in small wagons. The rails were movable and we built a new layout, our own grown-up train set with a sharply inclined ramp at one end. Half-a-dozen of us would haul a truck to the top of the slope, block the wheel with a lump of wood, and climb aboard. Then we'd knock away our wooden brake and brace ourselves as the wagon built up speed, pretending we were a troop train on the way to the Front. The trucks were always coming off the rails and spilling us out head first among the rubble. Then, bruised and bleeding, we'd put the truck back on the rails, push it up the slope, and try to kill ourselves all over again.

Bernard Mules from Somerset Road has since become a life-long friend. In the early days, though, he played Rommel to my Montgomery. But not as regularly as I would have liked him to have done. We didn't get to play British Army versus the *Wehrmacht* very often, because, unless I bribed him with something to eat, Bernard refused point-blank to be a German. As a compromise we'd split our gang into British and Yanks, and invariably manoeuvres degenerated into pitched battles in which supposedly loyal allies engaged in hand-to-hand fighting, battles to the death, or worse.

There'd be Bernard and me; Jeffrey Fryer and Michael Steggles who lived across the road; my cousin Yvonne Brown, two years older than me, who lived with us during the war; Doreen Lipscombe from next door; and towards the end of the fighting, John Evans, a new recruit from the flat above ours. We were all heroes except Doreen and Yvonne, who as mere girls, had to take secondary roles. They had all the bit parts in our make-believe dramas and cheered their heroes back from triumph as we paraded by.

The big craze was collecting shrapnel, the jagged bits of bomb and shell metal that cascaded down in molten showers every time the *Luftwaffe* raided London. When Lieutenant Henry Shrapnel invented the stuff in 1784, he couldn't have realised that 100 years after his death it would become a valuable form of currency for kids like me. A really coveted fragment, especially if it had a continental seven or a swastika on it, could be swapped for a spud gun or even a Dinky car. Even ordinary chunks could get you a go on someone's bike.

We used to go out on patrol the morning after every big raid to collect as much shrapnel as we could carry. The technique was to take a bucket of sand, a shovel, and a glove with you because a lot of the metal was still glowing from the night before, and too hot to handle.

The best gathering places were the gable ends of houses where the hot metal had pitted the walls and then dropped to the ground. Over the years I assembled such a large hoard that our back garden, untidy at the best of times, began to resemble a scrap dealer's yard. My mother threatened to give it all away, until, in my last big coup as a shrapnel mogul, I managed to swap it all for a rabbit hutch.

Another highly collectible treasure from the raids was something we used to call 'window' – the litter German planes scattered in the air to try to bamboozle our radar. It was black papery stuff, but if you burned the black away thick silver foil was underneath. We prized it highly, and used to go out rooting round the district like truffle hounds to bring back great piles which we'd cut up into bookmarks, paper chains, and Christmas decorations. I'm such an obsessive hoarder I've got some of that 'window' still knocking about somewhere in my studio on Eel Pie Island.

I can't recall ever being terrified of the war. Hitler was a bogeyman, like those unconvincing fairground figures they try to scare you with on ghost trains. I simply wasn't old enough to comprehend his evil. Being a regular picture-goer, Walt Disney frightened me far more. That sequence where Snow White makes her entry into the enchanted forest gave me more nightmares than the Führer and all his Nazis. I knew my parents worried daily about the outcome of the fighting, but their concerns passed straight over my head. They say it requires a great deal of inexperience to be beyond the reach of anxiety, and being as green as gooseshit, I was.

For the little snotnoses rampaging around Byford's Yard it all seemed like a big adventure, and we had the time of our young lives. More than anything, the Germans were figures of fun. Hitler was no more to be feared than his mysterious pal on the posters, the Squanderbug. Adolf was scary like the caricature villains in cartoons were scary, and we used to sing rude songs about his goolies, and march around imper-sonating Lord Haw-Haw – 'Jarmany calling, Jarmany calling' – as if they were both characters in a film.

At one stage a rumour went round the Southall grapevine that the Germans had a deadly plan to drop poisoned sweets on us. The more we discussed Hitler's humbugs and Goering's gobstoppers, the more diabolically imminent their arrival seemed. Some dismissed it as black propaganda put round by the Ministry of Health to safeguard our cratered teeth. But my parents took it seriously and threatened us on pain of death never to eat any sweets found in or near bomb sites.

Not that their warning kept us indoors. We traipsed round all the likely places searching for Hitler's deadly biological confectionery. If we had found any we would have been far too cowardly to have touched them. Warnings about the likely consequences had been painted in such lurid Technicolor detail we were more than convinced of the danger. Instead we gorged ourselves on Ovaltine tablets, and took ghoulish delight in imagining long lingering deaths from poisoned fruit drops. Our search went on for weeks. Just the sighting of one venomous toffee would have been a priceless addition to our treasury of war stories. But nothing so much as a dodgy sweet wrapper was ever found.

I did, though, get to see one of Hitler's secret weapons, and at a range that was too close for comfort. Most of my schoolmates were adept at spotting the shapes and outlines of enemy aircraft. Any kid worth his salt could tell in an instant the difference between a *Junkers*, a *Dornier*, a *Messerschmitt*, and a *Heinkel*. One paint-fresh morning in 1944, the clouds were high, the sun was warm, so Jeffrey Fryer and I decided to bunk off. We set out for school bright and early and, as was often the case, never got there. Instead we wandered across a patch of scrubby land we used to call Clay Fields. From there it was a short detour to the Cut, which was our name for the Grand Union Canal.

There were several places along the canal where its banks had given way and crumbled down to form little beaches. We planned to muck around on one of these sandy spits. Maybe take our shoes off, go for a paddle, see if we could trawl up any drowned dogs floating by. I was the type of child my parents warned me not to play with.

We started off by skimming a few stones. We'd just got round to thinking about going in for a dip when we heard an aeroplane approaching. We both ran along the bank looking up to see it streaking high above us. We'd never seen anything quite like it before. It looked as though it was on fire and was making funny phut-phut noises like an underpowered motor bike.

It droned across the sky and we ran along the towpath hoping to see the pilot bale out. Then the engine cut out altogether and the aircraft dived straight into some houses several rows back on the other side of the canal. There was a crump, like the bang a big book makes when you drop it on the floor. We both felt the blast from the explosion as a cloud of smoke, dust and debris billowed up over the place where it had come down. We were shocked by the violence of the explosion and thought we'd better creep back to school. We tried to sidle in after playtime and kept quiet about where we'd been, but a teacher had noticed our late arrival and we both got the slipper.

That night dad said that two old people had been killed by a flying bomb as they sat in their kitchen. They were amongst the first of 6,000 Londoners to suffer the same fate that summer. He said it was a V1 rocket, or doodlebug, and called it 'Hitler's last throw'. As it turned out it was Hitler's next-to-last throw. The V2 rocket, the precursor of space probes, claimed 3,000 lives in September 1944.

Victory on 8 May 1944 meant a riotous party for VE night. Grown ups danced in the street and got up to all sorts of hanky-panky in front gardens. Magically all the street lights came on again. A piano was dragged from a neighbour's house to wobble on a makeshift stage built from milk crates and bits of plywood. And the ding-dong went on all night.

We made a bonfire and burned effigies of Hitler and Mussolini. Long-hoarded delicacies suddenly emerged from larders where they had been hidden for years. A barrel of beer magically appeared, set up in the middle of the street. All the adults got silly with drink, and the children ate themselves sick. VE night was the first time I'd ever eaten jelly. I was strangely disappointed. I'd been told that jelly melted in your mouth, but this tasted like fruit-flavoured glue.

My dad dressed up as Adolf, with boot polish tins for medals. Several other men were equally bent on making fools of themselves – and the word doesn't seem misplaced – by swapping their trousers for frocks. There were a couple of Carmen Mirandas and a Vera Lynn, who all seemed to be enjoying the chance to wear make up and wriggle into frocks a little too much. But the cross-dressing doesn't seem to have affected the birth rate because in February and June of 1946 there were two waves of VE and VJ babies. I suppose it was predictable: sex was one of the few things that wasn't rationed.

At the VE party there were commemorative photographs. All the adult survivors, gaunt-faced and porridge-complexioned, bared their dentures for the cameras, with their children ranged beneath them on the kerb. I sat next to Bernard Mules and Jeffrey Fryer, wearing a party hat and my best smile for the pictures. But I didn't really want the war to stop. I'd enjoyed it and felt I was going to miss all the excitement.

CHAPTER THREE

ARTHUR DALEY IN
SHORT TROUSERS

A S A SEAT OF LEARNING MY FIRST SCHOOL DIDN'T SET MUCH
STORE BY CLEVERNESS. I think the prime aim of our
teacher in form one at Lady Margaret Infants School was
to drill us all in the art of sitting up straight and keeping
quiet. Key areas of the curriculum involved putting our hands on our
heads, or our fingers on our lips, while our teacher got out a pin so we
could all strain our ears and listen for it to drop.

She was called Miss Batt. The frumpish word Batt hasn't got much
poetry about it, but her face was a letter of recommendation that
mollified all resistance to her unlovely name. On the very first day, late
in August 1943, gazing adoringly into her enormous blue eyes and
admiring the honeyed strands of her hair, I was hopelessly smitten. I
thought Miss was her first name, and for weeks it puzzled me that so
many of the other women teachers seemed to have been given exactly
the same first name. One of her earliest lessons involved showing us how
to grow mustard and cress on damp blotting paper, and over the weeks
my fondness for her germinated faster than the seeds in the cupboard.

I never found out what her first name was. In those days the rank
and file were brought up to be very respectful towards the likes of
doctors, lawyers, and teachers, anyone in fact who had a car or a bit of

learning. They were automatically regarded as people of mark in society, belonging to a far higher category than the rest of us, and for raggedy-arsed kids to have known their first names would have been tantamount to an infringement of their status.

I suppose I must have learned something at Lady Margaret's, if only the words of 'Jesus Wants Me for A Sunbeam'. But our sing-song recitations of times tables and the chanting of the phonetic alphabet – 'g is for gas mask' – were no more than dull intervals between the excitement of the air-raids.

The inspectors from today's Office for Standards in Education would not have approved of some of the mumbo-jumbo Miss Batt passed on. She equipped us for life with such indispensable notions as: 'If your shoes squeak they are saying that you're walking properly,' 'Never swallow the pips of any fruit or a tree will grow inside you' and 'Classical music is much better than it sounds.' I still carry these thoughts with me like talismen and I thank dear old Batt for being the first person to tell me that serious music is worth persevering with: Wagner really is better than, at first, he sounds, and I'll always be grateful to her for pointing that out.

There were no shelters near the school and when the sirens went we used to sit on rush mats in the corridors. We cowered below tall windows, the glass criss-crossed with brown sticky paper as a precaution against blast, while Miss Batt tried to take our minds off the likelihood of being wiped out by reading aloud the stories of A.A. Milne.

Even then I realised that the goings-on in *The House at Pooh Corner* were far too arch and simpering for the barbarians in Infants One. An unhygienic, squinty, adenoidal crew, we sat trying to comprehend a story that had so little to do with our daily lives in wartime Southall it might just as well have been set in outer space. The first time we tried to play Pooh-sticks in the Grand Union Canal Jeffrey Fryer and I ended up fishing the corpse of a new-born baby out of the water. Grisly events like that, tiddley-pom, never happen, tiddley-pom, in the snug and ordered world of Piglet and Eeyore.

But in one respect, at least, I had something in common with

Winnie-the-Pooh. My spelling, like his, was wobbly. It was good spelling, but it wobbled, and the letters got in the wrong places. I compensated by making my handwriting so bad I hoped the teachers wouldn't be able to tell whether or not I could spell. By the time I left infant school I could just about read the few words linking the pictures in my comics. But my spelling remained extravagant guesswork and I couldn't even write my own name.

As much as I liked Miss Batt, increasingly the classroom felt like a prison where children were confined because we'd been captured by the schools' attendance officer and summoned to attend. The school board official who patrolled our district was a consumptive shadow of a man who used to shout weakly through our letter-box while mum and I hid behind the settee, pretending to be out. 'I know you're there, you're listening to *Workers' Playtime*.' In the end we took pity on him and answered the door.

Mum had started keeping me home because of the daylight raids, thinking I'd be safer with her hiding under the stairs rather than at school with Miss Batt whispering who dares, while Christopher Robin was saying his prayers, and the *Luftwaffe* were swooping low over the chimney-pots.

Even when she did pack me off to school, if I thought I could get away with it, I only stayed for the part of the curriculum I enjoyed most, playtime. When the whistle blew and ranks of grudging children began to march into class, I'd skive off to explore the neighbourhood with my mates, our eyes on the main chance.

I might have been a complete dunce at lessons, but on the streets I became a junior wheeler-dealer, Arthur Daley in short trousers. Work was fun, provided it wasn't the work I was really supposed to be doing, school work. Like Noddy Boffin, the golden dustman, I built up a thriving business sorting through other people's rubbish, snapping up the junk they'd cleared out and recycling it at salvage centres. There was a big drive on to collect waste for the war effort and you could make sixpence for every bag of old newspapers, cardboard, bones and rags. For metal, you earned even more. During the last years of the war I collected so much scrap that the Mayor of Southall gave me a medal, praising my public spiritedness for doing something that had become a nice little earner on the side.

Every time I board a flight today a slogan from those days comes unbidden into my head. 'Two thousand aluminium saucepans make one aeroplane.' Somehow air travel feels a whole lot safer, and my nerves much more settled if I reduce the dicey aspect of aviation to the homely image of pots and pans. I reckon between us my mates and I in Southall must have collected enough saucepans to make half a bomber.

It was while rooting through a squalid mound of rubbish heaped beside the air-raid warden's post at the end of our street early in 1944, that I discovered a rusty box. Its contents were to allow my parents the first possibility of pride in my achievements. Until then mum and dad had lurched between kindly embarrassment and apologetic resignation as the evidence mounted that their son was even dimmer than the blackout.

So far my schooling had merely reinforced the notion that if brains were dynamite I didn't have enough to blow my nose. On the evidence of my first school report academic skills had eluded me completely. After six months of trying I wasn't even able to recite the alphabet from memory. Miss Batt had written in her best copperplate: 'Trevor needs to pay more attention, and not play the fool.'

I squatted down beside my find and bashed open the lid of the metal container with a broken chisel. Inside, preserved against damp, was a familiar cardboard box that held the most coveted toy in every schoolboy's green-with-envy treasury of desired objects. I removed the precious lid, scarcely able to believe my luck, for there, laid out in neat, oily formation, was an almost brand new collection of Meccano.

I already possessed a few odds and ends of Meccano at home. But my parents couldn't afford more than the basic set, a 'Number One Outfit', so I didn't have enough components to make anything really complicated from my puzzle of nuts, bolts, wheels and washers. But the contents of the box must have been a 'Number Ten Outfit', the de luxe model of the range, complete with an electric motor, a clockwork engine and enough pulleys, wheels, whatsits, thingummyjigs and doodahs to make any young lad feel he'd hit the jackpot.

There was no question of letting my precious haul of Meccano stay where it was, waiting for the crusher and a new life as a Wellington bomber. My need was greater than Mr Churchill's. Reasoning that it wasn't really theft if you took something that had already been thrown away, I hid the precious box underneath a few bundles of cardboard. It was too heavy to carry, so I would have to return and collect it later.

I hurried home to our shed to fetch a trolley I had made out of old pram wheels, anxious in case someone else bagged the treasure in my absence. But it was still there when I returned, breathless, ten minutes later. Not caring who saw me, I loaded my booty onto the trolley and pulled it home in triumph, aided and abetted by a group of fellow truants who, by then, had twigged what I was doing and wanted to stake a claim.

Frank Hornby's invention of Meccano has since been overtaken by modern plastic construction kits, but in those days it was one of the most envied names in the toy-shop window. It was described as a new hobby for bright boys. But in my case the new hobby made a rather dull boy realise at last that he wasn't so hopeless after all. I never read the instructions that came with my filched Meccano set. The fact that I could barely read at all didn't matter, because I found I could write the most beautiful designs with the components taken from Frank's box. Straightaway I found that my talent lay in my hands. The puzzle of odd parts made very little sense in themselves, but when assembled into different shapes they came alive in the most extraordinary way to become boats, cars, bridges and cranes; in fact any object my excited mind could conceive.

For the first time in my life I had found something I was really good at. All my mates would crawl around my mother's living room lino at number 202 working with me on the most bizarre designs that would take over the whole room for weeks on end. One of the first things we made was an elaborate system of clockwork cable cars that spanned the room on a series of lines traversing from picture rail to skirting board and back again.

My dad would be sitting trying to read a paper when a cable car would go clicking and whining past his headlines on its way to the snowline that was our picture rail. Then, having forgotten about the series of wires criss-crossing the room, he'd almost garrotte himself when he got up to fetch a bottle of pale ale from the scullery. He pretended to moan, but he had a smile as wide as a Hammond organ when he said to my mother: 'Not bad is he?' He was a kind man, and generous with his praise, but it was the first time in my life that I had ever given him a reason to be genuinely proud of me.

The skills I learned then mucking around in our living room with those nuts, bolts, struts and plates from my Meccano set still come in handy in my work as an inventor. Playing with those bits and pieces was the first educational process I had ever thoroughly enjoyed, and whose lessons I retain today. I could barely read the plans and instructions, so I ignored them and let my fingers do the walking among the components. Then with a blend of fantasy, sorcery and lateral thinking, me and my mates created a collection of weird and awesome inventions. Unconsciously, I was following Edward de Bono's edict: 'Think sideways'.

Building flights of fancy with our Meccano, we were inventors without knowing it. An inventor doesn't have any plans or blueprints to work from, just an idea that's straight out of left field. Proving that a concept can work is the first thing he has to do. So he builds a prototype through trial and error, improvising with whatever bits of junk, wire or nails happen to be around. That's exactly what you do with Meccano, except of course there is no need to cut, drill, weld or shape anything because there's always a handy component in the box to represent the idea you're working towards. Nearly six decades later odd bits of Meccano still come in handy when I'm tinkering with an invention. And Mr Meccano, Frank Hornby, though I never met him, was the first teacher who ignited my enthusiasm for making things and inspired me to use what brains I'd been given.

It was around this time I discovered something else I was good at – swimming. I took my first strokes in the rancid waters of the Grand Union Canal. It was a question of instant learning because I jumped in out of my depth and the only way to avoid drowning was to windmill my arms in a frantic splash back to the safety of the bank. But I had proved beyond doubt that I was buoyant and, being totally without fear, in water I felt like a child of nature.

Within a few weeks I'd become proficient at a variety of unorthodox, extemporised strokes, which didn't cleave much of a path through the water but at least kept my head above it. One day my father was playing cricket for the Civil Defence team at King George's Field, along Lady Margaret Road. It was a hot day, a slow batting pitch, and I was soon bored, so I wandered off beyond the boundary down to the canal to have a swim with my mates.

My mother came searching for me half-an-hour later. When she spotted me splashing around on an inflated car inner tube in the sewage-coloured water she went spare. In a voice loud enough to halt traffic a mile away on the Uxbridge Road, she ordered me back to dry land. She had a point. The canal water had so much human, animal and chemical effluent in it, it had the sludgy consistency of lentil soup. If you swallowed a mouthful it tasted like something you'd sit in to remove a tattoo.

I cried and kicked up a fuss, so my parents decided that if I liked the water that much I'd better learn to swim properly in a municipal pool. My first visit to Uxbridge Baths was with my cousin Derek Bass, who was about seventeen at the time. He lived around the corner from us in Denbigh Road with Auntie Ethel, mum's sister, and Uncle Bert. They were always considered much posher than us because they lived in a semi-detached house and were one of the first families in the area to purchase a radiogram.

We cycled there on a very hot day in September 1943 when I was still only six. I was riding my tricycle and it took us hours to get there. By the time we paid our entrance fee and went to the cubicles I was tired, sweaty and irritable. The clamorous open-air baths weren't half as welcoming as my friendly neighbourhood canal. I didn't like the reverberating noise, the chemical smell, or the shrill whistles and overbearing manner of the bath attendants.

In spite of Derek's coaxing I hesitated for ten minutes, standing iron-willed and unbudgeable on the side of the pool, refusing to get in. Eventually Derek lost patience, grabbed me round the waist and threw me in the deep end. It was warmer than the canal, and as soon as I touched the water I was in my element. I held my breath, bobbed back to the surface and then splashed to the side of the pool using one of my impromptu strokes. I clambered out just in time to see the chief attendant telling off my cousin. After a long lecture he chucked Derek out of the baths before he'd had a chance to get wet.

While Derek was seething outside, waiting for me to join him, I swam my first width. From then on swimming became my sport and I started going to the baths three times a week.

In spite of the war or, on second thoughts, perhaps because of it, my first six years were golden and untroubled. Adults were mostly pre-occupied with other things and members of my gang were left to our own devices, roaming the streets aglow with mischief, as wild and innocent as puppies. Ignorant of any alternatives to war, raised in dangerous times, lacking food, I was never short on love.

Then suddenly time accelerated on me. The carefree, sunny web of childhood was broken by an event that for years I buried. Something happened that I couldn't tell my parents about. As much as I loved them, I thought they would never believe me. It was better left unsaid.

CHAPTER FOUR

A VERY SPECIAL BOY

T HESE DAYS I DON'T GO TO CHURCH. I tell people I'm a
Seventh Day Absentist. I have no fears about missing out on
heaven. In my reckoning it will be inhabited by saloon-bar
know-alls, that tedious race of sanctimonious bores I've
been trying to avoid all my life. On the subject of the afterlife I'm at
one with Nietzsche. In heaven all the really interesting people will be
missing.

But when I was growing up I used to attend church three times
every Sunday: morning Eucharist, evening service, plus regular doses of
Sunday school in the afternoon. Occasionally I was allowed a morning
lie in, or to skip Evensong to play out in the park, but I was never
permitted to miss Sunday school. During those soporific hours after
we'd eaten the wartime version of roast beef and Yorkshire (mostly
Yorkshire on its own with a bit of gravy) my parents needed me out
of the house so they could read the *News of the World* in peace and have
a lie down. Whenever anyone inquired why such God-fearing folk
should read a scandal sheet my mum used to say they only took it
because of its superb pigeon racing coverage.

The event that turned me against the church and churchmen
happened in 1943, and it is still deeply etched in my psyche.

It was a bright September afternoon in the church hall. The Sunday school scripture class had been doing a lesson on the Old Testament: Joseph's coat of many colours and the Pharaoh's dreams. I answered well, and our teacher, a clergyman, was so pleased he said he'd got a special reward for me. The others made their way home, whooping noisily as they tumbled out of the room.

What happened next could be one of those lurid cases my parents spent their Sunday afternoons reading about in the *News of the World*. I asked the teacher what sort of prize I was going to get. Like all kids I was a sucker for presents.

'Not yet,' he said. 'Later. First of all we have to play a dressing up game.' He went to a cupboard and got out a surplice. It was snow-white, freshly laundered. He flashed me an ingratiating smile and said: 'Put this on.' I was about to pull it on over my clothes. But, as casually as if he was asking me to post a letter, he said: 'No, take your clothes off first.' I hesitated and he smiled: 'There is no need to be afraid. It's just a game.'

The weight and authority of his request was such that taking off all my clothes seemed quite a natural thing to do, almost a privilege.

Then he said that we were going to say some prayers. He made me kneel down and I joined my hands while he led me through the Our Father. After the amen he started stroking my hair and saying how lovely and blond it was, and what a good boy I was. Then his fingers started probing.

I said: 'Don't.' But he kept touching me, repeating: 'I won't hurt you,' in a voice that wasn't much above a whisper. I wanted to ask him to stop but couldn't get the words out. His tone was so prim and dignified that what he was doing seemed to take on an almost ritual formality.

Suddenly I was aware of the oppressive atmosphere of the place. It was creepy, and I didn't want to be there any more. I asked if I could go home but he ignored me. His fingers were still exploring. I began to whimper. I was very frightened and started to tremble. That seemed to annoy him. I asked if I could go home again. But he did not reply.

A bluebottle head-butted a window pane. As anxious as I was to escape I was sharply aware of conflicting smells. Scented soap on his fluttering hands. Lavender polish on the floor. Mildewed hymn-books. The trapped heat of an Indian summer day.

'Don't be afraid,' he said, 'you are my very special boy.' His smooth, oily voice still slithers through my dreams.

Next thing I know he was hauling up the surplice past my shoulders and ramming it over my head like a hood. Then he was on me and into me. Pressing me down and crushing out my breath. It wasn't so much the pain of his thing in me, but the fear of bearing his weight and being unable to breathe.

That moment is held in my memory like a freeze-frame in a film. I wriggled my head round, desperate for breath, held down by the bulk of his body. I felt his hand clamped over my mouth and I panicked, struggling for air. Gasping, sweating, I thought he was going to kill me. I tried to roll over but he had me pinned to the floor.

The process was messy and noisy. My face was smeared with snot and saliva. I didn't know what he was doing, but I sensed it was wrong.

He made it seem like a grand gesture though, as if he was doing me the great favour of confirming me in my faith. While he was doing it to me he recited verses from the Bible, bits of prayers, muttering the name of Jesus. Holy words poured out in a blasphemous litany. Maybe he thought that if he said them often enough it would come true, and I would believe that what was happening to me was somehow heaven-blessed.

Then suddenly all was still again. He released his hand, and I rolled over on my back. We lay close together gasping for air like swimmers breaking the surface after a length under water.

I was crying. Through a mist of tears I could see a bookcase of New Testaments, dog-eared, covered with dust. A box of scouting equipment, ropes, tent pegs and billy cans. A tea chest full of stage props. A lectern on a low platform from where he'd just read us the Scriptures.

He turned a blank face upon me, then looked away. His thin hair was ruffled. His clerical collar underlined a raw Adam's apple. 'This is our secret,' he said. 'You mustn't say anything to anyone. If you tell your parents it will be a very bad sin.'

His warning frightened me. But the real terror wasn't of him, or the pain and shame of what he'd done to me. What I feared most of all was that my mum and dad would find out. From that moment I concentrated on keeping it a secret. I felt shut in like an accomplice in a major crime that had to be hushed up at all costs. There was nowhere to go with my story because I was sure no adult would believe me. Why accept the story of a boy who made a habit of exaggerating everything, rather than the word of a man whose job it was to remind people that telling lies was a sin?

'You'd better be getting home,' he said, casually. There was a pause. 'I want us to be friends.'

I didn't reply. 'Hurry home then,' he added. 'And I hope I didn't frighten you?'

I heard myself saying: 'No.' It was as though the weight and authority of his status, his refined voice and fine manners, had paralysed me. I went to the lavatory to clean myself up. I tore squares of newspaper from a hook in the cubicle, wet them, and dabbed away the evidence.

When I got back to the hall he was waiting to lock up. He watched me as I put my clothes back on. Looking at me while pretending to look past me through a window. I handed him back the surplice and he folded it under his arm.

'I'll see you at the same time next week. We are doing the story of Noah's Ark.'

I couldn't get out of Sunday school, and the next week I was there again. As much as I hated it, the same thing happened again. It seemed, in a strange sort of way, almost a duty. Something I had to let him do, in spite of the guilt and resentment, because I was his favourite.

There seemed to be no escape. As a child I felt I didn't have the right to question what he was doing. I'd been raised to respect adults and to think that what they did was always for the best. I tried to blot out my feelings by saying to myself: 'It must be all right, he's a grown up.'

I'd gone to Sunday school on my scooter. Now I pushed it back home fearing an inquisition from mum and dad. Wondering whether they'd be able to tell what had happened from the way I looked.

Between my lashes were the beginnings of more tears. I dried my eyes again. I tried to look normal, to keep my expression calm. I plotted how to make sure they wouldn't find out. Tea was on the table when I came in through the back door. I forced myself to eat it, in case they thought I was sickening for something and examined me. After the meal I spent a long time crying in the lavatory, hoping mum and dad wouldn't hear and ask me what was wrong.

I couldn't get out of going to Sunday school. Mum said there were no excuses and I had to keep up my attendance if I wanted to earn my diligence certificate. To get back at him I started to muck around during his scripture lessons. I began to answer back and give him a lot of cheek. Whenever he was around I went out of my way to misbehave. Belligerence took the edge off my sweetness and eventually he lost interest in me. He must have found another victim because after November he did not trouble me again.

That lonely, sickening experience stole something from me for all time. I felt as though I was suffocating in the darkness of silence. Though nothing showed, I wasn't the same child I had been, and never regained the same state of carefree innocence. I'd been changed irrevocably.

To compensate I built a protective shell around myself that's still there today. Not wanting to let on how much I'd been hurt, I shielded myself in cocky isolation. I became a show off, a bit of a card. I developed a resolute jauntiness, like someone forcing himself to be cheerful. Sometimes I wanted to weep, but that wasn't the role I'd chosen to hide my hurt, so I frantically played the fool, blaring out my shaky confidence like a perpetual fanfare.

Those events have left me deeply cynical about organised religion. I don't mind other people believing, but I can't. That man robbed me of my virginity and any trace of religious belief I had. He left me with the lasting conviction that the first and only Christian died on the cross. It's hardly surprising that now I have nothing but disdain for men of the cloth. In my book your average clergyman should wear his trousers back to front as well as his Roman collar.

There is a postscript to this wounding episode in my life. After I revealed in a newspaper interview that I had been molested as a child,

I received a letter from John Powis (a pseudonym), a friend I had known for years. He said he had read the article and it seemed we had more in common than a thirty-year friendship because he too had been abused, in his case by two Scoutmasters in Osterley.

'It seems to me that many people have these demons affecting their lives, unknown to their friends and family, and the perpetrators of these crimes in most cases get away scot-free,' he wrote. 'I've known you for thirty years, yet I didn't know about your demons and you didn't know about mine.

'Perhaps your way of dealing with them was eventually to tell the world. I started dealing with it six years ago when I found that whenever I heard about a child being abused on the news, I would burst into tears. I sought help and during counselling managed to start talking about my experiences. Isn't it sad that our generation found it impossible to talk about what happened to us, and that so many children of our generation were so vulnerable?'

The plundering of our innocence cast long shadows. John got on with his life, and I got on with mine. But fifty-odd years later the pain is there, duller, but still nagging away. Whatever people say about time healing, or forgiving and forgetting, there is no antidote to evil like that.

CHAPTER FIVE

UP THE SHED

T HE DIFFERENCE BETWEEN PRIME NUMBERS, MIXED NUM-
BERS AND CUBE NUMBERS THEN BEING AS ALIEN TO ME AS A
DISCOURSE IN FLUENT SWAHILI, IT IS HARDLY SURPRISING
THAT I FAILED MY ELEVEN-PLUS. A simple arithmetical sum,
or an English composition entitled: 'A day in the life of an umbrella',
had roughly the same effect on my brain as a squirt of Mace nerve gas,
reducing it to dumb-cluck paralysis.

My parents called in academic reinforcements in the shape of a
round, cheerful tutor called Bill Neame, but none of his extra lessons
in Maths and English managed to penetrate the dark halls and empty
attics of my mind.

By this time I was a pupil at North Road Juniors, a barrack-like
place near Southall High Street. On the day of the examination my
mother dressed me in a crisply laundered set of clothes, in the forlorn
hope, I suspect, that the immaculate state of my turn-out would hold
some sort of sway with the authorities and mark me out as a grammar-
school type. Though my vest and pants might have merited a place at
Southall Grammar, unfortunately the boy wearing them didn't, and I
was consigned along with the other also-rans to Dormer's Wells
Secondary Modern School.

I can remember sitting in the examination room trying to reduce a mixed number to an improper fraction, sucking my pencil and looking round at everyone else writing feverishly, and knowing then that I might just as well pack up and go home because I wasn't going to pass. Not that I really wanted to go to grammar school. Long before examination day I suspected that all my real friends were destined for Dormer's Wells. I didn't fancy being separated from them, and my wish was granted. The following September, 1948, that select band, whose lips moved when we were doing silent reading, all met up again in the playground of the secondary modern.

The British education system has always relished winnowing out successes from failures, categorising them, setting them apart, and the earlier the better. Soon, I expect, we'll be conducting such tests in the womb. In my youth it was accepted as the norm that those who passed the eleven-plus would go on to get white collar jobs, while the rest of us would have no alternative but to get our fingernails dirty on building sites or at factory benches, or for the girls to find some sort of temporary haven before marriage as a shop assistant or doing shampoos and sets at Maison Hazel.

My mother had sketched great plans for me. The main aspiration was that I would reach her pinnacle of pious respectability and become a 'One thousand a year man'. She wanted me to land a job, it didn't really matter what sort, which involved wearing a suit and tie and the regular purchase of season tickets. She had a reverential, almost supplicatory attitude towards those in receipt of luncheon vouchers. Until that nasty business when they were used to purchase sex at Cynthia Payne's brothel in Streatham, luncheon vouchers were, for her, the *sine qua non* of honourable employment. Conversely, anyone who ate in a works' canteen was beyond her pale. No matter that all his working life my dad had eaten in a works' canteen, mother had pinned her hopes on better things for me. (On her Geiger counter of poshness you also got a very high reading if your home was furnished with venetian blinds, rather than curtains.)

I didn't miss the grammar school education so much as the trappings of a grammar school education. I would have enjoyed swanking about in the flashy red and black blazer and ostentatious headgear our local grammar school went in for. I regretted not learning Latin, playing rugby, and wearing a braided cap, not because I particularly wanted to do any of those things, but because they were the trappings that went with eleven-plus success.

My mother would have loved boasting about my progress with the Latin ablative absolute, but it was not to be. Of course, had I studied Latin I would have made no progress whatsoever with ablative absolutes, gerunds or gerundives. But poor mother was never given the chance to worry on that score, and when the letter came through our door announcing that I had been selected to pursue a secondary modern education, I sensed that her disappointment at my lack of achievement was greater than mine.

The trappings I ended up at Dormer's Wells with were a very different load of trappings indeed, with the accent on practical skills like woodwork, metalwork, and dexterity with tools and machines. To start with I didn't want to know. In class, when I bothered to listen, I was disruptive. Teaching me must have been like trying to communicate with a slab of tripe. When I was twelve, however, my father bought me a lathe for my birthday. It was a Myford A1. It's long since been replaced by a more up-to-date model, but my first lathe taught me so many lessons that for sentimental reasons I've hung on to it and found a space for it under the bench in my workshop.

On the spotty cusp of my adolescence, the arrival of that inspirational gift marked a line of separation between the difficult, mutinous schoolboy and a new, more mature me. The lathe gave me hours of enjoyment, learning and discipline, and helped me manifest, outside the stifling strait-jacket of the school curriculum, that I had a lively instinct for making things.

I became a regular subscriber to *The Model Engineer* and read each edition as though every word in it was Holy Writ, from the diary notes 'Smoke Rings' right through to 'Novices Corner' and 'Queries and Replies'.

'Queries and Replies' was written in the almost mystical language of engineering, an idiom I spent hours deciphering and committing to memory.

Question: 'How,' asks A.G.M. of Allerthorpe, 'does one hob in a lathe? I imagine that the hob is made in a similar fashion to making a tap, it is then placed in the chuck, or better still in a collet, supported by the tailstock centre. The gear flank is then mounted on the boring table at centre height on the spigot. The lathe is started in slow back gear, and the flank fed into the job. Is this correct, and will the hob then turn the flank?'
Reply: 'We confirm that the method of hobbing gears in a lathe is carried out in the method you suggest.'

Ah, yes. In a fog, I'd puzzle over the query for a couple of minutes, trying to work out what on earth it meant. Then I'd ask dad to give me a practical demonstration on my lathe, and after he'd shown me a couple of times it all became crystal clear.

Re-reading my bound copies of the magazine today (I taught myself how to bind books and bound them myself) I think what an anorak I must have been. It seems extraordinary to me how, at the age of twelve, I could have become so engrossed in impenetrable subjects like the operation of the displacement lubricator or pantograph calculations, when at school the teachers were barely able to persuade me to open a book.

At Dormer's Wells I was regarded as a difficult and pigheaded boy. But 202 Lady Margaret Road, homely as it was, was home. There I was a completely different boy, because I was happy. My traumatic experience with the clergyman had made me distrustful of strangers. I had decided the world was against me. Apart from the swimming pool, the only place I really flourished was in the sanctuary of the maisonette with my parents, the two people I felt I could wholly rely on.

Dad's shed was at the end of our garden and together we spent hours in it as he demonstrated the basic skills and vocabulary of engineering. Dad's shed was like a shrine. Earth floor, but everything the best and neatly in place: gleaming tools, diamond-sharp chisels, the serrated teeth of every saw shining.

Under his guidance, I did all my learning by doing. My schoolroom became the tiny, meticulously kept workshop in the hut where dad presided, a sorcerer among his paraphernalia. There I gradually began to understand that knowledge helps you make things, that poring over books is worthwhile when there is a practical end result. The niceties of most subjects eluded me, and they still do, but those treasured sessions in our shed taught me the value of learning, and as a consequence I began to pay more attention at school during the lessons that I, young know-it-all that I was, deemed to be tolerably worthwhile.

I started using my lathe to make small household items out of wood: egg cups, candle sticks, and napkin rings, even though our household didn't boast any table napkins. Then, when I'd mastered the necessary basic skills, I turned some simple metal ornaments and ashtrays for my mother.

The most ambitious thing I did was to build a 1.9 CC compression-ignition diesel engine. It was a normal two-cycle motor without electric ignition, in which the very high compression ignited the fuel. I still have the article containing the instructions, written by a couple of Dutch engineers, Schepel and Buwalda. Over a couple of years I consulted the book so often that it now falls open at the familiar pages of plans that are foxed with fifty years of ageing.

Making the model engine took hundreds of hours of work. It was a great technological challenge for someone so young and, at the same time, a small scale project, because the engine only weighed five-and-a-half ounces and was just over three inches high. But it could swing a nine-inch diameter propeller at 5,500 rpm both clockwise and counter-clockwise, and fly a model plane with a four-foot wingspan.

With my dad always on hand to correct me when I went wrong, I turned all the engine parts myself. It was a simple enough engine, but the grade of precision had to be very high, especially for the cylinder and piston. All the dimensions had to be carefully observed, and that meant lots of false starts, rejected parts, curses and new beginnings.

Most of the metal was cannibalised from other machines. The cylinder which had to be made of unshrinkable tool steel was part of an old motor car axle; the crankshaft, in chrome nickel steel, was an old valve of a large diesel motor; the needle valve in the carburettor was a length of steel piano wire.

I spent long winter nights, turning, boring, filing, tapping and reaming parts for the engine. The critical stage came when I began to turn the piston down to its accurate diameter and then polish it highly so that it fitted perfectly, without side play, into the cylinder. It was important to get it right because without high compression the engine wouldn't run.

I had turned the cylinder very accurately, leaving an extra 0.006 inches to 0.008 inches for grinding. Next I spent night after night turning the piston to the accurate diameter and polishing it until it gleamed. Then I offered them up together. It was a tantalising moment.

'Careful not to take too much off,' my dad had warned.

'That's OK,' I had said with all the naive confidence of a novice. 'It will fit perfectly.'

But it didn't. There was so much side play between the piston and cylinder you could almost hear the rattle. My heart dipped. Hours of work had been wasted. So I had to start again, learning as I did a valuable lesson in patience and accuracy.

A month's work later I was ready to fit the new piston. I had tested the measurements more carefully this time, but I was as nervous as an opening batsman on a pair when I tried them out again. They fitted. Relief. I let out a loud leaky-gasket sigh. Dad was smiling stupidly.

'I told you it pays to take your time, Trev,' he said. 'Slow but sure wins the race every time.'

It hadn't been what most boys would have regarded as fun. I'd been doing so much rubbing down with emery paper I'd almost erased my fingerprints and my hands and face were grimed with oil and polishing paste. But I derived immense satisfaction from getting it perfectly right.

Building the carburettor was just as tricky. I was supposed to make several components, a fuel tank, a needle valve with a screw for micro adjustment, a plug tap and a fuel tube. Impatient to get the engine flying, I took a few short cuts by using parts from an old petrol motor, and had it all fitted together in under a week.

Making that tiny engine taught me the value of being methodical.

Everything had to be done with painstaking care and order or the engine wouldn't work.

The newly assembled motor, as in most cases, was at first too stiff to run under its own power, so I had to drive it on the lathe by taking off the driving disc and mounting the crankshaft end in the chuck, oiling and polishing it all the time. Before attempting to start it I had to take it apart again and clean every part. Then I had to put it back together and use liquid seal on all the flanges and bypass covers. Only after all that – a couple of years' work in total, more of an addiction than a hobby – was the engine ready to fire up.

For fuel we used an ether-petroleum, oil and castor oil mix to a proportion of 45%-45%-10%. We put a few thimbles of fuel in the tank and fixed the engine in a vice as we tried to start it for the first time. We called mum up to the shed and she sat in a deckchair we'd set up for her, clucking with expectation. She'd brought a thermos of cocoa with her, delaying the big moment by insisting we all have a drink of something nice and warm. One of mother's housewifely rules was milky drinks before bedtime.

Dad and I dawdled over our drinks, reluctant to arrive at our moment of truth. I didn't expect the engine to start first time. But if we couldn't get it to start at all, what a let down it would be. After our two-year incarceration in the shed it would have reduced me to tears. Dad too probably.

Mum forced us into action. She tired of her last cold mouthfuls of cocoa, upended her cup and soaked the dirt floor with chocolate.

'Well get on with it then Orville and Wilbur,' she said. 'I've got some ironing to do.'

Dad turned the flywheel a couple of times. I squirted a few drops of juice into the exhaust port and opened the needle valve a quarter of a turn. Next I enlarged the chamber slightly by turning the compression screw.

'OK, now give it a good sharp flip,' said dad.

I put my finger against the propeller and knocked it hard. The engine stuttered and fell silent.

'There's probably too much fuel in the cylinder,' dad said. He turned the propeller a few times by hand, loosened the vice and held the motor on a slant to blow out the excess fuel.

When I flipped it again, the engine belched smoke but started first time. Mother laughed and said: 'Chocks away.' It gave a few short spurts of power and faltered. Dad adjusted the needle valve and it settled into a steady whine, high-pitched and angry, like an army of wasps trapped in a bottle.

'Well done Trev,' dad said. 'What do you want to do next?'

'You said you'd show me how to make gunpowder.'

Mum picked up her tray. 'Don't you dare, Cecil.'

She left us to what she called our 'fiddle-farting'. The engine was still racing as she marched back to the house and her ironing.

CHAPTER SIX

DON'T TRY THIS AT HOME

SINCE LOADED FIREARMS WERE STRICTLY FORBIDDEN AT SCHOOL, MY FRIEND DAVID 'PUFF NUT' PURNELL AND I SPENT A GREAT DEAL OF OUR SPARE TIME TRYING TO MANUFACTURE THEM AT HOME. Our preoccupation with explosives and weapons was understandable because, until we were eight, bangs, bombs, and tracer rounds curving across the Middlesex sky were a nightly occurrence.

We resembled the London children in the story reported in the *New York Times* in 1942. Their teacher brought a seashell to school and asked her class to name it. None of them could. 'It's a shell,' she explained finally.

'That's no shell,' one boy told her. 'Shells come out of guns.'

We belonged firmly to that tradition, and our self-imposed task in 1951, Festival of Britain Year, was to build the most powerful piece of ordnance in Southall. My father, bullied to silence by mum, refused to give David and me the recipe for gunpowder. So we became members of the local library. We planned to borrow books about ancient Chinese explosives and Roger Bacon's formulae for the magical black powder. We discovered that the first military use for gunpowder was in AD 673, when the defenders of Constantinople used 'Greek fire' against the attacking Saracens. And that the English Franciscan friar,

Roger Bacon (in about 1294), was one of the first people to write a scientific account of gunpowder. The library contained more than we wanted to know about the Gunpowder Plot, but very little information about gunpowder itself. When we pressed the head librarian for more details, some actual instructions for making it perhaps, she got rather twitchy. 'There's a new Captain W.E. Johns in. Why don't you borrow that?'

'No thank you, miss.'

We knew that gunpowder was a mixture of granular ingredients (I am deliberately omitting the names of the chemicals because I know how easy they are to obtain). We knew that you never ground up more than two ingredients simultaneously, in case the mixture exploded on you. What we didn't know were the proportions you mixed them in. So, like all science brats, we began a series of experiments.

Our first trial run involved the obvious mixture of one third of each ingredient. The resulting powder burned with a disappointing 'phuttt', the dampest of damp squibs. Over a couple of weeks we perfected our formula until we were blending proportions of 10%, 15% and 75%. We mixed that together, dampened it down with a drop of water, and ground it smooth. We pressed the resulting paste dry, and then broke it down again until it was like coarse sugar. And we had gunpowder.

Our next task was to get our black powder to fire a missile. We found about five feet of half-inch lead gas pipe, bashed the end closed with a hammer and bent the fold over on itself. I made a tiny hole with a hand drill three inches from the blocked end of the pipe. That was our rudimentary howitzer, and highly dangerous too. (Don't try this at home, children.)

The first time we fired it was on a Wednesday night after school in the summer of 1951. Puff Nut poured some of our powder into the gas pipe, ramming it down with a length of cane.

'That's not enough powder,' I said. 'That won't even fire a pea.'

'If we put in too much the pipe will explode,' said Puff Nut.

We compromised by putting in more gunpowder than he thought was wise. But less than I wanted.

Then we tamped down the gunpowder with a wedge of paper, before loading our weapon with a steel ball-bearing. We packed in the ammo with more paper, and fixed the gas pipe into dad's bench vice, which was just by the door of the shed.

Then all I had to do was pour some more powder into the hole I'd drilled and screw a spill of paper in with it. I adjusted the pipe in the vice so that it was pointing up towards the roofs of the houses in our row.

'What are you aiming at?' asked Puff Nut.

'Nothing really.'

'You've got to aim at something or you won't know whether or not you've hit the target.'

I went back to the vice and lined up the pipe, working out the trajectory so that it was more or less aimed at one of our neighbour's chimney-pots.

Then we had an argument about who was going to fire the contraption. In the end I let Puff Nut do it.

'Make sure you wedge open the shed door,' I said, 'otherwise you'll blast a hole in it.'

Puff Nut lit the spill of paper with the box of Swan Vestas we always carried with us. As soon as it began to fizz he ran back to where I was crouching behind a couple of tea chests at the far end of the shed.

The paper spluttered for a few seconds and we held our breath. Just when we thought it hadn't worked and popped up our heads to see what was happening, there was a great 'thwop' as the gun fired. We could hear a sharp crack as the ball-bearing hit something with tremendous force.

We got up and hurried out of the shed to examine our target. One of the chimney-pots on the Hardwicks' house was missing.

'When old man Hardwick sees that there'll be hell to pay,' I said. I took the length of gas pipe out of dad's bench and stood it out of sight in a corner of the shed. 'We'd better not be around when he knocks on our door.'

We both rode off on our bikes, down to the bicycle speedway track the local dads had made for the Southall All Stars and mucked around there for the rest of the evening.

Old man Hardwick never played hell because he could never work out how his chimney-pot had disappeared. But for a while Puff Nut and I adopted a lower profile, working on less hazardous projects. We made an electric motor from seven nails, two staples, two tintacks, a wooden base, three yards of insulating tape, and thirty yards of insulated copper wire. The commutator, armature, and field coil magnet were all made from nails bound with copper wire, and the brushes were two six-inch pieces of bare wire bent into a particular shape. Attached to a cycle lamp battery we used the engine to drive various Meccano models.

This simple experimental dabbling, not much more than trial-and-error messing about, was, I suppose, the start of my journey of exploration through the world of science. It wasn't earth shattering stuff, all the readers of *Boy's Own* magazine and *Eagle* comic were doing similar projects in those days. But those experiments I performed with simple everyday objects taught me how and why things happen, and showed me that life can be a voyage full of surprises and amazing discoveries.

I lived on the same side of the road 200 yards from Puff Nut. We saw each other every day and chatted endlessly, but thought we needed to be in constant communication with each other. This was long before mobile phones, and most houses in our street weren't connected to the Post Office telephone network. So Puff Nut and I built our own communications system. We worked out that if you joined two sets of ear phones with copper wire, and spoke into the ear pieces you'd be able to have a conversation.

We tried it out in the street, stretching out 200 yards of wire along the pavement and shouting down the apparatus. It worked. The reception was muffled but we could hear each other. Two distant drowning goldfish. So we decided to set it up permanently. That meant unravelling our copper wire across the dozen or so properties that separated our two homes and all the neighbours thought we'd gone barmy.

It called for some tricky negotiations.

'What are you doing in my garden Trevor Baylis?'

'I'm just putting a wire along your fence Mrs Cosgrove.'

'Why?'

'I want to talk to David Purnell.'

'Well go and knock on his door if you want to talk to him.'

'But I want to talk to him in the middle of the night. What we're fixing up is like a telephone.'

'That wire's not electric is it?'

'No, Mrs Cosgrove, it's just a wire. There's no electricity in it at all.'

'If my cat gets a shock, Trevor Baylis, I'm going to come round and complain to your father.'

The wire between my bedroom and Puff Nut's trailed across garden fences, over pergolas, around greenhouses, and a couple of sheds into Puff Nut's downstairs bedroom. It sat next to his bed on the utility tallboy. We thought it was a marvellous feat of engineering and the eighth wonder of the world. But having set it up, we couldn't think of much we wanted to say to each other.

'Hello Trevor, have you had your tea yet?'

'No, Puff Nut, not yet. Have you had your tea yet?'

'Not yet.'

'Oh.'

'Oh.'

After such witty opening gambits our conversations tended to peter out. All our effort fixing up the wire ended in the discovery that we had no earth shattering confidences to exchange with each other.

'Hello Puff Nut, I've had my tea now.'

'Yes Trev, so have I.'

'I'm going to listen to *Dick Barton* now.'

'So am I.'

Fifty years before the arrival of mobile phones we were sharing the same empty conversations mobile phone users have today. About the only thing I never said to David was the stupefying catch phrase: 'Hello, Puff Nut, I'm on the train.'

We used to chat to each other down the wire in the small hours when we were supposed to be asleep. The system's one big failure was that you couldn't turn it off, so you could hear everything that was going on at the other end. One early morning I was the unseen eavesdropper on a noisy Purnell family dust-up that was being waged all around David's headset.

Puff Nut was a wizard at chemistry. We never used to buy fireworks, we always made our own rockets and roman fountains with magnesium flash powder, experimenting with potassium chlorate and copper sulphate to create bangs and different colours. In our shed laboratory we used to experiment with highly dangerous and volatile chemicals, with no protective spectacles or gloves to guard us against spillage. In those days wearing protective clothing was thought to be nambypamby. We didn't want to seem cissies to the other lads, so we risked blinding ourselves.

We used to etch glass with hydrofluoric acid. The acid was so ferocious we carried it in a bottle lined with wax. If we had spilled the fluid on our hands it was so caustic it would have burned through to the bone. What we got up to was enough to give a Health and Safety Officer the screaming abdabs. But we knew it was treacherous stuff, so we learned to treat it with respect and take care.

It was Puff Nut who told me about the carbide-in-ink-wells trick. If you put a few grains of carbide in an inkwell it activates the ink so that it spurts out all over the desk. Then if you put a match to it, the inkwell lights up in a greenish, blueish acetylene glow, like a homemade aurora borealis. That prank earned me more lines, detention and stripes from the cane than any other misdemeanour during my time at school.

Puff Nut's family took £10 assisted passages to Australia when he was fifteen. Our 200 yards of copper wire wouldn't stretch as far as Melbourne, and after an infrequent exchange of letters we eventually lost touch. For all I know he might have made a fortune in communications, dangerous chemicals, explosives, or all three, but whatever he's done I hope he's done well.

Another great friendship blossomed around then, one that endures

today. It was with a son of the circus, Johnny Pugh. His father Digger
Pugh was a tough operator, raised in Australia, who had enjoyed the
kind of unique career you normally only read about in boys' magazines
like *Hotspur* or *Wizard*. He had flown with the Royal Flying Corps
during World War One, then he earned his money as a bare-knuckle
fighter before becoming a circus tumbler. He fought under the name
'The Pocket Hercules', and he claimed to have drawn an illegal forty-
three-round contest in the United States in the 1920s against a man
with the ring name 'Pancho Villa'.

After World War Two he was one of the first impresarios to bring
stock-car racing to Britain. At the time I met Johnny, his dad was
running an agency that booked novelty and acrobatic acts into circuses
and variety theatres.

John Wallace Llewellyn Digger Pugh was a small square man whose
spirit was as large as life and twice as outrageous. He had the habit of
calling all people, even those he had scarcely, or never, met by their first
names. So when he started talking about Ben, you had no idea whether
it was Ben, as in Benito Mussolini; Ben, for the tenor Benjamino Gigli;
Ben Hur, Ben Turpin, or Ben Lyon.

In the 1930s he'd been part of a trampoline tumbling act called
'The Wallabies' and had performed before Mussolini and Adolf
Hitler. He once started talking to me about Adolf. I assumed he was
referring to the German dictator until it suddenly became clear that
he meant the film actor Adolphe Menjou. For a while I wondered
what Hitler had been doing in a supporting role in 'Dancing in the
Dark'.

I met Johnny one day at Heston swimming baths. All the lads used
to queue up for the three meter board and show off by doing complicated dives. We'd play a game called 'Follow Me' where successive boys
would try to outdo each other by attempting more and more elaborate tricks. It could get quite scary because we kept adding tucks, pikes,
somersaults or full twists, until hitting the water cleanly became almost
a physical impossibility. It was a matter of pride not to bottle out of
trying to go one better than the bloke before, so there were some
spectacular belly flops. By the end of each session most of us had red

marks all over our stomachs where we'd smacked down hard entering the water.

Johnny was very good at the game. He won it the first time I met him, and went on winning from then on. We got to talking and he said his dad had taught him tumbling. He told me both his parents had been in the circus, and his stepmum, Sheila, had been an acrobat in an aerial ballet. He lived at Alexandra Gardens and invited me to call round.

When I first visited Johnny's house it was like entering Disneyland. The ordinary suburban back garden on the edge of Hounslow was set out like a circus ring. There was a trapeze suspended from a lofty metal frame, a trampoline, and tumbling belts rigged so that novices could be taught the rudiments of circus skills. Digger Pugh was undeniably a man who knew every aspect of life under the big top, as versed in how to ride a water-smooth silver stallion as the very moment between feeds of raw meat when the lions would be at their least dangerous.

By now I was swimming for Middlesex schoolboys, devoting three hours every day to training at Heston Baths. Any spare daylight hours were spent running and weight training, or round at Johnny's house where his father started teaching me acrobatic skills in their back garden. He worked me on the trampoline and in the tumbling belt. Within a couple of months I was up on the high trapeze, learning all the demanding drills. How to hang from it by my legs and then swing up into a sitting position. Picking up the perfect timing that was needed, getting to know the rhythm of the swing as I gripped the crossbar. Counting until the moment when, in theory, I would let go. There was only one trapeze, but in my mind I was already flying across to allow the catcher to grab my wrists before I fell.

Johnny was like the brother I always wanted, and Digger became a supernumerary father. Once I'd met them I became a constant visitor to Alexandra Gardens. I was entranced by the stories of bare knuckle fights, rogue elephants, circus jealousies and vengeful roustabouts. It was life lived with glamour on the gaudy edge of show-biz raffishness that I had not encountered before. In a recess of my mind I half fancied running away to join a circus. But most of all I wanted to grow up like Digger Pugh. The character he'd chosen for himself wasn't afraid of anyone or anything, and I wanted to be just like him.

CHAPTER SEVEN

AQUA CRACKERS

WHEN YOU'RE SWIMMING THE BACKSTROKE, UNLESS YOU'RE YARDS AHEAD, IT'S DIFFICULT TO KNOW HOW WELL YOU ARE DOING IN A RACE. The drill is not to turn your head and look around because that increases the drag on the water and slows you down. All you can do is look up towards the fragmented segments of daylight dancing in the roof, sneaking glances at the opposition out of the corners of your eyes.

It was a tight finish, but I felt strong. Three of us were matching stroke for stroke, churning the water into effervescent white. There was nothing to separate us when we were ten yards from the end wall of the pool. Going under the flagged ropes I made one final effort, forcing my arms to push me to the end, paddling six strong leg kicks to each arm cycle. I was willing myself to win. My aim was to swim through the wall rather than just to it. I'd spent hours of training getting it right in my head. A positive mental approach. Overcome the temptation to decelerate in the last few strokes. Don't just touch the wall. Strike it.

We all hit the wall together. Three hands smacked the bath end in a flurry of foam. I bashed my fingers so hard into the tiles I cut my knuckles. I sank back into the water, seeking solace under the bubbling surface, the muscles in my arms and shoulders buckling and groaning.

I held on to the edge of the pool, heart thumping, lungs shuddering in protest. I looked around. The crowd was on its feet, clapping wildly, drumming the floor with their shoes. They'd just seen the best race of the 1953 Amateur Swimming Association's National Championships.

I dived under the ropes and hugged the swimmer in the next lane. 'Who won?' I asked him.

'No idea. Could be either of us,' he said, his face grey with effort. He glanced towards his coach hoping he could confirm the result. The coach shrugged and semaphored he didn't know.

I shouted to my trainer Ted Hardy, but he didn't know either. 'It's close,' he said. 'I wouldn't like to call it.'

The crowd in the Derby Baths, Blackpool, had gone very quiet. The place was filled with the kind of silence that comes just before a jury gives its verdict. I crossed my fingers and hoped for the best. I thought I might have won. But after five minutes of whispered deliberations the judges said I hadn't. One tenth of a second covered the first three home in the 110 yards British Junior Backstroke Final.

Derek Davies of Bristol was declared the winner in 1 minute 14.6 seconds. I clocked exactly the same time, but the referee ruled that my final lunge 'fell short by a finger tip'. Graham Sykes of Coventry, who went on to represent Britain in the men's backstroke in the 1956 Olympic Games at Melbourne, was placed third, one tenth of a second behind us.

I was disappointed because in the first heat I had swum the fastest time of the championships: 1 minute 14.4 seconds so, in theory, I should have won the final. This was before the introduction of electronic timing and the photo-finish. Tight decisions were worked out with a stop-watch and the naked eye. No wonder the judges had taken more than five minutes to deliberate and had called in the championship referee before making up their minds.

In second place on the podium all I could think about was the unfairness of it all. 'How can they give us both the same time and yet place him first?' I said to myself. 'Maybe if you had bigger hands or longer arms you could have won.'

John Humphreys, a member of my club, Heston SC, sent me a letter of congratulations when I got home, with this piece of advice: 'Hint for future major events – Don't cut your fingernails.'

Earlier that year I had attended a two-week training course at Loughborough College. It was for swimmers between fourteen and seventeen who were regarded as Olympic hopefuls for Melbourne, 1956. One coach, analysing my backstroke, had commented: 'Fast stroke. Head rather high and feet rather low. Some good promise here. Very light physique.'

That last phrase just about summed up why I never made it to the Olympics. A swimmer with a strong physique generating more power will generally beat a smaller opponent. All the smaller swimmer can do is to try to compensate by improving his technique, correcting his movements until he is swimming mechanically perfectly. But there comes a time at the highest levels when most swimmers have had their defects corrected and their technique is almost flawless, and so the whole equation comes back again to physique and power. In swimming, a good big 'un should always beat a good little 'un and, as I stopped growing when I reached five foot five-and-a-half inches, I never developed into a good big 'un.

I spent most of my teenage years training five hours a day trying to prove that dictum wrong. I used to get up at 4.15 every morning, summer and winter, and cycle down to Heston Baths for a three-hour session in the pool. Very early in the morning or late at night were the only periods in the day when public baths were available for serious swimmers to do their training.

The season would run from mid-September to mid-August and the daily schedule would go on relentlessly for eleven months. The aim was to improve your technical ability through stroke drills, while also developing endurance, and building your strength and muscles by exercises in and out of the water. I'd be doing very long straight swims of 2,000 to 3,000 yards, mixed up with short rest repeats, ten 200-yard swims with ten seconds' rest. Then later in the day I'd put in two hours of exercises, running, stretching, and using weights.

Ploughing up and down a lonely swimming pool can become as

good a way as I know to bore yourself to death. The tedious symmetry of length after length when nothing happens and you're isolated in a cocoon with nothing to liven up the relentless monotony. It's awful. Like *Waiting for Godot* in six feet of chlorinated water.

There are drills you can do to break up the grind, like combining the arm action with the leg action of another stroke, or one-length sprints with a walk down the pool back to the start. I used to enliven my sessions by competing against myself in my head. I kept a written record of how many lengths I did every day: fifty-five, sixty, sixty-two. Each session I'd try to break my record, or achieve the same distance in a shorter time. But it was pretty dull all the same, and only dedication kept me going.

I've never felt fitter, or hungrier than after those morning training sessions. I'd come out, glowing with innocence and health. Winter frost or breezy spring sunshine, the mornings felt so good I wanted to shout and thank somebody for them. I used to pretend there was a canal direct from the swimming baths to my house. I'd be cycling along in a rattle of broken spokes, but in my head I'd be swimming all the way home to demolish a huge breakfast.

There was an unchanging routine to every morning. I would start swimming at 4.45 every morning, devour my breakfast three-and-a-half hours later in four minutes flat, and arrive at school ten minutes late for assembly. Every day for going on two years I had my name taken by the lateness monitor, and every day I got the cane.

For some perverse reason I never told the school why I was late. I had made some bloody-minded resolution with myself not to tell them about my swimming. It was only after a letter arrived at Dormer's Wells selecting me to represent Middlesex Schools that they realised I could swim at all, let alone swim well. But after that they took pride in my achievements and the daily canings stopped.

My first advanced training course was at Loughborough College after I'd started work. I reported there with my cardboard suitcase and ration book on 4 April 1953 with thirty-three other teenagers from all over Great Britain. Any thoughts that it would be like a spring holiday in the Leicestershire countryside were given a jolt when we arrived at the college to be greeted by Max Madders, the man in charge of training. He marched in front of us in the manner of a censorious headmaster and laid down a set of rules that wouldn't have been out of place at a remand home. I still have an old *Daily Mirror* cutting about that training fortnight. It was headlined: 'A swim-kid's life is all cold water.' And it was too.

Most of it was poured on us by Max Madders during his opening address. 'You have been sent here because you are promising swimmers,' he said. 'Some of you will be in the British team at the next Olympics. You are here to work hard; therefore, no romancing, no dates, no dancing. Just concentrate on swimming and Melbourne.'

We spent three hours a day in the pool, swimming three miles in one long session. The coaches could follow our movements through glass panels underneath the water and correct any faults they spotted. When we weren't swimming we filled our day doing physical training, exercises with weights, running, walking, getting physiotherapy and massage, and attending lectures. The whole course for the lot of us cost the Amateur Swimming Association (ASA) £500. It was a figure that rather shocked the *Mirror* reporter. 'It may seem expensive,' he told his readers. 'But compared with the money the Americans and other countries spend on Olympic swimming preparations it's only like a generous subscription.'

The ASA's concern about improving the competitiveness of British swimming was understandable. Although we pioneered swimming as a competitive sport, the lack of indoor pools here and our mediocre climate meant we had languished, not winning any Olympic medals since 1908. In fact our first medal for forty-eight years came at Melbourne in 1956. Unfortunately it wasn't mine – I wasn't even there. It was the gold won by Judy Grinham in the Ladies 100 metres backstroke. She was a close and dear friend, as was my team-mate Margaret Edwards from Heston who won a bronze in the same race.

The star in my stroke at Loughborough was another sixteen-year-old, Haydn Rigby, from Southport. The best time I clocked there – 1 minute 17 seconds – wasn't far behind his, and it seemed to please all the coaches.

I've kept the letter I sent my mother after my first week there. I don't know why Max Madders was so worried about an outbreak of 'romancing' on the course, the concerns in my letter were much more innocent. 'We are given free Horlicks before our swims,' I told her. And my postscript was wonderfully naive. 'Will you please send me some sweets,' I asked mum, 'because there aren't many shops open round here.'

I was the Middlesex and Southern Area 100-metre backstroke champion in 1953–54, and I represented Great Britain in numerous international galas up to the age of seventeen. The BBC's *Sportsview* was a mid-week must for sports enthusiasts, bringing the action right into people's living rooms for the first time. They mounted their outside broadcast cameras everywhere, often at places I was swimming, like the King Alfred Baths at Hove, or the Marshall Street Baths in London.

Distant relatives used to get a surprise when they switched on their brand new televisions and suddenly saw me stripped off and ready to dive in. Television was still an astonishing novelty in those days and to come face to face on the box with a member of the family was, for some of them, almost unbelievable. My mum's cousin Elsie was so amazed to see me on television she dashed off a six page letter. 'I switched on television last night and there was Trevor getting ready for his race. As you can bet I was shouting for him all the way. I had no idea what was on and you can guess I got quite a surprise. You must be very proud of him. How old is he now? He was just a little mite when I last saw him.' And so on for five more breathless pages.

Sadly, all those hours of training and myriad lengths of the Heston pool never made me the champion I wanted to be. I worked hard. I was determined to succeed. But I reached a plateau and, try as I might, couldn't improve my times. My opponents' performances left me trailing, not far behind, but still in their wake, so I never quite made it to the top. I'll always regret not going with our swimming team to Melbourne. I am a patriotic sentimentalist and I would have loved to have been there. Puff Nut Purnell's family had settled in the city, and he wrote to me outlining all the fun we'd have and the things we'd do after I won my medal. One of the saddest letters I've ever had to write was to tell him I wouldn't be going.

But the sport did give me a lot of fun. In May 1954 I was part of an Avondale SC team from Southgate, North London, which went up to give Cambridge University Swimming Club a work out just before the Blues gala against Oxford. There were races in all the strokes, a relay, a water-polo match, followed by dinner at the Hawk Club. We won the gala easily. Then we all trooped off to their elegant dining room for a meal. There was a nice starter, some good rare beef, ripe Camembert, washed down with a deluge of claret, topped off with port and cigars strong as jute matting for those that wanted them.

'Do you always eat like this just before the gala with Oxford?' I asked their backstroke swimmer who was sitting next to me.

'No, a week before the gala we go into really strict training,' he said. 'We cut down on the port and cigars.'

I joined Ealing SC and took up water polo. It can be a tough sport, with lots of bodily contact. It's like being mugged under water. Professional boxing with the added danger of drowning. I was one of the faster swimmers whose job it was to swim to the middle of the pool at the start of the game to try to gather the ball. In one match against a team from North London I got to the ball first, just before the swimmer from the other team. As I passed the ball back to one of our players, I accidentally caught my opponent in the mouth with my elbow. He gave me a hard look but didn't say anything.

About a minute later we were treading water next to each other, with the play yards away. He smiled, gave me a fierce punch on the nose and said: 'Don't bother about the ball, let's just get on with the game.'

I was also one of the first people in Britain to see a demonstration of synchronised swimming. It was the late summer of 1953 at the Marshall Street Baths and the star of the show was an American girl named Beulah Gundling. She was the US solo synchronised swimming champion who was touring Europe to promote the new, so called, sport.

Her arrival here begged several questions. How can you have solo synchronised swimming? If you're alone in the water who do you synchronise with? The lovely Miss Gundling gundled the length and breadth of the pool confirming that a beautiful girl in a wet swimming costume can raise the ambient temperature by at least ten degrees.

Everybody loved her. I loved her. But I wondered what on earth her aquatic ballet had to do with sport. Not so much the dying swan, more the drowning duck. Maybe that's where I went wrong. I might have won more medals if I'd worn a nose clip and learned how to breathe under water and waggle my toes in the air. Which, in a way, I did.

I was part of a comedy diving act, the Aqua Crackers, with three pals of mine: Tony Wilcox, David Beale, and Brian Shorey. We used to do all sorts of silly stunts from the five-metre and three-metre diving boards: trick dives, pyramids, and clip-on dives like the 'horse and jockey' in which the horse bounces up from the three-metre spring-board to be met by another diver coming down from five metres who 'rides' him into the water, yelling like a cowboy. The last is a very tricky dive to pull off; if you don't get the timing perfect there's a nasty mid-air collision. The highlight of our act was a complicated comedy routine which involved me wearing women's clothing and being set alight. I'd come down from the five-metre board spinning like a Catherine wheel and douse the flames in the pool.

When I was seventeen the trick went badly wrong. I was on holiday with my parents at Totnes in Devon and I noticed a poster advertising a gala at Paignton Harbour. The stars of the show were to be a comedy diving troupe called The Aquazamis. I rang the organiser, who I'd met while swimming for Britain, and asked him if I could take part in the show. Basically I wanted to watch The Aquazamis work and filch a few of their gags.

I arrived at the gala with my comedy costume wrapped in my towel, eager to meet The Aquazamis. Twenty minutes before they were due to go on they still hadn't arrived. Then there was a phone call. They were stuck on the Honiton by-pass and wouldn't be able to make it.

The organiser was panicking. There was a full house watching the gala and he had no act for the big finale. I told him I'd work something out. I chatted to four divers from the Paignton Swimming Club and we sketched out a programme of comedy routines. One of them even nipped home on his motor bike to pick up a couple of clown outfits.

The show went very well. Until my fire dive. I always wore women's clothes and a blonde wig for it because they offered more protection from the flames. I was supposed to be a cleaning lady sweeping the springboard, telling off the other swimmers for making the place untidy. One of them creeps up behind me and lights the hem of my dress with a spill. I don't notice until the flames have got a good hold, then I rush up to the top of the five-metre board and dive in.

I'd done it dozens of times before and never come to any harm. But in the rush at Paignton all I could find to soak my dress in was trades vehicle oil, which unknown to me then, has a very high flash point. As soon as the bloke put the flaming spill to the hem of my dress I went up like a napalm bomb. Running round the pool to the five-metre board I was a fireball. My wig was alight, the dress completely burned away, and I could smell my own hair starting to singe. Suddenly the ladder to the top seemed to be 100 feet high and I had gone into slow motion. The crowd loved it. They didn't realise anything had gone wrong.

I launched myself into space. It seemed an age before I hit the sea. Then I was in the salt water of the harbour, cooling down, thankful that the flames were out at last, and hurting like hell. I swam to the edge of the harbour and climbed slowly up the steps. My face and side were very sore, skin was flaking off, and I was badly burned under both arms. I was having a holiday romance with a Dutch girl called Karen who was very concerned and wanted to take me straight to the first aid tent. But I still had one more dive to do, the comedy flight in which all the divers come off the board in quick succession doing different tricks.

I did the dive, we took our applause, and if the organiser ever noticed I looked like I'd been flayed alive, he never said anything about it. By the time Karen got me to the St John Ambulance tent I was shivering uncontrollably. Big strips of skin were hanging off me and you could see the flesh underneath. The first aid lady examined me, looking as though the first thing she ought to do was treat herself for shock.

I was taken to Totnes General Hospital where I sat in a cubicle feeling very sorry for myself while a nurse from Limerick gave me a large piece of her Irish mind. She used word the eejit a lot and told me: 'I've got better things to do with myself on Saturday afternoons than patch up silly herberts who dress up as women and set fire to themselves.'

Karen got in touch with my parents at the boarding house in Totnes and they got a taxi to the hospital. When they arrived on the ward I was sitting up in bed covered in slimy stuff and gauze swaddling clothes. As soon as she got there my mother started crying. All she could see was a pair of eyes staring at her through the bandages they'd wrapped me up in, like the Invisible Man. Just before they left my dad said: 'Look on the bright side Trev. At least you didn't kebab your wedding tackle.'

Mother was worried about permanent scarring, but although my burns looked horrific for a couple of days, they soon healed up. They kept me in hospital over the weekend, and after they changed my dressings on Monday morning I was discharged.

Forty-five years later I still enjoy the water. I go for long invigorating morning swims in my pool at home, only now I use the regular, repetitive lengths to concentrate my mind and give myself some thinking time. It's curious when you look at the history of swimming and notice the inventors who have been keen on the sport. Leonardo da Vinci was the first person to design flippers. He also sketched out the first hand paddles made from two oval palettes.

Benjamin Franklin, whose experiments with a kite led to the invention of the lightning rod in 1752, was one of the first great early swimming experts. On a Thames boat excursion in 1726 he took off his clothes, dived in and swam from Chelsea to Blackfriars. He was offered the chance to run a swimming school over here but returned to Philadelphia because he was homesick.

I often use the quiet concentration of my morning swims to think over problems I'm having with my inventions. Did Leonardo ever swim his version of the trudgen up the Tiber while pondering over a snag in his design for the submarine? Or did Franklin perfect his lightning conductor while doing the backstroke across the Potomac? I like to think that perhaps they did.

CHAPTER EIGHT

INDIARUBBER MEN, SNAKEGIRLS AND BEARDED LADIES

ONE AUTUMN DIGGER PUGH TOOK JOHNNY AND ME TO MEET WALLY TEXAN, A KNIFE THROWER WHO OWNED A TUMBLEDOWN COLLECTION OF BUILDINGS SOMEWHERE OFF THE BEATEN TRACK IN ESSEX THAT SERVED AS WINTER QUARTERS FOR A COLLECTION OF CIRCUS ACTS.

When we found it down a rutted track the place was all mud and corrugated iron. A small welcome party had turned out to greet the celebrated Digger. They were an endearing group, an exotic, mournful collection of types that might have been hired from a casting agency for a Fellini circus movie. There were a couple of dwarfs who told Digger they had a Christmas booking for *Snow White*. A girl contortionist with specs and a body like knotted flex. And a once-handsome woman who was the target for Wally's knives, her ruined beauty now slightly frayed around the edges.

'How's the eyesight Wally?' asked Digger. Wally gave him the kind of rueful smile that suggested that maybe it wasn't as good as it was.

Digger was there to audition an act he wanted to fill a hole in a variety bill at the Sunderland Empire. It was an Ali Baba routine in which a pretty girl writhed with a snake while dancing to languorous music. As she coiled herself around the serpent, a bloke dressed as a Caliph swiped the air close to her permanent wave with a scimitar. The girl got into a large basket with the python and the Caliph pierced the weave with about twenty swords. After a few passes around the basket, he withdrew the swords, making a great play of how sharp they were. Then, hey presto, the girl and her pet emerged unharmed and they all took a bow.

It didn't seem much of an act to me but Digger obviously thought it was good enough for Sunderland. He sat appraising it like a buyer at an auction and finally gave it the nod.

'Forty quid for the week Ralph,' he said to the Caliph. 'And make sure the snake doesn't misbehave, they've just redecorated the dressing rooms.'

In the woods nearby we found the cages of a menagerie where a collection of bored animals were spending the winter. Wally's glamorous daughter, Joan Rizaire, who had a sharp-shooting act, showed us a mule that was supposed to be unrideable, but all the time we were there it was sound asleep.

There was a covered sawdust ride under a huge Dutch barn where they practised their routines. A rough ring was marked out with straw bales. In the middle they'd set up a trampoline. A tumbling harness, attached to a pulley in the roof, was dangling above it.

Johnny started bouncing on the trampoline, showing off all the tricks his father had taught him. He was so good he didn't need the safety gear. Then Digger told me to have a go. He suggested I wear the harness, but I said no. I wanted to outdo my pal and was trying too hard. Going for a somersault I lost my rhythm, landed off line and bounced off the trampoline. It was a nasty crash. I caught my foot on the metal stay as I flew over the edge and landed awkwardly, flat on my belly in the sawdust.

I was hurt. More than that I had lost face. I told them I'd sprained my wrist and best call it a day. The truth was I had cold feet and I didn't fancy taking another heavy fall. Digger realised the mishap had put the wind up me. Other people might have taken the soft option and let me give in. But he told me to get straight back up on the trampoline and try again. 'If you don't do it now Trev,' he said, 'you might as well pack it in altogether. You won't ever be good at anything if you start behaving like a wet sock the minute something goes wrong.'

I was reluctant, but I squared my shoulders and got back up.

'Wear the tumbling harness this time,' he said. 'It will give you more confidence.'

I put it on and worked back up to speed while he held the rope on the harness. 'Go on Trev, you can do it,' he said.

I hit the spot once, twice, perfectly in time. I began to count myself into the move. Three. Four. Now. An adrenaline rush and I'd done it. A perfect double somersault.

Digger was smiling. 'There you are, it didn't hurt did it?' I kept practising. By the end of the session I was performing the trick without the harness. 'Well done mate,' he said when I jumped down from the apparatus. 'Surprised yourself didn't you? But we all knew you could do it.'

He was as hard and rough as an uncut diamond. He reminded me in a way of Jimmy Cagney, full of pent-up energy, tough and unshakeable. Digger had the ability to inspire such certainty it restored you to your true proportions and lifted you skywards. All the way home my feats on the trampoline were the sole topic of conversation.

Digger was so small he had to have wooden blocks fitted on the pedals of his Jaguar so he could reach the brake, clutch and accelerator. When he and Johnny turned up at our house to take me on our circus jaunts you could barely see his head over the steering wheel of his XK120. He was a very good driver, but a ferocious one. His big problem was that he never accepted he could be overtaken.

Once we were going through Ascot, just by the race course. He was taking us off to a meeting with one of his exotic acts. He was driving quite normally, about ten miles over the limit, but that was his usual practice. Suddenly we were badly cut up by a man in a Bentley who swerved right in front of us. The driver of the Bentley made the bad mistake of winding down his window and swearing at Digger as he overtook.

Digger wasn't the sort of man it was wise to swear at. He tucked in behind the Bentley until it had to stop at a set of traffic lights. The red signal lasted for about fifteen seconds and in that time Digger got out of his car, walked up to the Bentley, stood on the running board, smashed his fist through the closed side window, and knocked the driver out cold.

Then he walked back, casually picking fragments of glass out of his fist. He got back into our car. When the lights changed he drove off with a squeal of rubber, leaving the man in the Bentley still spark out. I'm talking here about a man who was only five foot six inches with his umbrella up, but he was completely fearless. As we got up to speed again Johnny and I sat there very quiet, shocked about witnessing our first example of road rage.

'He shouldn't have sworn at me,' Digger explained. 'But it was a good punch. Did you see it? They all go if you hit them right. Remember that.'

I kept listening for a bell, expecting a police car to appear in the rear mirror any minute. Nothing happened. After the high excitement, the rest of the day petered out to anticlimax. The act we went to see – Juanita and her Amazing Borzois I think it was – couldn't match the drama generated by Digger's explosive knuckleduster right.

We paid several more visits to the circus farm in Essex. Each time welcomed by more of Digger's unlikely acts: Indiarubber men, snakegirls, bearded ladies, and a weird collection of captivating freaks and sideshow curiosities. He operated at the outer rim of show business among the performing seals and clowns in spangled tights. About as far away from theatrical knights and command performances as you could get.

One of the colloquial meanings of the word circus is disturbance, scene of lively action. Life as lived by Wally Texan and company was certainly far more vivacious, romantic, and impulsive than anything I'd known in Southall. For a start none of them used their real names. Doreens metamorphosed into Doritas as soon as they put on spangled scanties. Stolid Bert Higgins suddenly became Bruno Kloosters and gained the imaginary rank of Captain when he stepped in with the caged lions. And they weren't merely caged lions they were 'Deadly dangerous black-maned Nubians.'

Every now and then things would erupt. There would be a huge operatic row followed by sentimental reconciliations. They made dreary Essex seem vital, racy and exhilarating. I imagined it would be an agreeable way to earn a living. A hint of danger, the spice of melodrama, and never in one place long enough for it to become stale.

I was coming up to fifteen, the age when compulsory schooling finished in those days. There seemed no likelihood of going on to college and I was starting to think about what I might do with my life after Dormer's Wells Secondary Modern. Though I was never as good as Johnny, I'd developed into a fair tumbler and Digger Pugh said that if I wanted a job, with his contacts he'd be able to get me fixed up with a circus.

I was tempted. But then, when I thought about it I knew my mum and dad would never approve, and so I said no.

Digger used to tell us the joke about the man who got a job mucking out the elephants at a circus. He meets a mate who says: 'How many elephants do you have to muck out?' He replies: 'Twenty-five.' His mate says: 'How much do they pay you?' He tells him: 'Ten pounds a week.' The friend is scornful: 'Ten pounds a week for mucking out twenty-five elephants? If I were you I'd chuck it all in and get a decent office job.' And the bloke says: 'What – and give up show business?'

When it came down to it I didn't fancy spending the rest of my life mucking out elephants. And there was a risk that that's what I would have ended up doing. In certain jobs there's no substitute for talent, and the circus is one of them. The real artists are few and far between. They are born, not made. It's no use just being adequate, or promising, if you cannot dazzle or entertain. Without the breathtaking quality to become a star, to fly a trapeze or walk a wire, hard work and all the other qualities are of no avail.

Like the man in Digger's joke, I would have loved it. Mucking out the elephants, helping to put up the Big Top, feeding the lions, selling tickets. I would have felt part and parcel of show business. For once, though, I did the sensible thing. Without a doubt I would have been seduced by the sights, sounds and smells of the circus, but I decided to look for what my mother would have called 'a proper job'.

My friend Johnny followed his father into the circus and became an acrobat. He now lives in Florida, and is the co-owner of The Clyde Beatty-Cole Brothers three-ringed circus. It is the largest tented spectacular in the world, and with his wife Bridget, Johnny tours across America with it. When the company celebrated its centenary in 1984 he sent me the souvenir programme. It was written in the same over-ripe language those circus stars used to speak to us in Essex all those years ago. 'Transcendent in opulent magnitude all under the big top just as your grandma and grandpa saw it.'

Johnny's acts included My Immba's Congress of Captive Baboons: 'Ferocious! Fearsome! Deadly! Known to attack leopards. Used as vicious "attack dogs" by North African Nazi troops, the reputation of these sinister simians precedes them. Here assembled before you are a captive congress of species, varied and rare, brought to you from around the world by the courageous My Immba. For the protection of your own, as well as the lives of your loved ones, please remain seated during this presentation.'

There was another splendid act, the 'lovely', of course, Michelle: 'Bizarre! Unusual! True youthful beauty and feminine splendor grace-fully and tastefully unveiled while dangerously suspended from the height of the Big Top's peak; her single lifeline against death's plummet – the strength of her own hair!'

Wonderful stuff. Staggering in its enormity! Awesome in its assem-blage! All the exuberant patter reminded me of the way the one and only Digger Pugh used to speak to me as a wide-eyed boy. Sometimes I wonder what would have happened if I had taken the job he offered me, but there's not much point in fruitless conjecture. I've never been one to bother about past regrets or future fears.

CHAPTER NINE
A BIT OF A CAD

IF THEY HAD GIVEN ME A JOB ASSESSMENT TEST AT DORMER'S WELLS SCHOOL THE REPORT WOULD PROBABLY HAVE SAID THAT MY APTITUDES AND ABILITIES WERE BEST SUITED TO SOME FORM OF EARLY RETIREMENT. I was in the B-stream in a B-grade school doing B-badly.

There was never any question that I would leave full-time education as soon after my fifteenth birthday as was possible. In 1952 work was plentiful. Even school leavers like me with no qualifications had the luxury of being able to pick and choose whatever form of employment we wanted to pursue.

After a round of interviews I had the offer of a job in the AEC bus factory at Southall earning £8 a week, a good wage in those days, or an apprenticeship with a soil engineering firm on £4 a week, with a one-day release to study for my Ordinary National and Higher National Certificates in Engineering. Guided by my parents, I chose the £4 a week job, and it proved a happy decision. The toad *work* proved an agreeable companion. Instead of squatting on my life, he let me stretch out and discover for myself the opportunities I had missed at school.

The company I joined had a name more suited to a firm of high class lawyers or up-market estate agents – Le Grand, Sutcliff and Gell.

In fact they were a firm specialising in soil mechanics and site investigations. After the war millions of pounds were being spent on rebuilding Britain. Le Grand and Co had been carrying out borings for water and trial holes for ground examination since 1872. When I joined them in the booming 1950s they had civil engineering contracts all over Britain investigating the bearing capacity of ground for large structures, the stability of road and airport surfaces, and the siting of dams. They also ran an electrical resistivity surveying unit to detect and evaluate potential water supplies, mineral deposits, and the contouring of hidden rock surfaces.

Fortunately for me Le Grand's had also managed to collect under one roof the largest group of oddballs, cranks and Bohemians ever to be levied in Southall. Principal among them was the man who became my mentor, John Arthur Joseph O'Neill Elliot. Except on the warmest of days he wore cavalry twill trousers, a blazer and a British warm overcoat to work. He could have been a British army officer who had seen better days. He was a natty dresser with brilliantined patent leather hair that matched his highly polished shoes. There wasn't an hour of the working day when he didn't have a Gauloise cigarette glowing in his fist. On his top lip and the fingers of his right hand he carried the luminous glow of nicotine stains.

He was one of the senior technicians and most of the knowledge I acquired at Le Grand's I picked up from him. The first skill I learned was how to make proper coffee. At home we only ever had Camp, the black treacly essence that tasted like nothing at all and came in bottles with a picture of a Sikh serving Camp coffee on the label. And on that label was another label until the Sikh serving the coffee disappeared into infinity up his own turban

At Le Grand, Sutcliff and Gell they had an elaborate antique coffee percolator you needed a degree in applied thermodynamics to operate. It took me my first two months there, and the threat of the sack, to master it. As the office junior, the making of the morning coffee was my responsibility. The firm's entire productivity appeared to depend on the complexion of the day's first vital brew. Make it too dark and they complained it tasted like licorice, too sepia and they asked if I'd forgotten to put in the coffee. It was like a Japanese ritual. The beans had to be ground to exactly the right texture. A precise measure of water had to be poured into the machine. And under no circumstances was I to allow the liquid to stew.

The final arbiter in all these matters was, of course, John Arthur Joseph, who sat for the first fifteen minutes of each working day offering advice from the desk where he was reading his copy of *The Times*. He had perfected the appearance of extreme busyness but he spent a lot of the time reading the paper or phoning his friends.

I would bring him the first cup and he would give his verdict. 'Not bad Trevor,' he would say. 'As cups go it's not quite the Mozart of coffees. But at least it's wet and warm.' As soon as his coffee was set in front of him he would start *The Times* crossword puzzle, and most days he would complete it before he'd finished his refill.

'Twenty-six across,' he would mutter, 'part in *Twelfth Night* – one playing it takes a bow. Five letters.' There would be a pause, as if tempting the dullards around him to provide the correct answer. A second or two later there would be a jubilant snort. 'Got you,' he would say. 'That kind of bow. Viola.'

I don't know how on earth he came to be working in Southall. He travelled to the office every day from his flat in Pimlico. The exact nature of his domestic arrangements there were an inviolable mystery. He had the air of a man who might have been cashiered from the services, or lost a senior position because of some undefined but shameful indiscretion. There was something of Captain Foulenough about him, and more than a touch of Flashman.

To my eyes, though, he was a genius, the first true intellectual I had ever met, and I basked in the glow of his daily pyrotechnic displays of knowledge. He would sit in a fug of French tobacco quoting Auden and Eliot. He always spoke of them in the same breath. At first I didn't realise they were poets. I thought the Eliot might be a relative of his. To me they sounded like some sort of music hall double act. Auden and Eliot, a song, a smile and a piano. Two musical cads, a bit like the Western Brothers, Kenneth and George.

One day he looked out through the smeared windows of our office at some threatening thunder clouds above the railway bridge and started to proclaim.

'The sky is darkening like a stain; Something is going to fall like rain, And it won't be flowers.'

I thought he'd gone bananas until he explained it was lines from an Auden poem called 'The Witnesses'.

He was the first person I ever met who could talk with authority and clarity on opera, military history, politics, literature, music, geography, food and drink, mythology, anything. Anything, that is, except sport. He loathed it. Each Monday morning he would grumble at his colleagues' interminable analyses of events at Stamford Bridge or Highbury two days earlier. 'Get the coffee on Trevor,' he would say. 'It might shut them up.'

John Elliot was the first person to make me fully aware of my lack of scholarship. He was witty and shrewd about things I'd never even heard of. He was a conjurer producing clever insights like bright silk hankies from a hat. His daily performances ignited something in me. Without saying anything, just by being him, he made me want to try to cultivate my fallow mind.

In the last couple of years at school I had started to work hard at the practical subjects, like metalwork and carpentry, and had made good progress; but arithmetic, algebra, differential calculus, and geometry stretched out before me foreign and distant, like vast uncharted seas.

I was so far behind the other day release students I had to go to evening school four nights a week, cramming to make up lost ground in subjects they were teaching us at Southall Technical College. I had to do a crash course to start the course, as it were. For the first time in my life I was doing homework, and found, to my great surprise, that I enjoyed it.

Dad and mum purchased a desk – one of those little bureaus that are too small to sit at comfortably, and haven't got enough room for all your books. I crouched at it late into the night, making myself familiar with Boyle's and Charles's laws, and trying to figure out how much heat is required to produce four pounds of steam from feed water at sixty degrees Fahrenheit when the steam has a temperature of 500 degrees Fahrenheit. (To save you the bother of working it out, the answer is 4,922.4 B.Th.U.)

A log-log slide rule became the emblem of this new-found diligence. I sat at my bureau fiddling with the rule until I'd taught myself how to calculate trigonometric functions and logarithms at a speed that surprised my dad. He'd tried to teach me before but I'd never concentrated long enough to learn. I suddenly discovered I enjoyed studying, that homework was not the chore I had dreaded, and that examinations, though still a formidable and exhausting form of self-imposed torture, no longer reduced me to ossified cluelessness. Most of all I realised my studies had a practical application at work.

Multi-storey flats were going up all over London and I used to go out with the senior staff watching them supervise drilling operations to calculate the depth of foundations needed for tall buildings. If you came across a sandy gravel bed the foundations would have to be piled below it into more stable clay. When your drilling found the ground water had a high sulphate content then the builders would have to take special precautions to protect the concrete they put down.

We also went out investigating the earth's crust using electrical resistivity surveying. Basically you pass a known electric current through the ground, and measure the difference of potential between two intermediate points. According to the pattern and spacing of the electrodes, you can use a formula to interpret the readings to evaluate water supplies, the contouring of hidden rock surfaces, and track mineral deposits like sand, gravel, clay, coal and ironstone.

One of the big projects I worked on was the survey for the foundations of the Shell complex on the South Bank of the Thames. Most of the workers building the huge Portland stone headquarters were Irishmen, gangs of indefatigable, soft-hearted lads whose capacity for hard work was only matched by their capacity for hard drink. During our time there they'd been a big help to me and Alan, the bloke I was working with, lending a hand to shift our gear around the site. So in our last week we offered to take a few of them out for a quick drink after work.

Just the one turned into a leisurely several. By about the fourth pub we were all fettled with Guinness. One of our Irish mates, a sandy-haired carpenter from Tuam called Noel, suddenly discovered he'd mislaid the top set of his false teeth. We all scouted round the bar, on the tables, under the tables, in the gents, on the pavement outside. Nothing. There wasn't a glimmer of a denture to be seen.

I offered to backtrack with him to the other pubs we'd visited to search for the missing teeth. We didn't have much luck. And it's hard keeping a straight face when you've got to ask yet another snotty barmaid: 'Has anyone handed in any false teeth over the bar?'

'What do they look like?'

'Teeth.'

We'd just about lost hope when we found them in a pub under the railway arches at Waterloo. There was no luck when we searched for them in the bar. It was a lost cause, we decided, and were going back to find the others. Before that we called in to the gents, just on the off chance. And there was Noel's top set, trapped in the gully of the urinal, in danger of being washed down the outflow, but held fast by the brass drain cover.

'There they are, Noel,' I said triumphantly.

He was so pleased at finding his teeth again, he bent down, picked up the dentures, and put them straight into his mouth.

'But what about the germs?' I said.

'Just buy me a whiskey,' he said, 'and I'll swill it around them.'

Next day everybody on the site knew all about it and were asking him if he had caught athlete's tongue.

I spent more than six years with Le Grand and Co, passing my Ordinary and Higher National Certificates in Engineering. The longer I was there the more I tended to mould myself on John Elliot. Within the office he was regarded as a supreme ladies' man. A bit of a cad. Some-one who through a combination of charm, flattery and wit exercised a mysterious hold over the female sex. He would bring in a photograph of an agreeable young woman and announce to the more impression-able apprentices that this was his target for the week. 'She's just my type,' he would say, giving us his Terry-Thomas leer. 'She's a girl.'

He would then outline his strategy for seduction. A few gin and Its, a bottle of Soave and a spaghetti bolognaise always featured high in his arsenal of weaponry. He would come in the following Monday morning with tales of high passion after late night espressos and honey grappas.

And, callow as we were, we always believed him. In the sex-appeal stakes he was no great shakes yet here he was doing better than all the rest of us put together. Apparently. Knowing no better, I concluded that sex appeal wasn't just a sharp haircut, a nice smile and solid torso; what put John Elliot ahead of the field was his intellectual chat, his way with poetry and his ability to complete *The Times* crossword puzzle. So I decided to use him as my role model.

I began to buy *The Times*. I'd wait until he had completed the crossword, and then copy his answers. I invested in some slim volumes of verse and sat up at night trying to commit it to memory, determined to out-Yeats him if I could. 'A pity beyond all telling is hid in the heart of love.'

To my surprise, it worked. Girls in coffee bars did sit at my table, lulled, off guard, because I seemed deeply absorbed in finishing the crossword puzzle of a respectable broadsheet. They chatted to me about poetry because they had noticed I was carrying the latest collection of Larkin. Then all I had to do was use one of my guru's chat up lines – 'Do you like jazz?' – and I was in. If I've become a bit of a cad myself I blame it on John Arthur Joseph O'Neill Elliot.

CHAPTER TEN

NUTCASE

I T WASN'T UNTIL 20 JULY 1957 THAT SUPERMAC HIMSELF TOLD US, IN A SPEECH AT BEDFORD FOOTBALL GROUND, THAT MOST OF US HAD NEVER HAD IT SO GOOD. Harold Macmillan was late saying it. I felt I'd had it good all the way through the 1950s. As soon as I started work in 1952 I began handing my mum a couple of pounds a week, but that still left me almost £2 for myself. In those days, for a young man free of all adult obligations, it seemed a small fortune.

Youth, for the first time, had money and was able to dip its bread in the gravy. Teenagers were regarded as a distinct group, often with more spending power than our parents. Most weeks I was able to put by £1, and there wasn't much doubt about what I'd spend the money on once I'd amassed enough.

This was the era of the eternally misunderstood, smouldering, soon-to-be deified James Byron Dean, when Marlon Brando was in his pre-barrage balloon days and still looked sleek and dangerous. Roaring around in black leather on motor bikes, or in Mod gear on motor scooters, was the way we could rebel and impose our wills on the adult world.

Unfortunately my plan to become a Brando-style Wild One and zoom around Southall on a high-powered bike got off to a false start. My parents were scared of the damage I might do to myself on a real motor bike, so, initially, they would only allow me to purchase a BSA wingwheel. This was an absurd little motor you encased within the rear wheel of a bicycle which augmented your pedalling with a puny amount of horsepower. It made me the laughing stock of Southall, Ealing and all points west. I remained a push-biker when what I wanted to be was a real biker with the full regulation leathers and lots of CCs under my throttle. The pathetic wingwheel made me disarmingly tame by comparison with the wild angel I saw myself as. My ludicrous appearance did nothing to disarm my mates though. They poured scorn on me whenever I ventured out in my gaberdine mac to tootle around the streets at a preposterous twenty miles an hour.

Big grins. Stepping out from behind trees. They'd wait near the crest of difficult hills and spring an ambush. Derisive shouts of: 'Roadhog!' would follow me as I chugged to the top, pink with embarrassment, trying to look unfazed, and failing. I took to leaving my bike and the infernal wingwheel in our shed and taking the bus everywhere, until I managed to persuade my parents to let me buy a real motor bike.

My parents' fears for my safety proved well-founded because I wrote off my first bike, an AJS 350CC scrambler, on Boxing Day 1955. Doing my full Brando rebel bit I refused to obey a red light near Southall Town Hall. I smacked into the side of a car and was thrown over its roof at about thirty miles an hour. I was fortunate enough to land on my feet before sprawling forward onto my outstretched arms. All I had to show for the accident were a couple of nasty grazes.

If I had pitched straight onto my head it would probably have been the end of me because I was wearing a helmet which didn't fit properly. It was a parachutist's tin hat I'd picked up at an army surplus store. The helmet described exactly what I was at that age. I'd painted the word 'Nutcase' right across the front of it.

My mates and I were all driven by the urgent necessity for intense speed. My next bike was even faster – a 500CC Triumph Speed Twin. We used to ride out to empty by-passes in outer suburbs and pretend it was the Isle of Man and we were Geoff Duke blazing round the TT circuit. Not minding where we went. Anywhere, so long as we could get there fast. Most of our jaunts would end up at the Ace of Spades, a bikers' cafe on the North Circular, where we'd linger over frothy coffees trying to look the business.

Roads were emptier. The fresh and pure sensation of flat-out velocity, so hard to imagine in today's clogged traffic, was easy to achieve. Sometimes I drive over familiar routes but fail to recognise them because once wide-open roads where we used to roar up to 100 miles an hour are now gridlocked bumper to bonnet.

In the winter it was like riding into an icy vacuum. My girlfriend, Valerie Taylor, would be on the pillion nuzzling into me, her face whipped by the wind. At weekends Box Hill in Surrey was a favourite destination. Valerie would sometimes arrive there so numb with cold she'd be unable to speak. I'd have to lift her off the pillion and pour two cups of hot tea into her to thaw her out. That's probably why our friendship lasted for more than two years. She was rarely warm enough to unlock her jaw and start an argument.

I eventually sold the Triumph, my helmet, and all my leathers to an old tumbling pal called Graham Tanner. One day, just after he bought it, Graham was sitting astride the bike parked up on the pavement in Southall High Street. He was wearing the helmet and a neckerchief tied over his face. A mate of mine, Dickie Birch, walked up to him, thought it was me, and said: 'Hello Trevor.'

Graham took off the neckerchief and replied: 'No, Dickie, it's me. Trevor's just sold me his motor bike.'

Dickie said: 'Well what's Valerie doing on the pillion? I thought she was Trevor's girlfriend.'

'She was,' Graham said. 'But Trevor threw her in with the bike.'

That's the way Dickie told the story to all our friends. The truth is slightly different. Valerie had a soft spot for Graham anyway. But, to be totally honest, she probably preferred the motor bike to either of us.

For months I had been scouring the small ads for a car so I could start driving lessons as soon as I was seventeen. I was just beaten to a 1921 Belsize open tourer. I wanted it for the registration number ND 1066. A week later I spotted a pre-war Austin Ten tourer in *Exchange and Mart* for £40 and snapped it up. For that money it was a fairly basic sort of vehicle, a tortoise of a car that I spent hours transforming into a hare. I jacked it up on bricks in the street outside our house and spent hours taking it apart, bathing all its innards lovingly in oil, and putting them all back together again. I took weeks adjusting and re-adjusting things to get every little judder of energy from the engine. After I'd finished souping up all the moving parts the car still made a noise like an over-excited sewing machine. But I loved her, and named her Janet.

She was a lovely old soul, full of character, and I customised her with a few odds and ends I picked up in a junk yard. She had a toilet seat strapped to the radiator, buffalo horns attached to the windscreen, and in the winter Janet's only source of warmth was a rubber hot water bottle labelled 'Heating'. I was strapped for cash at the time so for the first six months I displayed a Guinness label instead of a tax disc.

One night I managed to cram thirteen people into the car, most of them nurses from King Edward's Hospital, Ealing. We fitted everybody in somehow, interlocked, intimate, like human sardines. I was sharing the driver's seat with a bony girl who operated the gear stick with her left hand while I pressed the clutch and shouted to her: 'Third gear next. OK, one, two, three. Now.'

All I could see in the rear-view mirror was the face of one of the nurses who was wedged between the front seats. The lovely Jane Grey, heavy make up on eyes that would have won the heart of a lemur. A mate of mine, Mike Dodds, who is now a TV producer, had somehow got pinned into the back and was in a position where he was permanently looking behind us. (Mike went on to marry the wonderful Anne and their son Lawrence is my godson.)

'Watch out Trev,' he announced, 'there's a police car on our tail. Don't do anything to attract their attention.'

'Ferchrissakes Mike. There are thirteen of us in a five-seater car. If that doesn't attract their attention they must be blind.'

'They're still behind us,' he kept saying, punctuating his running commentary with cries of pain. 'Sod it, I've got cramp. They're still right behind us and there's two coppers in the car.'

As the car lurched and swayed across Ealing Common I tried to make sure I wasn't violating any regulations in the highway code.

My father, Cecil Archibald Walter Baylis, as a young lad.

Dad met my mum, Gladys Jane Brown, at a church-hall dance and it was love at first sight. They were married on 16 June 1934.

Born the day after the coronation of George VI, on 13 May 1937, I was my parents' first and last attempt at procreation.

I was baptised Trevor Graham. I later realised that very few people of note have been called Trevor ...

202 Lady Margaret Road, Southall Garden Village.

During the war I was too young to feel afraid of Hitler and his bombs, but exactly the right age always to feel hungry.

At the seaside: early family holidays on the coast were the root of my love of water and swimming. With me in the photo above are my mum and dad, my cousin Sheila and Auntie May.

My mother was a keen Thespian and is pictured here, second from the right, in a local amateur production. I'm sure I inherited my showmanship from her.

I was never a very good student, much to my mother's disappointment, though I discovered a talent for 'tinkering' and built my first engine when I was thirteen.

The other thing I was really good at was swimming and I won many trophies and medals and represented Britain in numerous international galas.

At Heston Swimming Club, with coach Ted Hardy (centre).

I'm standing on the trapeze and my great friend Johnny Pugh is hanging down. His father, Digger, soon had me dreaming of running away to join a circus.

Janet – my beloved car – and friends. I'm just visible in my deerstalker hat.

Perfecting our acrobatic and balancing skills in Johnny Pugh's back garden: Johnny is standing on my shoulders.

'Check your speed. Don't wander over the white line. Watch out for that cyclist. Who are you trying to kid Baylis? You're carrying twelve passengers in a car that's got a Guinness label stuck on the windscreen. How well you're driving isn't an issue.'

'They're pulling out and overtaking now.' It was Raymond Glendenning continuing his blow-by-blow summary from the back seat. 'They're waving us down Trev. I think they want you to stop.'

By now I knew they wanted me to stop because I could hear them ringing their bell. As the police car came alongside, the copper in the passenger seat was pointing his finger towards the kerb and inviting me to pull over. What made the situation even more absurd was the fact that I'd taken to wearing a loud check cloak and deer stalker, and smoking a droopy meerschaum pipe. (The influence of John Elliot again.) After the policemen had unpacked us from the car, counted us a couple of times, and got us all lined up on the pavement, the senior bloke produced his notebook and came over to me: 'All right Sherlock,' he said, 'give us the full S.P.'

We stood on the pavement, a group of sheepish youths, awash with Brylcreem, trying to look nonchalant, and lovely mascara'd panda-eyed girls, preening in their cotton blouses, paper nylon petticoats and stiletto heels, while the policemen did their job. They gave the car a thorough going-over, checking the treads on the tyres, lying on the pavement to look at the chassis, testing the springs, the lights and the windscreen wipers. They even lifted up the bonnet to examine the engine.

Of course one of the first things they spotted was the Guinness label stuck where the tax disc should have been. 'This label might be valid in Ireland, son,' the senior copper said, 'but it's illegal over here.'

They were a decent couple of blokes who were impressed by the car's condition. 'It's in very good nick for an old car,' the younger ginger-haired one said. 'Did you do all the work yourself?' They were both car fanatics and we ended up talking more about camshafts and spark plugs than we spent going over my motoring offences. They put the fear of god into me with the prospect of court appearances and big fines, but, apart from giving me a lecture, they took no action at all.

'Where are you all off to anyway?' By now the senior copper had put his notebook away.

I told him we were going to a party in Webster Gardens.

'That's only up the road,' he said. 'Tell your mates they'll have to walk the rest of the way. And don't even think about giving them all a lift home.'

I was so relieved I told them the party would be going on until the early morning. I gave them the number of the house and invited them to drop round after their shift if they fancied it, and, astonishingly, they both did. If all this sounds very Dixon of Dock Greenish, that's how things were in the 1950s. The friendly local copper who saw old ladies across the road and clipped delinquent lads around the ear really did exist. Over the years since then everyone, police and public, have become much more intemperate. That's one of the things I regret as I get older. These days you're likely to be spreadeagled against a wall and told: 'You're nicked,' just for forgetting to renew your library book.

I got hooked on jazz, with its hint of anarchy and art-school insurrection, and spent hours in record shops, or 'melody bars' as they called them, listening to obscure bands that were being re-formed by forgotten old men in New Orleans. It became a point of arcane dispute amongst us whether it was possible to tell the difference between Bunk Johnson's pre-false teeth and post-false teeth trumpet playing.

I used to drive for miles taking my mates to see the revivalist bands that were being formed over here, Mike Daniels's Delta Jazzmen, Denny Coffey and His Red Hot Beans, Mick Mulligan's Magnolia Jazz Band. We'd stand in the darkened back rooms of pubs in a hectic flush of beer, BO and California Poppy, eying up the crumpet while the musicians tried to convince us we were in the red light district of N'awlins during the Mardi Gras bacchanalia, instead of a Charringtons pub in Hounslow on a smoggy night in November.

Larkin got it wrong. Sexual intercourse didn't begin in 1963 between the end of the Chatterley ban and the Beatles' first LP. For some of us it started just after we'd heard Humphrey Lyttelton's 'Bad Penny Blues' and purchased our first CND badge. Although nobody uses the word any more, 'necking' still manages to make it into the dictionaries. 'Clasp one another round the neck, engage in amorous fondling.'

There was lots of amorous fondling in the Austin Ten. For nice girls necking was permissible, but anything further was severely discouraged. By the girls and their mothers, obviously. But principally it was discountenanced by the obdurate construction of their undergarments.

The most successful form of contraception in my youth was made of rubber. I'm not referring to the condom, I mean that impassable unmentionable the roll-on. My happy back-seat fumbling mostly fumbled no further than a passionate embrace because for years I never worked out how to get beyond the girdle. A girdle was unopenable, unfathomable, like a rubber Fort Knox. A horrible unaccommodating garment that snapped at your fingers, testy as a swamp alligator. Whoever invented it deserves to be strangled by her (or his) own pantie-girdle.

Until I was called up for my National Service in 1959 my most permanent relationship with a member of the opposite sex was with my car, Janet. Her finest hour came late in 1956 during the crisis that followed British, French and Israeli action against Gamal Abdel Nasser in the Suez Canal Zone. While the world raged against us, petrol was put on ration.

Anthony Eden's climb-down, our humiliating defeat, and Britain's new status as a second-class power was hardly a talking point among my friends. What we discussed long and ardently was, how were we going to get to Harrow to hear Ken Colyer's band when there was no petrol for my car?

My friends were very down until I reassured them that petrol wasn't the only liquid fuel you could use to drive a car. I gave them a little lecture about it. There were other explosive mixtures which, compressed in the cylinder and ignited by an electric spark, could make a gas which would expand and thrust the pistons downwards, and through the connecting rods impart a rotary motion to the crankshaft which would then drive the car.

'What have you got in mind?' asked Mike Dodds.

'I don't know yet,' I said, 'some sort of combustible juice. I'll have to do a few experiments.'

I went up to my dad's shed and began to mess about with formulae. Mike Dodds was there in his role of faithful ally, getting in the way.

I purloined a tumbler each of scotch and gin from my parents' drinks cupboard and mixed the alcohol with some turpentine and cleaning solvent. The smell was disgusting. But when I tried it out on the tiny engine of a model aeroplane it worked.

'But will it work on your car?' asked Mike.

'I don't see why not.'

'What if it ruins the engine?'

'In that case I can always strip it down and build another engine.'

We found three more people who wanted to hear Ken Colyer as much as we did. 'How badly do you want to go?' I asked them. 'Enough to buy a bottle of Scotch?'

They all did and I brewed up a potent cocktail from five bottles of Johnny Walker, some turpentine, amyl acetate and a drop of Castrol R oil.

It worked. After a few stutters of complaint I managed to get the engine going with the starting handle. Janet got us there and back, sounding very ragged, groaning like buggery and belching out clouds of smoke, but nippy as ever.

'She's a bit like us,' I said to Mike. 'Quicker on liquor.'

CHAPTER ELEVEN
WE DID IT HIS WAY

AT MY NATIONAL SERVICE MEDICAL I WAS DECLARED A1. It happened like this. I stood in a long line of naked mothers' sons before a man in a white coat who claimed to be an army doctor. He didn't look like one. For all we knew the man in the white coat could have walked in from the bacon counter at Sainsbury's in Ealing. He displayed a rather approximate and cavalier grasp of the science of human anatomy. He went in for asking questions about one part of your body while he was meticulously examining another.

'Show me your tongue,' he said.

I showed him my tongue and he poked it with one of those lolly stick things and looked down my throat. 'Any history of piles?'

He removed the lolly stick and I spoke: 'You can't see them from there can you?'

He gave a little sneer of a laugh, and said: 'Watch it son. Underneath this white coat I'm still an officer.'

He took hold of my testicles. 'Any history of mental break-down?'

'Not lately sir.'

'Don't try to be funny. Hearing?'

'Pardon?'

'You're not taking the mickey are you son?'

'No sir.'

'Can you hear my watch ticking?'

'No sir.'

'Good, I'm not wearing one. Recent illnesses?'

'I had a virus the other week sir.'

'Virus? You're not a malingerer are you son?'

'No sir'.

'Have you left a sample?'

'Not yet sir.'

'Good. Pass some water before you go.'

'Yes sir.'

'You look right as rain to me. But you'll be notified of your medical grade in due course,' the quack said.

As I walked back to where my clothes were piled on a chair, he was parting someone's buttocks and asking: 'Are you colour-blind?'

It was 1959 in a drill hall in Acton. I'd been summoned there by a buff-coloured letter informing me that in accordance with the National Service Act I was required to submit myself to examination by a medical board. When I put my clothes back on I had to complete a twenty-minute written test. It asked me questions like: 'What is the next number in the sequence two-five-eight?' It was obviously designed to weed out brigadiers from potential privates in the Pioneer Corps. I toyed with answering the question: £1.10s. 6d., but I didn't want to end up a brigadier so I took the exam seriously.

Five weeks later I got my enlistment notice and a three-shilling third-class rail warrant from Southall to Chichester. I'd been selected to do my basic training with the Royal Sussex Regiment at Roussillon Barracks and was told to report there on 5 November. It was a Thursday; all new intakes started their army life on Thursdays.

I was out of step as soon as I got inside the main gates. The bloke checking off a list asked me my name. 'Baylis, mate,' I said. 'I'm not your mate,' he replied with feeling. 'See these stripes, they mean I'm Sergeant to you.'

Being an only child I'd been brought up as a bit of a mother's boy. She cleaned my shoes, did my washing, pampered me. She'd bring me a cup of tea and a biscuit in bed at seven in the morning and if she thought I looked like I needed a few more hours, she'd let me lie in until eleven and ring work to say I was off colour. I'd come to rely on her large maternal presence – she had hips like a front row forward in her middle years. Her fussing and affection had become my cushion against life's discontents. But I soon learned that a soldier's best friend is not his mother, it's his rifle, and the news came as a bit of a shock.

I became aware that army life wasn't going to be like home in the Quartermaster's stores when I was being issued with my kit. 'Gentlemen, if any of this stuff fits you then you must be deformed,' we were told. I was stuffing my drawers: cellular, green, other ranks, two pairs; and my blouse: battledress, khaki, other ranks, one; into my kitbag: shapeless, heavy, other ranks, one: when the question of footwear came up.

'Boots?' the Lance Corporal said. 'What size?'

'If it's all right with you I'd prefer a shoe,' I said politely, 'and I take a seven-and-a-half.'

The Lance Corporal glanced at the culprit who'd had the temerity to speak. It was like the scene in the workhouse where Oliver Twist asks for more. He exchanged looks with the Quartermaster who was standing one pace behind him.

The Quartermaster viewed me with the deepest suspicion and spoke, not to me, but the back of the Lance Corporal's pitted neck. 'Lance Corporal Ewence I think you're dealing with the sort of person Doctor Spooner would have referred to as a shining wit. Tell him that unless he's excused boots there's no such thing in Her Majesty's Army as shoes, let alone half sizes.'

The Lance Corporal gave me a pair of size eight boots. As I moved down the line the Quartermaster muttered: 'Christ, they'll be asking for suede brothel creepers next.' I didn't say anything, I was still trying to work out who the hell Doctor Spooner was.

I made another ricket after I had collected my bedding and was scuffing along a corridor with my kitbag in one hand and a mattress balanced on my head. I saw someone with a stripe on his sleeve and asked: 'Is someone going to show me to my room now?'

He went so red in the face I thought he was going to rupture a major artery. He said the word room three times, increasing the volume each time. Then he said it again. 'Room! This isn't the Ritz Hotel. You're in the Royal Sussex Regiment now. Where do you think you are, on your daddy's yacht?'

I found the way to my Nissen hut. There was a stove in the middle of the barrack, hardly big enough to take a shovelful of coke. The place was draughty, permanently cold, and had the same cheery ambience as a public convenience. The air was blue with swearing and Player's Navy Cut. My comrades in arms were huddled on their beds, acned, whey-faced and miserable looking. A radio tuned to Luxembourg was playing the week's number one record. 'Travellin' Light' by Cliff and the Shadows. There was one free bed at the end of the room and I took it.

The bloke in the next bed said he was Benjamin Evans. He was painfully thin, his face the sort of deathly white that made you think he'd just given his pallbearers the slip. I told him my name. 'I'm from Wales,' he replied, 'but you probably guessed that already.' His accent had 'Land of my Fathers' written all the way through it like a stick of Aberystwyth rock.

I put my kit into some sort of order and made my bed. I tied up all my civilian belongings in a brown paper parcel and addressed it to my mother. It was a symbolic moment. I was wrapping up my old life and sending it home to mum. I was no longer an individual, I was a number: 23648702. I sat on my bed keeping very quiet. Adam Faith was now on the radio singing: 'What do you want?' Well for a start, I didn't want to be there. All I could think about was the two years of army service that loomed before me like a high dark hill. I still had 730 days to go.

Just when I was thinking things couldn't get any worse, they did.

Our orderly, Corporal Greer, made his cheery presence felt by entering the hut and laying down a withering barrage of four letter words. Over the next five weeks he was frequently to take the name of the Almighty in vain and amaze us with his effortless command of profanity. He had raised the use of bad language to an art form. Four letter words peppered his every utterance in a sullen, repetitive and brutish way. He managed to create whole sentences in which swear words, stripped of any sexual connotation, were used as noun, verb, adjective, and adverb. I once heard him tell the Regimental Sergeant Major: 'Sergeant, the fookin' fookwit fookin' fooked the fooker.' He was talking about a rifle that one of us had managed to jam.

The purpose of his visit was to inform us that he was a stickler for getting things absolutely right. 'In the army there are two ways of doing things,' he announced, 'the wrong way, and my way.' All through our basic training he never let us forget he wanted things doing: 'My way.' Long before Old Blue Eyes took up the refrain, 'My Way' was Corporal Greer's unwavering theme.

He looked around the room with a glance of utter disdain. 'What do you fookin' think this fookin' place is? A fookin' Chinese brothel? Get it tidied.' He then demonstrated how everything, from the lacing of our boots to the making of our beds would have to be done 'My Way'. He began our introduction to the rampant and completely arbitrary rules of army life. How we had to stamp our army numbers on the lower left hand brace of our braces, not the right one. How we had to fold our sheets and blankets every morning in a certain symbolic way. How vital it was to keep the hut's coal scuttle highly polished.

'But why Corporal?' Poor old Evans asked the question that all of us were thinking about.

Greer approached him with a gleam of triumph in his eyes. The bully had found the prey he was to fasten his claws into for the duration of our basic training.

'Who the fook are you?'

'Evans sir.'

'Don't call me fookin' sir, I'm only a fookin' corporal.'

'Sorry Corporal.'

'Listen to me Evans. Over the next fookin' five weeks you're going to learn how to do things my fookin' way. And what fookin' word isn't in my fookin' vocabulary Evans?'

'I don't know Corporal.'

'The fookin' word why.'

After Greer had fooked off we all shuffled down to the cookhouse for our evening meal. It was stewed leeks with a topping of congealed and rubbery cheese.

I sat next to Evans and tried to cheer him up. 'This grub should be right up your street Taff.'

'Why's that?

'Leeks. Your national emblem.'

'I've never tasted them before.'

The conscripts playing with, then pushing away, their mess tins of lukewarm vulcanised leeks had arrived at the depot looking like a typical cross section of British youth. Former public schoolboys wearing cravats wanting to put their names down as soon as possible for officer training and daddy's old regiment. Teddy boys with tattoos and duck's arse haircuts trying to look streetwise. Skilled tradesmen, Borstal boys, married men with a couple of kids at home, illiterates, layabouts and graduates. Now we all looked the same in our scratchy uniforms and sadistic hair cuts: apprehensive, utterly fed up, beginning to feel the dull pain of army life and the inoculations we'd had that afternoon.

Evans hadn't enjoyed his first taste of the Welsh national emblem. 'Come on Ben,' I said to him. 'My mum gave me a couple of quid when I left home. I'll buy you a beer in the NAAFI. 'You're not teetotal are you?'

'No,' he said, 'I'm not that Welsh.'

I bought us a couple of Cream Label stouts. We poured them slowly to a rich head. Ben told me he was a butcher in civvie street and engaged to be married. 'It's a bugger this National Service. I can't save for the wedding or anything. And I'm worried about affording the fares home. I've heard we only get two free rail warrants a year.'

I started to read some of the bumph that had come with my two army bibles, my AB 634, part one, my Soldiers' Service Book, and part two, my pay book.

'How much are we paid?' he asked.

'About thirty bob a week,' I told him, 'that's what it amounts to after deductions.'

'Christ, I'll never get home.' Poor old Taff stared at his boot toes and looked like a chained collie. I got us some more Cream Labels. By the end of the evening I'd spent most of mum's two pounds and we were both bloated and quietly pissed.

When we got back to the Nissen hut a few of the lads who considered themselves officer material were working on their boots. When they are issued the leather of army boots is pimpled and dull. Army lore requires recruits to burn off the pimples with a heated spoon and then work in layer after layer of polish, shining the surface until the boots gleam as black as the seven ball on a snooker table. The fact that this renders them completely useless as waterproof footwear is neither here nor there. Military equipment isn't meant to be useful, it's meant to dazzle the enemy with an unsullied sheen.

All the eager beavers were spitting on their toe caps and rubbing the polish in tiny circles hoping to impress Corporal Greer. The rest of the billet were getting ready to settle down for the night. A few blokes were already asleep, some were sitting on their beds writing letters home, the other half dozen were crowded round the radio listening to pop music, pretending they were in a coffee bar somewhere, anywhere but Roussillon Barracks.

One of the music lovers was sitting on Taff's bed, clicking his fingers and trying to look flash. He was one of the ex-teddy boys. He was named Warren and liked to be called Bunny. He was muscular, running to fat. A lairy, lippy and sourfaced South Londoner who thought he was a hard case. Ever since the army barber had run the clippers through his Tony Curtis, he'd been spoiling to take it out on somebody.

Taff asked him to move.

'In my own good time,' he said, 'this is my favourite record.'

He'd noticed how the Corporal had picked on Evans and he too had marked him out as a victim.

'But that's my bed,' Taff said politely.

'I know it is.'

Taff didn't quite know what to do. He went to his locker and fiddled about, pretending to put his gear in order.

Bunny remained sitting on the bed, grinning in triumph at his pals. Another record came on the radio. He stayed where he was.

'You said you were going to move.' Taff was hovering at the end of the bed.

'No I didn't,' coming it for his mates, 'this record's another favourite of mine.'

While all this was going on I'd gone back to my space and was lying on my bed. I thought maybe I'd better show willing and Brasso my buckles and buttons. But then I thought better of it and lit my pipe. I'd just about got it fired up when there was a commotion around Taff's bed.

'I want to get my head down.' By this time Taff's voice was pleading. His pasty face had gone a blotchy red and he was on the edge of tears.

'You'll just have to wait, won't you?'

I took the pipe out of my mouth and said very quietly: 'Why don't you pick on somebody your own size?'

Warren looked at me and said for the benefit of his mates: 'Christ, who's the fugging toff with the pipe?'

By this time I'd had enough of the army and Bunny for one day. I got off my bed, walked over to where he was sitting and nutted him. He went down, poleaxed, disappearing into the space between two beds. When he stood up there was so much blood pouring from his nose it looked like I'd hit him with a shovel.

There was a sudden hush in the room. Bunny said: 'I was only having a laugh mate.' Then he staggered out to the wash-house to clean himself up.

I went back to bed and smoked my pipe until lights out.

The next morning Warren had a nasty cut on his nose, a black eye and was very subdued. When Corporal Greer saw the injuries he gave him an old-fashioned look. Nobody said anything. And the funny thing was, by the end of the week, five other blokes had taken up pipe smoking.

CHAPTER TWELVE

A LACK OF
MILITARY BEARING

O UR CHEERLESS BARRACK ROOM WAS COLD, NOISY AND INSANITARY. It was like trying to sleep in an icebox against a continuous broadside of snoring and farting. Every morning we'd be woken at six with the same cheery reveille: 'Wakey, wakey. Hands off cocks and on socks.' Urged on by the Corporal's obscenities we'd spend the next sixteen hours until lights out in a daze of frenzied cleaning, pointless chores, drill, physical training, map reading, field craft, weapons instruction, and education.

The education consisted mostly of hideously graphic medical films. There was one detailed Technicolor study of venereal disease which reduced even Warren and his guffawing mates to shocked silence.

When the lights came up Taff looked paler than ever. 'Trev,' he said, 'that's the best argument I've ever seen in favour of pocket billiards.'

If Greer, like most corporals at basic training, was harsh, the man who gave him lessons in malevolence was Sergeant Kavanagh. He was a mulberry-faced fusspot with an obsession about the state of our webbing. He made you feel that the only thing keeping the Tartar hordes behind the Iron Curtain was the deterrent value of our immaculately blancoed webbing.

At one inspection he stood behind me and I could feel his breath on my neck as he bent close to inspect my turn out.

'What's all this filth Baylis?'

'I don't know, Sergeant.'

'I'm talking about your kit Baylis. Did you clean your webbing?'

'Yes, Sergeant.'

'When? Last week? It's absolutely, diabolically filthy.'

'But I cleaned it last night, Sergeant.'

'Excrement of the ungulate, Baylis.' He enunciated each word, savouring its texture.

'Pardon me, Sergeant.'

'Bullshit.'

Most of the time I got by without attracting too much flak, though my style of marching did not meet Sergeant Kavanagh's strict aesthetic demands. Once our squad was pounding up and down the parade square trying to master an intricate turning manoeuvre when he happened to catch sight of me. 'Christ,' he screamed, 'swing your right arm properly Baylis, or I'll tear it off, stick it up your arse and have you for a toffee apple.'

Taffy laughed so much he tripped himself up and fell over. And we all had to stay out on the square for an extra hour of drill.

Although the state of my uniform generally left a lot to be desired, I kept forgetting to salute the officers, and I was absent-minded in the 'Sir' department, by the time the passing out parade came round I'd got used to taking orders from loud-mouthed dipsticks. After a while all their sarcasm and abuse washed over me. They still shouted the odds, but I'd learned to turn a deaf ear.

My swimming training had made me very fit, so the physical part of the course was a breeze. I used to annoy Corporal Greer by winning all the cross-country runs. Once I came in so far ahead of the others he thought I'd taken a short cut and made me run the course again, this time with him beside me making sure I took the correct route. Though I'd been round once already, I ran shoulder to shoulder with him all the way. Long before the last half mile he was breathing like a man about to make a dirty phone call, but I eased up about 100 yards from home and let him pull away and win. He never let me forget he'd beaten me. But after that, apart from the ritual swearing, he was the pussy-cat purring, and I could do no wrong.

On the day of my initial services medical in Acton I'd had a long chat with a military type who asked me what branch of the forces I preferred. I'd told him the RAF. He said that was an excellent choice, and asked me why I wanted to become a Brylcreem boy. It was then I made my mistake. 'I think it will be a lot cushier than the army,' I said. His face clouded over. He wrote something against my name, and said I would be hearing from the Board in due course.

So I should have known better when, towards the end of my basic training, I was asked to attend a selection interview for the Intelligence Corps. I didn't know what the Intelligence Corps did but it sounded a cushy number. Why they'd selected me as a potential candidate, one of three in our intake, was also a mystery. The other two were men with university degrees and three languages between them. Thus far in my army career my only manifestation of cerebral activity was a couple of attempts at *The Times* crossword puzzle.

I was interviewed by an officer with a double-barrelled name who was the spitting image of the late Malcolm Muggeridge. He had receding hair and such a bulging forehead he seemed the embodiment of a man whose brains had gone to his head.

We chatted in a desultory way about my interests. I said I liked jazz and that seemed to strike a chord with him. We talked about Louis Jordan's Tympany Five and his 1951 hit 'Saturday Night Fish Fry'. It was beginning to look like I filled the bill. If all it took to get into the Intelligence Corps was an ability to talk about jump blues saxophonists, I was home and hosed. But then he asked me why I wanted to join the Intelligence Corps.

'Well I suppose the shoulder flash has got a lot to do with it,' I supposed.

'What do you mean?'

'I'd imagine a uniform with the word "Intelligence" sewn on the shoulders is quite good for picking up certain types of birds.'

He looked at me as though I'd made an attempt to steal the regimental silver.

'For some girls the idea of going out with a bloke in the Intelligence Corps could be a big turn-on. They don't like to think they're getting involved with a dickhead do they?' I said.

'I wouldn't know,' Malcolm Muggeridge's face clouded over. He wrote something against my name, and said I would be hearing in due course. I didn't get in.

I doubt whether I would have got very far even if I had been inducted into the mysteries of the Intelligence Corps because my political opinions at the time were such that all the NCOs had me labelled a red. Without really knowing much about political theory, two years earlier I had declared myself a Marxist. A strong whiff of Communism gave you a distinct edge with certain types of arty girls who used to frequent jazz clubs wearing CND badges. Although my Marxism was closer to Chico, Harpo and Groucho than it was to Karl, Vladimir Ilyich and Che; not having many earthly goods I wanted to share them with the world.

My girlfriend at the time was a ravishing student from Austria called Geri Mayer, whom I'd met the year before when she was on holiday in England. She had given me a tiny framed photograph of herself to hang on the dashboard of my car with the message: 'Denk an mich fahr vorsichtig,': 'Think of me while you're driving.' I'd fixed it to my locker in the billet at Roussillon Barracks. One day the Padre was doing his rounds, checking out whether the squaddies' views on the Trinity were doctrinally sound, when Geri's photo caught his eye.

'Who's this?' he asked me.

'My girlfriend, Padre. She's Austrian.'

'Fraternising with the enemy, eh?'

'The war ended fourteen years ago, Padre.'

'I know, I was there.'

After our passing out parade most of my intake were split up. Taff was happy because he was going on a drivers' course, closer to Wales. 'Look both ways before you hit something,' I said as we made our goodbyes, and I never saw him again.

I'd been selected to do a course at the Eastern Command physical training depot at Shorncliffe, near Folkestone. After the initial shock of bull and square bashing, National Service settles down to twenty-two months of calendar watching. When an army isn't fighting there's nothing to do but wait, and waiting is a boring business. Rather than idle away the rest of my time in the forces learning how to look busy while doing absolutely nothing, I thought I might as well try to do something I would enjoy. So I put in for an ACCI course to become a physical training instructor.

There were two competing platoons on the course at Shorncliffe. I was in 72B. You were paired off with a bloke from the other platoon who was roughly your size and weight so you'd have a rival in the various athletic activities. I was put up against an amiable bloke called Brian Ackerley.

We were just about evenly matched when it came to gymnastics, weight lifting, and running. In the swimming I could beat him by half a length in all the strokes without exerting myself. My big bugbear was boxing. We used to do everything timed to three-minute rounds. Three minutes of skipping. Then a bell would go for a minute's rest. Then three minutes on the heavy bag. More rest. Three minutes of sit-ups. A breather. Then a session on the speed ball. I enjoyed that part, AOK, but the session always ended with the two of you getting into the ring for a scrap, and, sod's law, Brian was the Amateur Boxing Association Southern Area welterweight boxing champion.

I was proficient at judo and unarmed combat. But for some reason, although I'm a championship-class shadow boxer, whenever there is a real live opponent in the ring with me I'm absolutely hopeless with my fists. The fact that I'm a southpaw might have had something to do with it. Every time Brian came towards me, snorting out his breath sharply through his nose the way boxers do, I had no clue at all about how to defend myself.

After a few days of each other's company Brian and I had become good mates. We used to escape from the camp whenever we could wangle it, take a bus to Folkestone and sit in a pub called The Cherry Pickers eating crab sandwiches. But each time we climbed into the ring the Company Sergeant Major Instructor (CSMI) would insist that Brian put on a good show. He even called people up to the ring to watch the savagery.

Whenever he caught me with a meaty punch, which was most times, Brian's instinct was to back away and let me recover. Meanwhile, just outside the ropes there would be the eager CSMI, Dick Gradley, blood-lust in his eyes, urging him in for the kill. Brian would come at me saying 'Sorry' each time he got me with a solid hit. An uppercut to the nose: 'Sorry about that Trev.' A straight right to the temple: 'Sure you're all right mate?' A left hook right on the button. 'Go into a clinch, Trev. I'll hold you up.'

There would be songbirds flying out of my ears, light bulbs going out in my mind, and all the while dear old Brian would be looking apologetic and trying his best to punch me friendly. Once, though, I did have him down on one knee. He was bending over me to see if I was still breathing.

After three weeks, just before permanent brain damage set in, I was switched to Queen's Barracks, Aldershot to complete the course there. Boxing didn't have such a high priority on the curriculum and I qualified half way down the list. After nine weeks away I returned to the Royal Sussex Regiment as an ACCI (physical training instructor). Promoted to the rank of Lance Corporal, they put me on a boat to Belfast and I did the rest of my National Service there.

Serving in Northern Ireland at the start of the 1960s was like being sent on one long outward bound course. I was able to get superbly fit, and spent a lot of time out in the fresh air and invigorating dankness of the rich green countryside. For eighteen months I was rarely out of my waterproofs.

The Unionist and Nationalist communities eyed each other suspiciously across the divides between their segregated neighbourhoods. But this was before the Troubles dislocated everyday life. There were no bombs or punishment shootings, armoured vehicles patrolling in a hail of missiles, or watchful squaddies on street corners with fingers on the triggers of guns.

A soldier in a British uniform was eyed watchfully. Even in civvies if you asked for a pint with an English accent in a republican bar it was a bit like a Western where a stranger in town wanders into the saloon. The place would go deathly quiet and the barman tried to avoid your eye. But you were served your shot of red-eye, eventually, and no one tried to draw on you.

If ever strangers attempted to bring up religion and asked me what faith I was I'd pretend to be an agnostic toying with Buddhism. I figured they wouldn't be inclined to harm anybody whose beliefs wouldn't permit him to harm a fly.

My job at Palace Barracks in Holywood was to take the knock-kneed, weedy, round-shouldered, skinny, fat, flaccid, asthenic weaklings who made up the pride of our battalion there and turn them into hard men. It was a task that involved lots of yelling and shouting, and for a while I felt as though I was mutating into the diabolical Corporal Greer. But then I got a grip on myself and reverted to the scruffy and unorthodox me.

During the week I'd work on the men's fitness, doing physical jerks, urging them round the assault course, teaching them unarmed combat, and how to survive by living off the land. At weekends I was supposed to keep them on their toes with activities like canoeing, pot-holing, orienteering and rock-climbing. It was like being a matey Red Coat in an establishment that was half Borstal Institution and half lunatic asylum.

One of the most difficult jobs was teaching young muscle-headed squaddies how to kill each other with their bare hands without actually ending up with half a dozen warm corpses on the gymnasium floor. I'd show them how to take out an opponent with the least amount of expense. 'Get your finernails in right behind their ears. Fine. Now press your thumbs deep into the eye sockets. Got it so far? Right. Now press the thumbs in still further and rotate. No Gill, don't bloody well actually do it. Private Postlethwaite is down to play scrum half for the Company XV tomorrow and we need him.'

The physical training instructors used to act as the enemy whenever the battalion went out on manoeuvres. Before every scheme the planners would consult the long-range weather forecast. Invariably it predicted rain, and in eighteen months it was never wrong. We'd all be trucked out in atrocious weather to somewhere remote, the Mourne or Sperrin Mountains, and play at being muddy soldiers for a week.

The troops would be told to target our base. They'd be given a map reference and come hunting for us. Our job would be to locate them, harass their flanks, and take a few prisoners. The poor bloody infantrymen would be living out of their packs, surviving off dehydrated rations and mountain water, sleeping in their bivvy bags, unable to do much more than nap, and having a thoroughly miserable time.

Their enemies would be better prepared. We had it down to a fine art. We'd bring tents, a few beers, and set up camp well away from the reference point the squaddies had been given. We'd hunt them across country, all gung-ho, and take them out with salvoes of thunder-flashes and stun grenades. Our little raids would be timed just before light when they'd be thoroughly pissed off by the conditions and softened up by the gnawing damp.

I once slithered around the edge of a bog and got to within a dozen yards of twenty soldiers. I could hear them effing and blinding to each other other in the dark.

'Any of you lads fancy a cup of tea and a nice hot pie?' I whispered.

Their answer was a volley of foul language.

'No, I'm serious lads,' I assured them. 'There's a nice dry tent only a quarter of a mile away. There's a brew going and we've got some Ormeau Bakery pies.'

'You serious Trev?'

'Never more so.'

I persuaded the twenty infantrymen to jack it in, and we stumbled across the sodden fields back to my tent. After they'd had their tea and a bite of pie, I gave them the bad news. 'Oh by the way,' I said, 'you're all dead.'

'Oh no we're not.'

'Oh yes you are. The pies were poisoned.'

'Don't be so bloody stupid.'

'OK, but you're still dead.'

'But that's not fair though.'

'I know. War never is fair. You've got two choices lads. Either you can complain to the umpire, or you can all stay here and have another cup of tea.'

They grumbled about dirty tactics for a while, but the dead men stayed on all night drinking my tea.

As I was in charge of adventure training I was able to indent the MoD (Ministry of Defence) for all sorts of supplies, just as long as I could prove they were all being used primarily for the soldiers' recreation. The wheels of army bureaucracy may wind very slowly, but they do wind, as I soon discovered when I began to place my long list of orders. If I could persuade someone in authority to sign my chitties, in triplicate, in the right places, nobody ever questioned what I was doing.

The secret was to camouflage the big items deep in the manifest amongst relentless pages of cheap and insignificant components. So after a long list of routine orders for nuts, quarter inch, fifty; woodscrews, two inch, brass, 500; eyelets, steel, three inch, twenty and a confusion of bolts, rivets, tintacks, nails, clamps and hinges, I'd suddenly hit them with the big one: capstan lathe, one. It worked. The CO, Lieutenant Colonel Pip Newton, was a busy man who could barely tell a jackhammer from a jackrabbit. I'd perfected the art of misleading him, and as long as I chose the right moment to ambush him, he'd been known to sign anything that was put under his nose.

One day I was sitting in my little office, the adventure hut it was called. I was having my elevenses when Terry Smith, one of the corporals from the guard room, came bounding in at the double.

'Trev, where do you want them to unload all your stuff, mate?'

'What stuff?'

'The stuff you ordered for the adventure club.'

'Just drop it outside. I'll get the lads to take it over to my workshop later.'

'But there's tons of it Trev. A convoy of lorries turned up at the main gate asking for you.'

'Is this some sort of wind-up, Terry?'

'If you don't believe me come and look for yourself.'

Sure enough, there were three three-ton trucks parked outside the guard house laden with gear – all the machine tools I'd ordered, a lathe, welding equipment, drills, circular saws, and a load of woodworking tools, plus timber and canvas for making canoes, ropes and climbing gear, aqualungs and diving kit. The works. There was even a box of safety helmets.

There was so much stuff I had to call out half a company to help unload it. As we were manhandling it all into my workshop and store room the CO came by and stopped for a chat.

'Baylis, you've got enough gear there to open your own factory,' Pip said.

'Yes, sir.'

'When's the first tank going to roll off the production line?'

All the men dutifully laughed at his joke and I said: 'We're going to be making some equipment for the adventure club, canoes and stuff like that. And a few of the men wanted to try to build a couple of go-karts.'

'Jolly good,' he said, 'carry on.' And I took that as the go ahead to keep on ordering materials.

I snorkelled as a boy and learned scuba-diving with mates from my swimming club, and now it all came in handy when I took up pot-holing. There are some awe-inspiring underground systems in Northern Ireland and along with a couple of mates, Private Derek 'Paddy' Lock, and an officer, Lieutenant Tom Enfield, we began to explore the limestone cave network in Fermanagh called the 'Marble Arch System'. Tom's real name was Thomas Byng, a descendant of one of the most distinguished military commanders during the Peninsular War. He was a Viscount, but he told us not to bother with the title.

We made an odd trio. The officer, Eton and Cambridge, with a coat of arms and a motto: 'I will defend', and two council-house other ranks. But we got on famously. With a group of students from Queen's University, Belfast, we were the first people fully to survey and map the Marble Arch System. The project got full backing from the army who provided us with inflatables and all the gear and apparatus we needed.

Some people have an irrational fear of penetrating deep underground. The thought of being trapped in a dark narrow gully as the water rises is a nightmare vision that keeps many safely on the surface. But the sharp surprise of squeezing up a narrow spout and suddenly tracing, in the shimmering light of your carbide lamp, the outline of a magnificent cathedral of limestone columns is one of the most enchanting moments of exploration I've ever experienced. For me it surpasses even the view from the top of a mountain, with the advantage that, deep underground, there is no wind buffeting around your ears.

Paddy, Tom and I used to spend most weekends working our way through the uncharted labyrinth of rimstone pools (pools formed when deposits in the water build up dams), crystal caves, vadose canyons, and causeways. Looking back at the primitive gear we used it's a wonder we all survived. We didn't have one wetsuit between us and I used to swim in my army denims. I'd spend ten minutes underwater plunging through icy pools trying to find an opening in the sump that might lead on to the next chamber. By the time Paddy and Tom hauled me back to their perch on a rock ledge I'd be blue with cold.

Once we were exploring a waterfall trying to discover whether there was a way through the system at the bottom of the narrow chute. We had a wire ladder which we slung down through the cascading water. They roped me up and sent me over the edge into the blackness. I got down about half-way before the cold got to me and I blew three times on my whistle for them to haul me up. 'It's like Niagara Falls down there,' I said. 'Cold as a witch's tit.'

Paddy went next. He got down further than me, but then called to come up because he was chilled to the bone.

Paddy and I were ready to pack it in for the day, but Tom wanted a go.

We tied the rope to him. 'Don't take any chances,' Paddy said. 'It's a bit iffy down there.' Tom gave us the thumbs up, and disappeared into the cascade. We made sure the rope was secure and braced ourselves as we watched him descend, his light shining up through the water. A few minutes later the rope stopped moving. 'I've reached the bottom of the ladder. There's still quite a drop below me. I'd better come up,' Tom shouted.

We kept the rope taut as he climbed a few feet up the ladder. Suddenly there was a tremendous jerk. The rope burned through our hands as we tried to slow his descent. The force of the water had taken Tom off the ladder. He was in free fall. We held on desperately as the rope ran out.

'Christ Almighty!' said Paddy, 'he's either hit the bottom or knocked himself out on the rock face.'

We shouted his name down the booming cataract. There was no reply. The two of us passed through a series of rapid emotions about the flak we'd get for having an officer go belly up on us. We could dimly see Tom's light way below us. We shouted his name again. This time he replied.

It was a nightmare pulling Tom's weight the twenty feet back to the ladder. We had to strain our nuts getting him back to where he could start climbing for himself. By the time he'd climbed and we'd pulled him back to the top of the waterfall we were all dead beat, our heads reeling from the effort.

Tom looked like a drowned rat, but apart from that he was serviceable. 'I'm grazed all over,' he said, 'but it could have been worse. Luckily there was a pool at the bottom to break my fall.'

Tom was a marvellous bloke, more like a pal than an officer. Since those carefree days in Northern Ireland he's succeeded to the family title and is now the eighth Earl of Strafford. He was always taking me to task, in his urbane and thoroughly polite way, about my lack of military bearing. He said I managed to reduce a quick march to a slow amble, and used to get courteously exasperated whenever I forgot to salute him. 'Well Baylis,' he once said, 'for a change you did remember to acknowledge me. But I think even you would admit that it was much more of a cheery wave than a salute.'

All the equipment the CO had airily signed for more than proved its value. I trained up a few of the blokes in basic engineering skills and between us we built a four-seater speedboat made from plywood and an old Ford V8 engine. It was one of the star exhibits at the Northern

Ireland Command arts and crafts exhibition at Holywood barracks and was singled out for special praise by the Chief Education Officer, Lieutenant Colonel C.H. Davies.

His praise came too soon. After the exhibition we took the boat down to Belfast harbour for its sea trials. We launched it down a ramp and gently eased it out on to a stretch of open water. I opened up the throttle and we shot across the harbour at such a lick you would have thought we were attempting to break the water speed record. After about 100 yards there was an ominous thump, the boat bounced a couple of times on the water, and broke up. We all had to swim for it. By the time we got to the harbour wall all we could see of our boat was a patch of oil and a few bits of plywood floating on the surface. The V8 engine had gone straight to the bottom. I figured the plywood hull we'd built simply wasn't strong enough to cope with the power of the engine. As I increased speed the tremendous vibration had shaken our flimsy hull to pieces.

'What happened?' one of the blokes asked as we stood shivering on the quayside.

'Don't ask me, mate,' I said, 'I'm not in the navy.'

Our next project was more successful. We built a couple of go-karts, turning some of the components on our lathe and using two old scrap motors as a source of spare parts. The battalion was so proud of our efforts that when the Minister of Defence, John Profumo, made an official visit to our barracks my group was wheeled out to demonstrate the go-karts for him.

A couple of us raced the go-karts round the parade ground and squealed to a halt in front of the Colonel and the Minister of Defence.

'It's jolly good fun,' I said to John Profumo, 'why don't you have a go?' He couldn't really say no, so after I'd talked the Minister and the Colonel through the controls they both zoomed off on a test run around the parade square.

Afterwards Lieutenant Enfield approached me in his usual diffident way and said that he wanted a word. 'It all went very well, Baylis,' he said, 'and the Minister was extremely pleased. But just one small point of etiquette. When you are speaking to the Minister of Defence you must always call him "Sir". You could also refer to him as Minister, or even Mr Profumo. But you should never do as you did and call him John, or even worse, mate. Got that, Baylis?'

'Yes, sir.'

'Jolly good.'

'And by the way, the Colonel wants to see you tomorrow morning.'

When I went up in front of the Colonel the next day he asked me: 'Baylis, who is running this Regiment, you or me?'

'You sir.'

'You wouldn't have thought that yesterday. You practically ordered the Minister of Defence into that go-kart.'

'I'm sorry sir.'

'We thoroughly enjoyed ourselves. But a word of advice. In future try not to take over the show.'

'No, sir.'

CHAPTER THIRTEEN

JUST THE SORT OF CHAP WE NEED

I T WAS FRIDAY AFTERNOON, ABOUT FOUR O'CLOCK, THE WEEK'S WORK DONE, THOSE WITH FORTY-EIGHT-HOUR PASSES ALREADY ON THE ROAD HOME, TIME TO KILL. Although I'd been through it once already I decided to check my paperwork again. It had taken me twenty-two months in the army to learn how to do nothing intelligently.

The phone rang. It was Major Cartwright, the CO's yes-man and drinks pourer. 'Fancy a trip abroad Baylis?'

'I've got a lot on my plate at the moment, sir.' The army's first rule for fending off painful surprises: never volunteer for anything.

'The CO's looking for a few likely volunteers for a little scheme he's got on the go.'

'I'm very busy, sir. Setting up a mapping course in Antrim.'

'The CO thinks you're cut out for this job Baylis.'

'Does he, sir?'

'Yes. Fit. Streetwise. Enterprising. Just the sort of chap we need.'

'But I haven't got a valid passport, sir.'

'Doesn't matter. For this little junket you won't need one.'

Three hours later I was walking down a long neon-lit corridor at Aldergrove airport with a man with an unpronounceable Polish name.

Outside we climbed into an RAF Land-Rover that took us through the drizzle to an old four-engined Shackleton parked in a distant corner of the tarmac.

I'd spun my story to a harassed RAF sergeant at the services check-in desk. He grumbled and told me I was asking for the impossible. 'Go away,' he said, 'you've got more bloody front than Harrods.' But I hung around, hangdog and pathetic, until he got fed up with me. He gave me the hopeless look of a man prepared, just this once, to placate a lunatic. When no one was around to see, he hustled me through a door to a briefing room and introduced me to a pilot who had his feet up on a desk. He said he was Jan something-or-other. One of those Polish names with no vowels in it.

'I can get you back to the mainland,' Jan said. 'Lyneham any good to you?'

'Great.'

The CO's little scheme turned out to be a test of initiative for three of us who happened to be stuck at camp for the weekend. We all heard about it so late in the day we assumed it was the result of a bet he'd struck on the golf course that lunchtime with a friend from another regiment.

The three handpicked go-getters were sent out from Palace Barracks at one-hour intervals with the objective of getting as far away from Belfast as we could travel in fourteen days. 'If you can hitch a ride to Australia so much the better,' Major Cartwright told us.

We were all dressed in civvies and each man was given a letter of explanation signed by the CO that was to be used only in case of trouble. Our valuables were taken away. All we had was a fiver each, a rucksack containing a change of clothes, and a few basics like soap, toothbrush, towel and shaving gear.

'But when we get wherever we're going, how do we prove that we've got where we say we've got?'

'Use your initiative Baylis,' said Cartwright, 'go to a police station. Get the local mayor to write you a note. Something like that.'

As an exit line, it was not very confidence building.

At the sharp end of the Shackleton, I was surprised to discover how basic it was on the inside. There were exposed wires running all over the fuselage and the aircraft had a ramshackle, Sellotape, canvas and wing-nuts feel about it. I sat behind the pilot, wearing a headset and a determined expression as he prepared for take off. All I needed to complete the Blériot effect was a white scarf and goggles.

'The plane looks a bit of a relic,' I said.

'But she's a dream to fly,' Jan said. 'You're not a nervous flyer are you?'

'I don't know yet. This is my first flight.'

To add to the air of unreality, I'd noticed there was a coffin tied to the bulkhead behind the flight-deck.

'I could have done without making my maiden flight sitting next to that thing,' I said. It was hardly an auspicious omen.

'Motor bike accident,' the pilot said, 'some poor sod with the Royal Electrical and Mechanical Engineers tried to jump a red light.'

The only other living passenger on the plane was an RAF Leading Aircraftsman called Geoff. He was on a forty-eight-hour pass. Cadging a flight was the only way he was able to get home to see his family. Once we got to the mainland he had to train it all the way from Lyneham to Leicester and then back again to Belfast before Sunday night. 'I'm only home for a few hours,' he said, 'but it's worth it just to sleep in my own bed for a change.'

I explained about my ludicrous mission and he asked me how far I expected to get. 'I'm aiming for France,' I said. 'A girlfriend has been spending the summer near Biarritz. I think I might try to track her down.'

I said girlfriend, but by that time she was an ex. I'd met Jane Grey when she was a nurse at King Edward's Hospital, Ealing. As Terry-Thomas used to say: 'She was an absolute scorcher.' We went out for eighteen months, but it's difficult to woo a girl when you're stuck in a barracks in Belfast. Her letters got cooler and more sporadic. A couple of months earlier she'd sent me a 'Dear Trev' letter saying the romance was off and so was she. She had packed in her job in Ealing and was planning to spend the summer working as a children's nurse in a holiday village on the Basque coast. She'd mentioned the names of a few camp-sites. I thought I might as well give myself a real test of initiative and try to find her.

The pilot made a perfect landing and I thanked him for being so gentle with me first time. He pointed to the coffin. 'If you can wait until I've sorted out the paperwork for that, I can give you both a lift to Swindon.' An hour later he dropped us outside the main railway station, where Geoff and I split up.

I'd decided to make my way to a port that had routes to the Continent. The first lorry that stopped for me on the A 345 was on its way to Southampton, so I settled for there. We got there at about three in the morning. The driver parked up near the dock gates and treated me to a yellow pyramid of scrambled eggs in an all-night cafe.

I was carrying my AB64 as proof of identity. As soon as people realised I was a soldier they couldn't have been more willing. They seemed to get a kick out of helping me. Being a soldier made me one of the family and my problems were their problems. As I was finishing my meal the driver called over a couple of his mates who worked the boats. They were stewards and offered to get me on board their ship which was sailing for France later that day. It was a vessel that had brought over some immigrants from the West Indies and was going on to drop off cargo at La Pallice, the industrial port of La Rochelle.

The lights of the *SS Irpinia* cosily glimmered in the dawn as the stewards led me boldly up the main gangway. They had no intention of smuggling me to France, they said. The captain was a pussy-cat. There would be no problems.

They took me to the purser. He rang the captain, who asked for me to be brought straight up to the bridge. He was a gaunt Scotsman of startling ugliness. His uniform was covered with cigarette ash which he kept trying to brush off with his cigarette hand, adding more as he did so.

The captain listened in silence, wafting ash as I explained what I was about. His unsmiling manner matched his appearance. He obviously didn't want to waste any words on me. I expected him to hear me out and then order me off his ship.

When I'd finished he gave me a cool disconcerting nod and looked me up and down. His mind was made up and I thought the worst.

'Well I'll say this,' he said at last, 'you look absolutely knackered. You'll be with us for eighteen hours, so I suppose you'd better have a cabin.' At last he allowed himself to smile. He appeared highly amused at the thought of pulling a fast one on the French authorities. He passed on a few instructions over the intercom, then he held out his hand. I shook it.

Like a spectator in a dream I was led down several stairways by one of the stewards who had brought me on board. He unlocked a double cabin and told me to make myself at home. He went away and brought me back a bottle of ice-cold beer. I drank lying back on the pillows of my bunk. Then I dropped the bottle onto the soft pile of the carpet and fell asleep. I hadn't shut my eyes for more than twenty-four hours.

The sound of the ship's engines woke me at six that evening. It was bright daylight. From the porthole all I could see was the glare of sun, sea, and a tumble of slow-motion foam. We were due to dock at two the following morning. I began to worry about how I would get ashore with no passport. I came up with no ideas at all and went to see the purser.

He gave me a note from the captain. It read like an order. I was to have dinner, a few beers in the crew bar, and then go back to bed. He would see me for breakfast at eight o'clock the following morning when we'd talk about getting me ashore.

As I had never been abroad in my life I had no idea how strict they were at passport control. I'd seen a lot of films in which all the officials were extremely zealous, examining documents, reading data, and studying you and your photograph closely before giving it back. In most of the films the border guards had been Nazis, but I couldn't imagine the French being much more accommodating. And bribery was out of the question. I only had a fiver.

The next morning the captain outlined a plan, which to me was simple to the point of being foolhardy. He said French stevedores had already started to unload the cargo of coffee and rum from the small forward hold. His crew were out on deck and on the quayside super-vising the operation.

'I'll take you down and introduce you to the French gaffer,' he said.

'You hang around helping the dockers for a couple of hours. Then when they knock off, just walk off the docks with them.'

'But what about the customs and immigration?'

'It's all taken care of,' he said. 'The man owes me a favour.' I must have looked very dubious because he added: 'Don't worry son. You won't be the first person to get into France this way.'

It was as simple as he said it would be. At the end of their shift I walked out of the port in the middle of a group of noisy stereotypical French dockers. It's the scene from the World War Two prison escape movie *Albert RN*, where they use a dummy as cover for the head counts. Except that I am the rather unconvincing dummy surrounded by a crowd of gesticulating French men in blue overalls. I had an anxious moment when we had to walk past the gatehouse, but the dockers didn't even have to clock out. The men in uniform waved them on their way with shouts of 'Salut' and 'A bientôt', and I walked through the gates with them trying to look suitably Gallic and Gauloise-stained.

The gaffer bought me a coffee at a cafe where he'd parked his motor bike. Then he gave me a pillion ride to the A 10 on the route south. I eventually got to Biarritz, but I never did find the lovely Jane Grey. I called at a few camp-sites around the tamarisk-covered headlands along the coast, but soon realised the likelihood of coming across her were marginally smaller than my chances of being offered a buckshee suite at the sumptuous Hotel Palais.

There were some wonderful sweeping curves of sandy beach. With the wind from the Bay of Biscay it made great surf and I had an exhilarating, intimidating swim out among the big waves. While I was drying myself on the sands I soon regretted it. All the exercise had made me starving hungry. I wanted to preserve my fiver, and the aloof late summer visitors to the resort weren't the kind of people to give hand-outs to a shabby English soldier on the scrounge.

I trudged back up to the Basque Corniche road looking for a ride to somewhere a bit less classy, where the people might be more generous. My next lift took me all the way to southern Spain, to within easy hitching distance of Gibraltar. But getting there should have earned me a medal for valour in the face of overwhelming odds. My long via dolorosa through the Pyrenees and down to Fuengirola was one of the most curious and frightening experiences of my army service. I thought every mile I travelled during those forty-eight hours would be my last. By the time the man driving the lorry dropped me from his cab I was paralysed with fear and drink. He was in marginally better shape: he was only paralysed with drink.

He was called Miguel and had stopped to pick me up in a pinkish theatrical dusk on the road out of Biarritz towards St Jean de Luz. He was driving a big pick-up truck and had collected a Ferrari that had been badly damaged in a smash at Bordeaux. He was very friendly and chatty and spoke good English.

'You can talk to me and keep me awake,' he said, and offered to take me all the way to southern Spain to the garage where he was delivering the wreck.

He offered me some cold tortilla and invited me to settle down in the bunk compartment behind his cab. I woke in the early hours of the morning and we'd crossed the border while I'd been asleep. He was playing loud pop music on the radio. I got back into the passenger seat to keep him company. He sat stiff and upright, occasionally singing along with the music. Through the windscreen I watched sudden headlights come and go, nodding off in the long stretches of darkness.

A dig in the arm woke me. He was offering me a swig from a bottle of wine. I took a mouthful and gave him the bottle back. He put it to his lips and drained it. He pointed to a crate in the bunk space and asked me to open another. They were screwtop bottles of rough red wine. I undid one and set it down on the surface between our seats. In less than an hour he had emptied the bottle. He kept taking one hand from the steering wheel to raise it to his lips as the lorry kept pace with a looming blur of traffic.

He indicated that I should open another bottle and he started on that one. He kept offering me the bottle. 'It's good wine,' he said.

'Yes.' I tried to keep hold of it, figuring the more I drank from each bottle the less he would be able to. But he grabbed it out of my hand when it was one-quarter full, and drank it down.

'Take it easy,' I said, 'you've drunk more than a bottle already.'

'I am a very good driver,' he smiled. 'On one bottle I drive very well, on two, maybe three, I drive even better.'

He selected another channel on the radio. It was playing Flamenco music and he started to beat his hands rhythmically on the steering wheel. We were on the main drag to Zaragoza. The traffic was heavy and he began to fume at the slower vehicles, seeking the earliest opportunity to swerve out over the central line and overtake, shrieking past: tyres, exhaust and horn baying.

He kept this up for another three hours, during which time I had opened another bottle. By now I was matching him mouthful for mouthful, trying to reduce his intake by drinking more than he did. My head was reeling and through the shimming heat of a Spanish midday I imagined every approaching lorry was aimed straight at us. I thought about asking him to stop and let me out but we were in the middle of a wide arid plateau miles from anywhere. We kept going for another hour, then he braked and pulled onto the hard shoulder of the dual carriageway.

'Time for siesta,' he said, and almost fell into his bunk behind the cab. I stretched out across the front seats and tried to doze, my head throbbing, cheap red wine corroding my insides. He woke five hours later and drove for 100 miles without drinking any more until we found a petrol station and restaurant by the side of the road. He filled the lorry with fuel, and said we also ought to refuel before the next leg of the journey.

He ordered us both plates of serrano ham, with fried eggs, and delicious peasant bread. He had three cups of strong black coffee. I thought he was trying to sober up, until he asked for a large brandy to be poured into the third cup. He talked about his job, how he earned a fortune transporting expensive wrecks around the Continent.

'I have driven in every country in Europe except England,' he said. 'The Germans are my best customers. They have very expensive limousines, and they crash them often.'

As he paid the bill he purchased a bottle of Spanish cognac. 'Brandy is a great consolation on a long journey,' he explained.

We followed the same ceremonial through the night as we ate up the kilometres towards Cordoba. Only on this stage of the journey there was a slurp of brandy between each bottle of red wine. I resolutely put away most of the drink myself, so there would be less for him.

He was driving recklessly fast. I kept closing my eyes as he hauled his squealing rig in and out of the traffic. But, even under the influence of numerous swallows of red wine and a top dressing of spirits, I have to admit he was a very good driver. He said he was a motor racing enthusiast and a fan of the great Fangio. In deference to my nationality he kept giving me the thumbs up and saying: 'Stirling Moss. Very good. But Fangio numero uno.'

The drunker he became the more he boasted about his safety record. 'No accidents,' he said proudly, slurring the words. 'No insurance claims. I am an excellent driver.'

We sped towards Malaga, along a winding highway, flints in the asphalt like burnished silver. The heat inside the cab was stifling. Miguel said he was thirsty. He turned his drink-boiled eyes towards me, brusquely motioning for another bottle to be opened. I screwed it open and offered it to him. I'd had enough. He'd beaten me. He slurped down a quarter of the bottle and handed it back.

It was mid-afternoon. We were driving through a vast sea of olive fields. 'A good place to rest,' he said, and brought the lorry to a standstill. We both climbed out and lay in the shade of a straggling vine. He had fetched the brandy with him. He sat against a mud wall slurping the last of the liquid consolation into himself until he was so consoled he fell asleep.

The chill woke us after dark. I hauled myself back into the cab. My brain was clenched like a boxer's fist, my mouth was dry, I felt embalmed with drink. He, by contrast, seemed quite perky. Before starting the engine he razored his stubble of black beard with an electric shaver and cleaned his teeth. By now reaching for the wine had become a reflex action with me, and when he switched on the ignition I turned to open another bottle of wine.

'No thank you,' he said gravely, still very drunk. 'I must be sober for my wife.'

It took us three more hours to get to Fuengirola. He was still driving furiously, tacking in and out of the traffic like a drunken skipper of an old sailing barge. I was by now familiar with this manoeuvre but it still scared the hell out of me. I kept my eyes closed every time we overtook. He dropped me just out of town on the road to Estepona. 'Thank you for keeping me company Trevor,' he said. 'We made good time didn't we?'

There was a hiss of air as he let off the brakes and pulled away. His last words to me drifted through the open window of the cab.

'Stirling Moss very good. But Fangio numero uno.'

At Gibraltar I blagged my way past Spanish customs, showing them my AB64 and explaining to the only one who had any English that I was a British soldier on an initiative exercise. The border guards must have been slack cogs in Franco's arbitrary system because they laughed and waved me through. From the Rock I put in a reverse-charge call to Palace Barracks in Holywood, and sent Colonel Newton a postcard of the barbary apes, countersigned by the local postmaster, to prove I'd got there.

That last assignment was the army's farewell present to me, part adventure holiday, part finishing school and crash course at the university of life. It was my first wide-eyed experience of so many things. I had never imagined what market day in a French town would be like until, on my way home, I wandered into one at St Emilion. I was so naive I wondered why all the place names had been so familiar, like Medoc, Sauternes, and Cognac. Then I made the connection and realised these were the same places where all that delectable drink came from. The names had much more poetry and grandeur about them than stolid English towns. St Emilion actually sounds rounded and delicious in a way that a drink made from grapes grown say in Dorking, or Chipstead, never could be.

I had trudged into St Emilion on a sunny but chilly morning and was surprised to see so many horses and carts converging on the town. People were setting up stalls on trestle tables in the square and I had never seen such beautiful richly coloured mounds of fresh green vegetables or ripe red fruits. I didn't realise that so many different types of cheese, or sausages, or fish existed, or that meat could be fashioned into such exotic cuts. They just weren't sold at home.

One of the fish men was on his own and trying to set up a red and yellow canopy over his stall. Everyone was busy erecting their own displays, so I held a rope, helped him sling the canvas over a wooden frame, and tied it off with him. He thanked me, and when he realised I was English, he gave me a fish. It was a red, aggressive looking thing with spikes on it. He wrapped it up, insisting I take it, and as I was skint I didn't argue.

That afternoon I sat in a river up to my armpits and had a shave. I had a fire going on the bank with some potatoes baking in the ashes. I'd picked them up from the cobbles of the market. Then I knelt over the flames, my red fish skewered on a stick, and cooked it in the embers. Everything about the meal was indescribably sweet, the fish and potatoes, the cool music of the river, the warmth of the sun as I had a doze, deliciously full. Everything had been so perfect that I savoured the aftertaste, just in case I never passed that way again.

On the way back from Gibraltar I'd done so many miles I'd become an expert hitch-hiker. I'd fashioned a small union flag into an armband to attract the attention of passing drivers. Four lifts had taken me back up the length of Spain. I started spending my fiver to buy food that was so cheap I ate like a millionaire. I slept off my long lunches, lying out in the sun among the goatbells. I was striding up the foothills of the Pyrenees, and dreading the climb, when my fifth lift slowed for me.

'We're going as far as Pau,' an English voice said from a big Rover. 'We can drop you off there if that's any good to you.'

It was Jean and her husband Don, an expatriate couple from North London who ran an antique business in Pau, the capital of Bearn on the French side of the mountains. They drove me there, chatting all the way, and put me up in their house for two days. They were tremendous hosts, showing me all over the historic town which, they told me, had been a popular resort with the British since 1820. They spoke of it as proudly as if it had been a jewel of the Home Counties, boasting that it had the first golf course ever built on the Continent (1856) and even had its own fox-hunt.

The terrace at the back of their house had a fantastic view of the Pyrenees, due south of the town. We'd gather there as the sun was going down to see its declining rays reflect pink and orange on the peaks thirty miles away. It was so beautiful it looked unreal, like a painted theatrical backdrop. We were looking at the sunset one night when Don asked me what I was going to do when my National Service ended.

'I used to be a soil engineer,' I said. 'But I want a change. After what I've seen and done in the past two years, I don't think I could stick working indoors.'

CHAPTER FOURTEEN

A BORN SHOW OFF

AFTER THE ARMY I WAS OUT OF WORK FOR SIX MONTHS. Having decided to do something more exciting than soil analysis I couldn't find an employer even vaguely excited by the prospect of employing me and I soon realised I had no idea what I really wanted to do with my life. I thought about reviving my old comedy diving act with a few mates, but in the bleakness of mid-winter the world of summer pageants and outdoor galas seemed a very distant prospect and, for the moment, I gave up on the idea.

I mooched around Southall meeting old friends, scrounging pocket money from my parents, feeling dispirited. As 1962 began I resigned myself to looking for a job in my old line as an engineer. I wrote an application to the Silvertown Rubber Company. By return of post they invited me for an interview. I thought it had gone rather well until the interviewer asked me what job I fancied at SRC. All I could think to say was: 'Yours.' Bad mistake. Daft answer. He gave me an edgy look and shuffled his papers. Flippancy was not the quality he was looking for. He told me I would be hearing from him soon, and I did. He turned me down in a three-line letter.

Time passed very slowly and nothing turned up. In April I saw an advert placed by a swimming pool company seeking a technical salesman. I sent them my CV, and their Managing Director, John Glazier, replied in a note asking me to meet him at Surbiton Town Hall.

Why Surbiton Town Hall? It seemed a bit cloak-and-dagger. Should I wear a carnation in my buttonhole so he would recognise me? I rang his secretary who explained John had an appointment with a council official in Surbiton that morning, and that he'd meet me at the Town Hall's front desk at 11.30.

I turned up ten minutes early wearing my electric-blue salesman's suit and sashayed around the foyer trying to look as dynamic as a man who could sell raincoats in the Gobi desert. John walked up to the front desk exactly on time. We shook hands and he said: 'Do you fancy a drink?'

'It's a bit early for me.'

'I meant a cup of coffee.'

I thought I'd blown it straightaway, but he gave me a king-sized grin. Over coffee we got on like old friends. He said that my engineering background would be an asset on the technical side of the job, which involved ironing out any mechanical blips customers had with their swimming pool systems. By the time I'd emptied my cup he'd offered me the position.

'Do you think you'll be able to sell people swimming pools?' he said at one point. 'You've never worked in sales before have you?'

'Look at it positively,' I replied. 'That means I've still got a one hundred per cent sales record. I've never once failed to sell anybody anything have I?'

I had landed on my feet. John Glazier was a good boss, and I stayed with Purley Pools for almost eight years, driving my company car, a Standard Eight, later upgraded to a Standard Ten, all over Britain. The company specialised in the first PVC-lined swimming pools, selling them to schools, local authorities and aspiring couples who wanted to keep one splash ahead of the Joneses. I found myself attending trade shows nationwide, putting up the pools, filling them with water and trying to enthuse people enough to install one in their back garden.

The pools were selling well, but I thought our sales routine was drearier than early closing day in Dunoon. It was the usual pitch.

Trying to stop people as they hurried past attempting to avoid eye contact with you. If they hesitate, close in. Flash your wide kiss-of-death salesman's smile. A firm handshake. Don't stop talking. 'This is our latest model. Would you like to see our brochure? Come and browse. I know you're in a hurry but would you like to take one of my cards?' And they would be off, stampeding away from your patter faster than jackrabbits from a prairie fire.

I have always admired the way spielers operate in markets, selling crockery with a quick line in patter that's often funnier than the material you hear from professional comedians. Fairground drummers – literally drumming up customers like W.C. Fields's huckstering elixir salesman – know more about holding a crowd spellbound than most West-End actors and front-bench politicians.

I told John our act lacked pizzazz. We needed to brace our salesmanship with a touch of showmanship. I kept pestering him and, on a quiet day at the Ideal Home Exhibition in 1963, he let me give it a try. I went into our little pump room, changed into a pair of swimming trunks, and started to swim up and down our pool.

I enjoyed my dip and was just about to climb out when John hurried over.

'Don't get out,' he said. 'We've started to sell swimming pools.'

So I stayed in the water and gave the punters a show, performing all the trick dives I could remember. I splashed them into submission, forcing them to stop and look at what the madman in the pool was doing, so John could hook more of them with his patter, steer them uncomplaining towards the brochures, and start to discuss easy terms.

Exhibitions began offering John cheap space with the proviso that I put on my swimming and diving displays. I started to think about production values, and gave the demonstrations more visual impact by dressing our stand with a few fake palm trees, setting up some staging beside the pool and introducing a few pretty girls in bikinis. The show soon became more like a water spectacular than a presentation of various dives and swimming strokes.

It proved highly popular; the wetter spectators got the more willing they were to buy our pools. But I wasn't a hit with everybody. One year I was putting on my usual performance, this time at the Chelsea Flower Show, larking about and splashing everybody with grotesque belly slops from the staging, when John beckoned me out of the water.

He looked at me sideways, indicating trouble. He had been joined by a woman official with a sour face. She pursed her lips and drew herself up to her full six foot, a mountainous woman in a woollen dress, that like her, was more plain than purl. She had the beady look of a regimental sergeant major who had just spotted an outbreak of slovenliness running wild among the other ranks.

'I'm afraid I'm going to have to halt your little show,' she said, putting a sniffy emphasis on the word 'little'.

'May I ask why?'

'This sort of thing just isn't done at the Chelsea Flower Show.'

'What sort of thing?'

'Splashing people,' she said, looking at me as if I was some dull oaf out on parole from a secure institution. 'It's hardly dignified, completely unsuited to the ambience of the flower show. And I'm afraid there have been complaints, several of them extremely vociferous.'

John and I apologised to her. There was no point in arguing, and anyway it's very difficult to mount a serious argument when all you're wearing is a striped Edwardian swimming costume. From then on whenever I wanted to make John laugh I would put on a plummy voice and say to him: 'I am afraid there have been complaints, several of them extremely vociferous.'

At the firm's headquarters in Godstone Road, Purley, they set me up a workshop where I carried out experiments, attempting to improve the pump, filtration and chlorination systems for the pools we installed. During my time with the company I devised more than fifty new components that were incorporated into the company's range of pool equipment. The work-space was not much bigger than my dad's garden shed and I spent many happy hours there ferreting away at mechanical problems, looking for ways to make the apparatus more efficient.

Apart from boyhood experiments, my very first inventions were created in my little rustic hut at Purley Pools. As daylight failed I'd still be working, full of that marvellous and unforgettable glow of satisfaction each time a good idea blossomed to brightness and I produced a device that actually worked.

In 1964 I built a completely automated chlorination system for the company that was twenty years ahead of the competition, using a chemical process to burn all the germs out of the water so bathers could swim in it perfectly safely as it was cycled and recycled round the system.

One of the most fascinating aspects of invention is how ideas can sometimes be recycled like swimming-pool water. Recently I've been puzzling over water purification yet again in an attempt to produce a cheap system for sterilising brackish water in tropical climates. My consciousness was suddenly awakened to the work I had done in my hut at Purley Pools thirty-five years ago, and I was able to call on some of the things I learned then to help solve a new problem in the Third World. When the inventor is perched on the edge of his chair desperately trying to think up new solutions, sometimes the answer lies in retrieving old ones.

But most of my eight years with Purley Pools I was out on the stump, selling pools at county fairs and agricultural shows. I became the only salesman ever employed by the company who could dive from a height of eighteen feet into three feet of water. I'd ask the crowds to stand back, unless they wanted to get soaked to the skin, and then announce my dive with the usual rigmarole.

'Children, this is a very dangerous dive. Under no circumstances should you ever attempt to try it yourselves.'

If you are an experienced diver it's quite an easy stunt to master. The golden rule is to start diving from no height at all and gradually increase it as you get more confident about what you're doing. Only a complete and utter nutcase would attempt to do it from eighteen feet at the first time of asking.

Indoors it was sometimes impractical to dive into the pool: people tend to behave ungraciously if you splash a couple of hundred gallons of water on the waxed maple floor of their precious gymnasium. So I perfected the art of diving onto a damp sponge. I used the word 'damp' as part of my pitch to the crowd; somehow there's more poetry in the phrase: 'Ladies and gentlemen, I will now attempt to dive from eighteen feet onto a damp sponge.' Dry sponge doesn't have the same bardic ring to it. In fact it was a dry sponge, a large offcut of foam rubber I had picked up at a junk auction. Diving onto the damp sponge was no more dangerous than diving into water, and one of my mates in the diving team gradually increased the height until he was diving onto the sponge from eighty feet.

The performing and selling side of the job was a doddle. But setting up the stand, erecting the pools, filling them with water, then draining, dismantling, and packing away all the impedimenta ready for the next show was a chore I grew to hate. Once, on the last day of the Holiday and Leisure Show at Olympia, I had a date arranged and I wanted to get the de-rig completed as quickly as possible.

The way we usually drained the pool was to pump the water through the filtration plant and run it, via a hose, to the nearest drain. But for some reason all the electricity had gone down and we couldn't operate the filtration system. Our stand was up on the mezzanine floor. We had done all the other jobs, everything was packed and ready to go. Dismantling the pool would be easy, a ten-minute task. But first, somehow, we had to make 8,000 gallons of water disappear.

I looked at my watch. I had this gorgeous girl waiting to meet me in half-an-hour at the top of Park Lane. So I used my initiative. I approached a bloke in a brown coat, part of a phalanx of brown-coated workers with wide brooms who were absently pushing piles of dust and rubbish past our stand. I explained to him we had 8,000 gallons of water to drain from the pool, that there was no electricity to run the filtration plant, and we hadn't got any gear to siphon it off. The bloke in the brown coat was a man after my own heart. While he pondered my problem, I told him I had a hot date and wanted to get away. I also slipped him a fiver.

He put the fiver in the breast pocket of his overall. He gave me a beatific, slightly stupid, smile and uttered the fatal words: 'Just let it go mate and we'll push it around with our brooms.'

I got out my jackknife and slit a big hole in the corner of the plastic pool. Then I legged it to the nearest exit just ahead of a tidal wave, running to escape before I was engulfed by a wall of water.

Charles Dickens, they say, didn't exaggerate, he merely observed. I wasn't there to do either. But the letter of complaint, when it arrived on John Glazier's desk the following week, spoke of water gushing down the up-escalators, of commissionaires abandoning their posts in panic, and a small lake forming in the car park as water sluiced out of Olympia. John remained surprisingly composed. All he ever said to me about the incident was: 'I am afraid there have been complaints, Trev, several of them extremely vociferous.'

It was a very happy company. For nearly eight years I woke every morning to my great good luck and drove off to my next agreeable engagement. I loved the job, it combined the security of a regular wage and a nice car with the swagger of show business. I'm an instant show off, just add water and stir. I can, and I'm not particularly proud of this, talk for England. Sometimes, when I'm up there on the soapbox in full flow, I can see my friends rolling their eyes, longing for the spring to bust on the talking machine. I think I must have got the talking gene from my mother. Rereading the fifty-year-old reviews of the Church Dramatic Club in the *Southall County Times and Gazette*, I see myself in every description of her.

In *Family Affairs*, a comedy by Gertrude Jennings, the reviewer noted in 1949: 'Gladys Baylis made her vulgarity a relieving touch amongst so much culture.' Without even acting, I've been doing exactly that for most of my adult life.

By 1964 I had moved into a flat in Thames Eyot, Twickenham, with an old swimming pal of mine, Tony Hutchings. He then earned his living as an artist, illustrating strip cartoons, and now lives in Andalucia where he writes and illustrates children's books.

Tony was a very handsome lad who bore a remarkable resemblance to Sean Connery. He was so like him he could have been cloned from 007, and he made the most of the likeness by perfecting Connery's sibilant Scots delivery of words like: 'Shaken not Shtirred', 'Pushy Galore', and 'Shpectre'.

All through the 1960s, tagging along with Tony Hutchings in James Bond mode was a wonderful way to get to talk to pretty girls. I went along with the illusion by pretending to be Sean's shy and retiring publicity agent. Once we were in a West-End club when a waiter came over with a bottle of champagne for us.

'We didn't order that,' I said to him.

'It's for Mr Connery,' the waiter said. 'It's from the gentleman over there.'

We looked across, and sure enough there was a customer smoking a big cigar and waving at us. I don't know who he was, some movie-mogul type, but he must have known the real Sean Connery. We didn't want to appear rude, so we smiled and waved back, and drank the champagne, raising our glasses to him as we did so. Tony Hutchings actually said: 'Cheersh!'

The prices in the club were steep and we couldn't afford to return the compliment and send a bottle of champagne to Sean's acquaintance. He's probably still thinking to himself. 'What a mean bastard that Connery is.'

Tony used to exhibit his paintings on the railings of Hyde Park and every weekend I'd help him ferry his pictures up there. Sometimes they were still wet, straight off his easel and we had to use two cars. I was driving a metallic-blue 3.8 litre drophead E-Type Jaguar then, a dream car. It was like a seduction scene on wheels, with far more machismo than I had.

One Saturday after I had dropped off Tony's latest masterpieces I drove down the King's Road. It was a beautiful blossom-littered May morning and I had the hood down, window-shopping the talent as the talent did its window-shopping. I was wearing a buckskin tasselled jacket and playing Steppenwolf's 'Born to be Wild' on the car stereo.

I passed a stunning-looking girl in a miniskirt. Drifting along on bare brown legs that seemed to go on for ever. She had a beautiful walk. She was with a tallish man and they appeared to be having an argument. Ten yards up the road I just caught a red light and cursed. I gunned the engine as I idled in the traffic, waiting for the green.

The passenger door clicked. The girl I'd just seen slipped into the seat beside me and said: 'Where are we going to then?' She had lovely green eyes and her name was Judy.

I went out with her for a year. Things like that happened in the 1960s.

CHAPTER FIFTEEN

DROWNING DUDLEY MOORE

'**D**UD IS AN AMAZING CREATURE. Due to his sadly deprived upbringing in Dagenham, he grew up sadly deprived of gills. You could say Dud is singularly lacking in the gills department. Well, doubly lacking actually. He hasn't got any gills at all. So you, Trevor, have to be on constant alert because one thing could lead to his mother and he'll sue.'

The monologue was from Peter Cook. Wearing a false beard and wetsuit, he looked a dead ringer for the German undersea adventurer Hans Hass. He was in the driving seat of a car half-submerged in an eight-foot-deep tank of water. I was alongside the car, paddling my flippers, trying not to laugh, ready with an air line to resuscitate the gill-less Dudley Moore. Dudley was trapped by his seat belt, already underwater, and blowing bubbles. As Dud grew crimson in the face, the studio's floor manager gave a signal to a crane driver. He hoisted the car clear of the tank, and with water spilling everywhere, Dudley breathed again.

The tank was in the car park at ATV Studios at Borehamwood where Pete and Dud were rehearsing a sketch for a TV special they were doing. It was 1969, and though I was still occasionally working for Purley Pools, I'd begun to do a lot of freelance stunt work. The sketch was a send–up of an item on the previous week's *Dave Allen Show* where a pedantic Swedish road safety expert had demonstrated how to escape from a car trapped underwater.

I had helped stage that earlier stunt too, and the bearded Swedish expert, a tedious authoritarian type, as dull and heavy as a Volvo car, had slowly bored Dave Allen and most of the audience comatose. In fact death by drowning would have been a more enticing prospect than listening to him tell you how to survive.

Peter Cook had watched the programme and was inspired to do a sketch in which he and Dud would send up the Swede's escape routine. But, while poking fun at the original demonstration, they still had to follow all the safety rules, and I was hired as a diving adviser and emergency backup.

The maxim was not to panic as the water level rose. Wait until the pressure inside the car equalled the pressure outside, so it was easy to open the door and escape. But Dud, being one foot shorter than Pete, would be half-drowned long before the water reached the required level. And that – such as it was – was the gag.

After a break Pete, Dud, and I were called back out to the car park to rehearse the sketch again. 'Quiet please everybody,' Cook shouted. 'This time we're going for a drowning.'

I had been a fan of Dud and Pete on television since *Not Only . . . But Also* began in 1965. It seemed odd to be working with them in a tank because so many of the sketches I'd seen them do in *Not Only . . .* had also involved underwater jokes – like Cook's character whose life's work consisted of teaching ravens to fly underwater, and the subaqua signature tune, with Pete and Dud still singing and playing as their piano was dropped into the Thames at the Tower of London.

They both approached the sketch in a totally disorganised way. They vaguely knew what they were going to do, but nothing was finalised on paper. Though the words might have been virtually ad–libbed, the safety aspect was worked out to the smallest detail. Dudley was going to be strapped into the car with his head – eventually – one foot underwater. I was wearing full diving gear and my job was to keep feeding him air from a line and quickly get out of shot so they could do close ups of him blowing bubbles and pretending to drown. It was an acting job he did very convincingly.

I sat chatting to them in the make-up room, watching as they improvised at the last minute, continuing a moronic dialogue in gobbledegook that was very funny, but which neither of them bothered to write down. They kept giggling and collapsing into laughter, and every time Pete got Dudley laughing he kept on going until he had him helpless in his chair.

They didn't seem at all worried by the possible danger of working underwater. They had just finished filming *The Bed-Sitting Room*, the surreal after-the-bomb comedy by Spike Milligan that Richard Lester had directed them in. Both of them had had to go up in a balloon with an expert crouched in the bottom of the basket to show them what to do. When they got up several hundred feet from the ground the balloonist said to Peter Cook: 'I wouldn't go up on a day like this.'

Peter Cook had told him: 'You are up on a day like this. What do you mean?'

The expert said: 'Well it's just for Mr Lester. But I wouldn't normally go up – we're at the mercy of the winds.'

As soon as the balloonist said that the balloon fell out of the sky. Cook damaged his knee and had to spend four weeks in hospital.

Just as Peter had finished telling me the story we were called back to the tank to perform the sketch. We climbed up the steps to the gantry that ran round the top of the tank and I said to Peter: 'I wouldn't go up there on a day like this. We're at the mercy of the water.'

The sketch went very well. The escape got a lot of laughs from the crew as we taped it. Peter Cook in his straggly fringe of beard gave us his leaden Swede, while Dudley Moore pretended to drown. Dudley kept taking breaths from my air line, blowing a spuming column of bubbles up to the surface. He might have risked dying of laughter, but he was never in any danger of death by drowning.

After the stunt was over and we were getting ready to pack up and go to the green room, Peter Cook started kidding me, claiming he'd dropped his wallet in all the excitement and it had gone straight to the bottom of the tank. He asked me to look out for it as we drained out the water and de-rigged.

'Being a man of my means I wouldn't normally bother you,' he said. 'But the wallet happens to contain an IOU from David Frost that has great sentimental value.' It was one of his elaborate fantasies, and in the hospitality room afterwards he kept asking after his wallet, until he tired of the joke and began an hilarious ten-minute diatribe about the elk vol-au-vents on offer in the buffet.

I had built the circular tank – sixteen feet in diameter by eight feet deep, holding 10,000 gallons of water – with a mate of mine, Dick Harris, who was a pilot with British European Airways. The tank was made of steel and toughened glass so spectators could see what was happening underwater. We prefabricated all the parts in my workshop and assembled it for the first time at the bottom of my parents' garden in Lady Margaret Road in 1965. It made an ideal display pool because it was easily dismantled and could be transported on the back of a lorry. I formed a company called Shotline Displays, named after the line weighted with lead shot which divers use for location purposes, and began to promote subaqua shows in my home-made tank.

A couple of weeks after the stunt with Pete and Dud, it was in action again at ATV Studios for an item in a David Nixon spectacular. David, one of the first illusionists to make his name on British television, had devised an elaborate card trick in which a large set of playing cards was dealt underwater by an assistant wearing an aqualung.

The eight feet of water added to the mystification. How could Nixon possibly influence the cards when he was outside the tank? It was a fairly routine trick, one I'd seen before, but doing it in more than a fathom of water made it seem more exotic and unfathomable. The trick certainly puzzled me. I sat through two rehearsals, and the recording of the show, and I still couldn't figure out how he did it.

Recording the routine was a long slow process. This was before the days of the 'yak-yak', the link which enables you to communicate with people underwater, so the director had to give instructions to David's wetsuited assistant via an elaborate system of semaphore through the glass sides of the tank, or by getting him back up to the surface. At one stage he got so fed up with the long delays he said to me: 'Trevor, you know the old show business saying: "Never work with children, or animals." I think you can add frogmen to the list now.'

David was a lovely giant of a man. In between rehearsals I even persuaded him to have a swim in the tank. He said magicians were always looking for new ways to present familiar tricks, and I suggested he ought to trying sawing a woman in half underwater. He laughed and said it reminded him of an old joke about the magician who tells his agent: 'I've got a unique act. I saw a lady in half.' The agent says: 'Unique? Every magician I know can saw a lady in half.' The magician replied: 'Ah yes, but I do it lengthways.' We decided that sawing a woman in half lengthways underwater would be a show-stopper.

From the mid-1960s onwards Dick Harris and I took our circular tank to shows all over Britain putting on displays with subaqua clubs, and diving teams from the marines, the navy and the paratroop regiment. In 1966, World Cup year, I took it abroad for the first time. It was packed into a British Rail container at Hayes and Harlington station, shipped from Harwich to Antwerp, and taken down to Cologne for the Photokina Exhibition, where I used the tank to demonstrate underwater photography.

Getting it there was reasonably cheap, about £120 each way for the whole load. I rang up the clerk at the Railways Board to enquire whether or not I could count myself as part of the load and get to Cologne for nothing. He told me I would have to buy a ticket like everyone else.

My first lodgings were in a flea-pit of a hotel close to the Rhine, which in spite of its name – The Hotel Zentral – wasn't near anywhere I wanted to go. I didn't speak a word of German and on my first, and only, night there I became involved in a bizarre incident straight out of a Whitehall farce.

There had been a meeting in the exhibition hall to discuss with the show's organisers what we could and couldn't do with our water tank. The Germans were paranoid that we'd splash the customers and after a lot of haggling we had to agree to reduce the level in the tank to six feet so that the water wouldn't keep sploshing over the top to drench the staid burghers of Cologne.

The meeting finished at gone eleven. I had a beer on my walk back to the hotel and didn't arrive there until getting on for midnight. I went straight to my room and started to unpack. The furnishings were covered in dust and grease stains. Everything was so grotty I decided to take a precautionary look at the bed. As I suspected, the sheets had been slept in before. When I looked under the pillows I found the previous occupant had left behind a frilly nightgown.

I rang down to the front desk and asked someone to come up. About half-an-hour later a porter knocked on the door. His English was worse than my German. We stood for several minutes speaking very loudly in our respective languages, making no sense of each other. In elaborate pantomime I indicated the bed. I threw back the bed-clothes and pointed to the grubby sheets. With appropriate gestures I also indicated the frilly nightdress. I picked it up and offered it to him, wanting him to take it away.

He stared at the nightdress, and suddenly a light of comprehension flashed in his eyes. 'Ich verstehe,' he said. He turned on his heels and walked out, leaving me still holding the nightdress and feeling rather stupid. Half-an-hour later, when I had finished my unpacking and was cleaning my teeth before turning in, there was another knock on the door.

When I opened it the porter was standing on the threshold looking pleased with himself. Next to him was a large woman with a lecher-ous grin on her face and a bust like a roll-top desk. They were both inside the room before I could stop them. He, smiling, with his hand out expecting me to tip him. And she making a beeline for the bed, where she picked up the frilly nightdress and held it against herself seductively.

The lady was no pin-up, more like Uve Seeler, the German centre forward. Except her hair was dyed bright orange and the lids of her eyes smudged with royal blue eye-shadow. Underneath all the paint, Polyfilla and Dulux gloss, her wrinkles sagged like crepe bandage.

For once I was completely at a loss for words. I couldn't believe it was happening. The porter was still hovering. She was pouting. I had my toothbrush in my right hand and a foaming mouthful of Gibbs SR. She sat on the edge of the bed, arranged her scarlet lips into a moue of desire, and said: 'Anything special you want me to do?'

'Yes,' I said. 'Get out of here. There's been a ghastly misunderstanding.'

She looked puzzled. Years in the trade had given her the idea that no man could ever say no. I did, several times, before the pfenning finally dropped and they left. I let her take away the nightdress as a souvenir, but it also cost me a fiver each to get rid of them. Right after breakfast the next morning I paid my bill and moved on to a boarding house run by a nun-like spinster who let sparklingly clean rooms to nice commercial gentlemen. But I checked the state of the bedding first.

I enjoyed the rest of my time in Cologne, doing the full tourist bit for a couple of days after the exhibition had closed. On a Sunday I walked through the marvellous park on the right bank of the Rhine, enjoying the fresh air and the view along the river. It got to lunchtime and I had a beer and a sausage in a local bar where I told the man who served me how much I had enjoyed my walk. He said that if the British had got their way the parks wouldn't have been as beautiful.

Immediately after the war the British had occupied the city, he told me, and straightaway looked round for a non-Nazi to run the city under their administration. Their choice was a former mayor, Konrad Adenauer, who had just been released from a concentration camp. The first winter after the war was bitterly cold and the British military governor ordered the mayor to have the trees in the city's parks cut down for fuel. Adenauer refused. He said the people of Cologne could put up with the cold for one more winter, but it would take 100 years for the trees to grow back. The blimpish British officer sacked Adenauer, but that didn't stop his progress. He became the Federal Republic's first Chancellor. And the park I had just walked through was still full of Adenauer's majestic trees.

One false move a few days earlier and maybe I wouldn't have been there to enjoy my walk by the tree-fringed Rhine. I got a fierce reception on the second-to-last day of the show when I arrived at the exhibition centre without my official pass. I tried soft-soaping my way through the front gate but it didn't work. I didn't have the right accreditation. The guard wouldn't let me in, and wasn't in the mood to discuss it.

It had started to rain quite heavily. I didn't fancy walking all the way back to my lodgings to pick up my pass, so I nipped round the block to try to creep in through the exhibition's back entrance. There weren't any security men in sight, so I walked round the barrier, took a sharp left and started to hurry through the downpour towards the doorway closest to my stand.

Suddenly there was a big shout of: 'Halt!' and the voice didn't sound as though it would brook much argument. I turned round and found a chisel-faced security man was pointing a gun at me. He came right up close, jabbering orders, still aiming his automatic at a point just below my wallet. 'It's OK. I'm not trying to escape,' I said. 'I'm just going in to work.'

He didn't lower the gun. I thought it best to smile at him and put my hands up.

'I'm English,' I said. 'I'm one of the exhibitors at Photokina.'

'Where are your credentials?'

'I've left them at my hotel.'

It hadn't been raining for much more than a minute, but we were both thoroughly drenched. My hair was stuck to my head, all my clothes were ruined. It was raining so hard, as he glared at me water was dripping off his nose like it was a leaky tap. It was as if someone had just flushed the celestial WC.

Our dramatic little tableau held its position, me with my hands held up towards the rain, and the guard still threatening me with his gun.

It seemed so ludicrous I started to laugh. 'Look mate,' I said. 'If you're going to shoot me, let's go inside and do it in the dry.'

By this time he'd had enough of standing out in the rain as well, so he walked me into the exhibition centre where eventually one of the organisers recognised me and verified my story. But the guard didn't put his gun back in its little pouch until he'd been assured I was on the level.

As I was already soaked to the skin, I thought I'd give early visitors to an exhibition something to remember. In my street clothes, without even taking off my shoes, I went straight to the tank, and jumped in. I gave the punters a half-hour display of trick diving, careful of course not to splash any of the good citizens of Cologne.

The only person I've ever met who has a louder laugh than me is the Labour MP for Grimsby, Austin Mitchell. He's got a hearty, hiccuping guffaw that, at full volume, comes close to the sound of a juggernaut straining up Richmond Hill. By comparison, my laugh is no more than a silvery maidenly tinkle. I met Austin early in 1969 when I took my display tank up to Queen's Hall in Leeds to give a demonstration of assault swimming and underwater ordnance with the Royal Navy.

I'd got a call from the Flamingo Park Zoo asking me to go for a swim with Cuddles, their Killer Whale. They thought it would make a good publicity stunt and had arranged for Austin, who was then a fresh-faced young reporter with Yorkshire Television, to film an item for their magazine programme *Calendar*.

'Has Cuddles ever swum with humans before?' I asked the girl at Flamingo Park Zoo.

'No, that's the whole point. We want to get him used to swimming with human beings,' she said.

'Just be aware that there could be problems,' I warned her. 'Cuddles might not like it.'

It was arranged that I would turn up at Flamingo Park, with some of the Royal Navy divers. The day chosen for the filming was freezing cold. There was snow on the ground, and a biting wind blowing in from the Urals. Ice crackled on Cuddles's pool as I talked things over with the crew. I got my wetsuit on and went in with Cuddles, who was as good as gold.

Austin Mitchell was looking on from the side of the pool.

'Austin, you ought to come in and swim with Cuddles,' I said. 'It would make a much better story.'

Austin wasn't too sure. 'The water looks freezing', he said.

'Cuddles is enjoying himself though.' I was trying to reassure him. 'It would make a great item for your programme.'

'Yes,' he replied, 'but you and Cuddles are better swimmers than I am.'

Austin had never done anything like it before. Understandably he was apprehensive. I promised him he would be perfectly safe. I got out of the pool, showed him all the safety procedures, and because I was so confident, he went along with it. He put on a wetsuit and we both plunged into the icy water.

Cuddles was so friendly it was like playing with a large, wet Labrador puppy. He loved our company and took us both on high-speed rides around his pool, in a stir and fume of icy water. He enjoyed having his tongue stroked. (Cuddles that is, not the future MP for Grimsby.) He'd open his mouth and allow you to put your whole arm in, past the rows of jagged teeth, so you could rub his tongue. It felt as if you were tickling one of those dimpled rubber car mats.

After we got out of the water, we went down below to look through the observation window in the side of Cuddles's tank. He swam down to take a look at us. He seemed to recognise us because he kept making noises like he was calling for us to come back into the water again.

The filming had gone well and Austin was pleased with himself. 'That was a piece of cake wasn't it?' he said when we'd both changed back into our street clothes.

'We were lucky he was so friendly,' I said. 'Sometimes they can throw their weight around a bit.' I didn't realise no one had told him that Cuddles didn't swim with humans every day.

Austin was aghast. 'You mean he could have turned on us?'

'He could have,' I said. 'Why do you think they're called killer whales? They're the ultimate ocean predators. In the wild they rip up seals and penguins for their tea. You saw his teeth. Cuddles could have had your arm off if he'd wanted to.'

He called me something unprintable. Then he took me for a drink. I've met Austin several times since he became an MP, and we always share a thunderous laugh over our swim with Cuddles. But I don't think he's ever quite forgiven me for it.

I suppose my swim with Cuddles must have lulled me into a false sense of kinship with aquatic mammals, because that summer I became involved in one of the most financially disastrous ventures of my career. With a couple of friends, Bernard Mules and Dick Harris, I was called in by a company called Orca to help them stage a performing dolphin show at Branksome Chine, near Bournemouth.

Delphinus delphis, bottle-nosed dolphins, are popularly noted for their grace, intelligence, playfulness and friendliness to man. Because of the curvature of their mouths they've got built-in smiles, and so audiences regard them as beguiling creatures. The four I got lumbered with were the exception to the rule. They were slow on the uptake, sulky, capricious and morose; the set of their mouths made it look like they were laughing at me for being a mug.

Bernard and I built a thirty-five-foot diameter ten-foot tank, with two observation windows in the side, and a big rake of seating around the pool. We set it up at the bottom of the chine, and waited for the summer holiday-makers to pour in. They didn't. We had made one elementary and costly error. There was no need for the public to pay us their entrance fees because they could see the entire show for nothing from prime balcony positions at the top of the cliff.

Not that there was much of a show to see, because the dolphins proved to be disobedient, and permanently stroppy. Getting them to come out and perform was harder than luring hibernating toads up from the bottom of a well. There was a vet on the payroll who gave them regular checks, and they were all perfectly healthy. They were simply prima donnas on a Maria Callas scale. They did their act after much coaxing and only when they felt like it – which I suppose was the ultimate confirmation of their high intelligence.

I could never chalk up: 'Next performance 3 pm' because I could never rely on them to do their stuff at 3 pm, or 4 pm, or ever. They refused to do anything to please the visitors, who anyway were perched up on top of the cliff enjoying the non-show for nothing. The one thing the dolphins would do willingly was eat. They must have been the hungriest dolphins in captivity because they were consuming nine stones of fish every day. What with the fishmonger's bills, the vet's bills, and no audience, the show was losing a fortune. Phineas T. Barnum's last words were supposed to have been: 'How were the receipts today in Madison Square Garden?' If I had hopped the twig during that disastrous fortnight I wouldn't have had any last words, because at Branksome Chine there were no receipts.

We pulled the plug after two weeks before the four dolphins cleaned us all out. They were sold on to a showman called Lew Holloway who ran an oceanaria at Margate. My four snouty beauties had gone, but their memory lingered on. For weeks I smelled of fish.

Later in 1969 the British Council asked me to take the diving tank out to Vienna for a trade fair to promote exports. The idea was to put on a stunt spectacular and try to sell the Austrians a few swimming pools at the same time.

I'd worked out the costs of transporting my gear there by rail, and decided it would be a lot cheaper if I bought a lorry and drove everything to Austria myself. I went to a breaker's yard in Hounslow and said I was looking for a cheap vehicle that was capable of carrying a four-ton load to Vienna and back. The trader offered me a good deal on an old furniture pantechnicon, a huge Bedford TK. He was going to charge me £200, but when I told him I only really wanted it for about three weeks, he did a deal and said that, provided I brought it back in good condition, he'd give me £150 for it when I returned.

It was too good an offer to turn down, but there was a problem. The largest vehicle I'd ever taken out until then was a short wheel-base Land-Rover. I had never driven a lorry and there were only two days of practice before I was due to set off via Harwich to the Continent. The van had been owned by a removals company called Chas. Emes' Removals. But Chas had obviously employed a cheap sign-writer because the letters were badly spaced, and the apostrophe was in the wrong place, so the side of his van read: CHASE ME'S REMOVALS.

My crash course in learning to handle the vehicle was exactly that. I'd try to be careful. Driving it with my foot on the brake in case of emergency, and hitting things. At first I couldn't get the huge van round a corner without putting the back wheels up on the pavement. Several items of street furniture got buckled and I smashed a set of 'Keep Left' bollards along the Uxbridge Road while I was trying to get used to steering the thing.

On the departure date, a Sunday, Dick Harris helped me load up the van, then he got a cheap BEA flight to Vienna, abandoning me to do the donkey-work on my own. I got to Harwich without mishap. Driving the monster through Holland and France was fine. But I had forgotten that lorries aren't allowed on German motorways on Sundays.

I crossed the border into Germany just beyond Strasbourg and was belting south along the main drag when a police car pulled me over onto the hard shoulder. I got down from the cab, assuming the role of harmless foreigner. The two traffic policemen looked me over, presumably exchanging the German equivalent of 'We've got a right one here,' because I was wearing a bobble hat. I thought my best bet was to dramatise my mission as much as possible. 'I've got to get this vital equipment down to Vienna,' I told the cops. 'It's an urgent delivery for the British Council.' My relentless use of the phrase 'British Council' must have done the trick because, after they had looked through my papers, they let me carry on.

I made virtually the same speech four times along the autobahn as four different patrols flagged me down, and the excuse worked every time. It must have left the traffic police with a strange view of the British Council. What vital mission is it, they must have wondered, that the British government entrusts it to a man in a silly knitted hat driving a sludge green lorry with the words CHASE ME'S REMOVALS badly painted on the side?

The next evening, I got off the autobahn too early, thirty miles from

Vienna, and hit trouble on a hilly B road. I'd just left a village when I came to a long steep hill that must have been one-in-eight. I tried to get up a head of speed to take it in one push, but half-way up the engine ground to a halt, made a sad despairing noise, and died on me.

There wasn't enough power in the engine to haul my four-ton load the remaining fifty yards up the hill. I was well and truly stuck. I made sure the brakes were full on, wedged the wheels, and walked back down into the village to seek help before it got dark.

The lads drinking their first beers on the shadowy terrace of the *bierhaus* thought my predicament a grand opportunity to work up a nice thirst and liven up a slow evening. They all trooped out of the pub and walked back with me to the pantechnicon. I'd already worked out that the only way to get it up the hill was to do a multi-point turn until it was facing backwards up the slope, and then reverse it to the top in the lorry's lowest gear.

It took us nearly an hour to turn the lorry round, with lookouts posted up and down the road to halt the on-coming traffic as I completed each lumbering manoeuvre. We'd let the traffic flow after each jerky shift of position, then hold it up again while I manhandled the steering wheel to take another bite at the turn.

There was a convoy of traffic choking the road half-a-mile back in both directions by the time I had the furniture lorry facing backwards up the hill. I was trembling with the effort, soaked through with sweat. My Austrian friends waved the traffic on and we let it flow for half-an-hour, drinking beers, me recovering my puff.

Then with lots of German 'left-a-bits' and 'whoas' I inched the lorry back at walking pace up the slope. Just over the brow was a side road where I was able to make an easy turn. Two hours after I had stopped on the hill, I was pointing towards Vienna again, sent on my way with a ragged cheer from the beer-drinkers, barking dogs, and village boys running behind me to wave goodbye.

I set up my display tank at the trade fair centre in the Prater. By night I slept in the removals van and by day entertained the Viennese crowds with three performances of the diving act. After all the effort to get there, and using their name so freely, my contribution to the

Platoon 72B, Eastern Command
School of Physical Training,
Shorncliffe, near Folkestone.

Becoming a PT instructor was my way
of dealing with the tedium of National
Service life.

Building the
four-seater
speedboat which
unfortunately did
not survive its
sea trials.

After the army I
worked for
Purley Pools for
nearly eight
years. My diving
and swimming
displays proved
very popular.
Here I am with
Carol Finnimore,
my ex-Ealing SC
team-mate who
added a touch of
glamour.

PURLEY POOLS

GODSTONE ROAD, PURLEY, SURREY.

TELEPHONE. BYW... 1322.

PURLEY CANDLE
FILTER
Nº 3 £304

The show soon became more like a water spectacular.

Pete and Dud: as a huge fan of theirs I had great fun working with them on this underwater sketch.

I also helped out with a stunt by illusionist David Nixon, which involved an elaborate underwater card trick.

The special tank being positioned in the car park at ATV Studios in Borehamwood.

Mucking about on the Serpentine on Christmas Day 1960.

The Boat Afloat Show 1970. I was given special dispensation and allowed to park my E-Type Jaguar on the kerb just outside the gates. (*Derek Pratt*)

Messing around in the water has been a constant theme throughout my life, whether water-skiing – barefoot – or performing a 'crucifix dive'.

'The clockwork radio I loved, the clockwork pacemaker I'm not so sure about!'

My favourite cartoon, which appeared in the *Spectator* in February 1997.
(*The Spectator*)

A proud day: with gong and radio. (*Michael Stephens/PA Photos*)

I have received many honours and am visiting professor of a number of universities. Who at Dormer's Wells Secondary Modern would have thought it possible?

Face to face with myself: being sculpted by friend and neighbour Emily Morgan. (*Randall Webb*)

British Council's export drive was negligible. In two weeks I didn't manage to sell one swimming pool. But I did get a bonus. The dealer coughed up the £150 he'd promised me for the van when I got back home.

CHAPTER SIXTEEN

AN EGYPTIAN IN BERLIN

FOR EIGHTEEN DAYS DURING CHRISTMAS 1970 I BECAME THE REINCARNATION OF RAMESES II. Appearing thirty-six times, I masqueraded as the illustrious warrior-king, achieving one last glorious hurrah for the Egyptian ruler of the nineteenth dynasty.

I must have been the only blond pharaoh with a cockney accent in the rich, meandering history of the Nile. Twice a day, matinees and evenings, my retinue and I put on an underwater escapology act in a Berlin three-ringed circus called Mensch, Tiere und Aufsehen (Men, Animals and Sensation).

My spot came immediately after the elephants, and there was certainly more mumbo than jumbo about my act. Since the ancient Egyptians believed that the heart was the centre of thought, I suppose I really ought to have had my heart examined for ever agreeing to do the season at all. Berlin in winter is hardly the place to do an underwater act.

To gloss over the deep chasm of my ignorance about Egyptian civilisation I had read up on the period and worked out a little historical pageant that had as much to do with the real facts as the average sausage roll has to do with a pedigree pig. We worked out an elaborate rigmarole about the Egyptian season of Akhet, the time of the Nile flood. To display his kingly qualities Rameses II came down to the river to undergo trial by water. My old mate Bernard Mules had built me a steel sarcophagus rich in gold, copper and precious stones, made from a couple of pots of metallic paint, a few bicycle reflectors and some sequins.

At every performance I was bound tightly with yards of rope, blindfolded, and then nailed inside this elaborately jewelled coffin, topped by a gold and blue funeral mask made of fibreglass. The sarcophagus was then lowered into fourteen feet of water, and remained totally submerged for four minutes before Rameses II broke free from his bonds, smashed his way out of his coffin, and splashed to the surface amid a roar of approval and applause.

Ever since my boyhood when Digger Pugh taught me the basics of circus tumbling I have always been a sucker for the trumpet blare and vibrant life of the Big Top. When I was in my teens he used to give me the freedom of a circus camp in Essex, and it was there that I fell in love with the exotic and dangerous world of showmen.

The 1970 circus occupied the Deutscheshalle in what was then West Berlin. To announce the grand opening, there was a traditional parade through the wide and windswept streets from the Zoological Garden railway station by the Kurfustendamm, along a winding route to the arena. I can appreciate why great painters like Toulouse-Lautrec, Renoir, and Seurat were all fascinated by the circus. There is a gaudy, freakish quality about it, a vitality that gets into your bloodstream and stays there for life. I was captivated by the sights, sounds and smells of the sawdust-ring the first time I walked into one at the age of fifteen. Even now the feeling of excitement still hasn't gone away.

My little entourage and I were at the heart of the parade surrounded by clowns on stilts, elephants trunk-to-tail, painted midgets, wild beasts in gilded cages, girls in spangled scanties trying to smile through clenched teeth against a biting east wind, and a brass band blaring out Johann Strauss.

I was feeling the cold myself because all I had on was a flimsy tunic, some gold body make up, a few bangles, and the red and white double crown of Egypt, made of cardboard. A couple of mates from my trick diving troupe, Johnny Crease and Alan Roberts, were decked out as priest and vizier. There was one shuffling mummy bound in thirty feet of off-white crepe bandage, and a quintet of blonde Nefertitis. They were played by five very buxom Berlin showgirls, who, as representatives of the opposite sex, were about as opposite as you could get.

It was starting to freeze. As our procession marched sedately through the cavernous boulevards even the caged polar bears began to look fed up. The exhaust fumes from the snarled up traffic had started to annoy them. The stinging cold made those of us without fur coats equally despondent. Before we got half-way to the Deutscheshalle the mummy claimed he was as cold as a well-digger's arse in the Tundra and broke ranks to put on a sheepskin coat. A little later our five Queens of the Nile claimed the nasty wind blowing off the River Spree had got right up their Nefertitis. They sashayed off to bring up the rear of the procession in the ringmaster's limo.

'You know, I think we're in for a white Christmas,' Johnny Crease said brightly. Immediately the air was blue with ancient Egyptian hieroglyphics. 'Fuck off,' we all told him.

Inside the arena it was still bloody cold. Spotlights and flares for a lighting rehearsal picked out the vaporous breath of men and animals. It was like standing in a big concrete fridge. To warm up we huddled among the steaming elephant stalls, overcoats draped over our shoulders, embalming ourselves with a bottle of schnapps.

I was brought up tacitly approving Molesworth's view of foreigners. The Russians are rotters, Americans are swankpots, the French are slack, the Germans unspeakable, and the rest as bad if not worse than the above. While the British are brave, super, and noble. Cheers, cheers, cheers. But in the circus, nationality doesn't seem an issue. There is no great sense of rivalry between the acts, more a feeling that everybody is there to ensure the show goes well and that the customers go home happy. I suspect the camaraderie is enhanced by the knowledge that most acts are only a slip away from disaster. And, in Berlin, mine certainly was, in more ways than one.

My first public performance went from child's play to panic stations in the space of ten seconds. I tried to stay calm. Professional. In control. Not like the voice on the squawk box.

'Abort! Abort!' It was Alan Roberts, my link-man on the surface, his blurted message distorted by static. 'Can you hear me Trev? Get out now.'

Something had gone terribly wrong. The sarcophagus was supposed to enter the water under control, lowered slowly and horizontally by a crane. But trapped in the darkness I could feel it pitching backwards. My feet were up in the air. It was entering the water at a crazy angle, like a wayward submarine.

'A shackle's gone on the rig. You're going in too fast, and you're going in head first. Get out now!'

There was a full house in the Deutscheshalle for the show's first matinee. I didn't want to cut the act short. Ticket prices were high and the audience wanted its money's worth. I couldn't lose face with the other performers, or risk getting the sack. I badly needed the cash.

The squawk box crackled again. 'Can you hear me? You're going in at a steep angle. A cable's slipped and we can't pull you out. Get out now! Repeat, get out now!'

There was no way I could speak to Alan. It was a one-way link. All I could do was lie where I was with my heart thumping. 'What's happening? Can you hear me Trev? Get out!' Alan kept shouting over the link.

Water was coming in through holes in the coffin. The tilt brought it rushing down towards my face. The coffin had become a drowning machine.

All it would take was to fire the hydraulic rams. They'd force out the nails holding the coffin lid, and I'd be out. But what if the coffin had come to rest upside down? I was totally disorientated, no longer certain about what my senses were registering. I lay there sweating as the coffin lurched and then came to rest with a thud on the bottom of the tank. By a fluke it landed the right way up. I put my hand up and could feel the space for the air-pocket under the death's head of Rameses. In normal circumstances there would be enough air trapped there to keep me breathing for more than four minutes.

I could feel the rush and press of water. Adrenaline flowed quickly through my veins, my pulse was up. I tried to stay calm, to control my breathing. I was using the oxygen too quickly. I had no idea how much more was left. I started counting. I must give the audience a bit of a show. If I surfaced too quickly they'd think the act was no good.

All this was going on in slow motion, while Alan was going hoarse on the squawk box. 'For god's sake Trev. Fire the rams and get out.'

I counted past fifty and started to go woozy. I felt the edges of my consciousness begin a slow waltz. I was going under. I'd got to get out. I must act now. I was on the edge of blacking out and losing it fast. I knew what I wanted to do. I wanted to fire the rams. But I couldn't get round to doing it. I'd got the clarity of thought of a knocked-out boxer trying to beat the count. I willed my limbs into motion but they refused to do what I told them.

Weary to the point of surrender, I urged myself to a big effort. I hit the button and nothing happened. The rams wouldn't fire. The water was lapping my chin and I was beginning to swallow mouthfuls. I held my breath, gripped by black and absolute terror. I didn't know what had gone wrong with the bloody rams. My strength was ebbing away, but I concentrated all my effort into bashing the control button one more time. This time the hydraulic rams did their job, and burst the lid off the coffin.

I pushed, shoved and kicked to get clear of the sarcophagus. It was only fourteen feet but it seemed a long way to the surface. My ears were drumming and I thought my lungs were going to burst. I broke through to the air, coughing and retching as I expelled water from my nose and mouth. The audience were going wild. Alan Roberts was in the water beside me.

'Are you all right Trev? What took you so long?'

I was sucking in air, unable to speak and trying not to vomit. I hauled myself up to the side of the tank and Alan and Johnny Crease helped me out. Huge applause was cascading round the vast auditorium and I bowed to the audience. The people in the posh seats at the ringside were going wild.

'Why didn't you come up when I told you?' said Alan.

'I couldn't get the hydraulic rams to fire.' Which wasn't an absolute lie.

'You had us all worried there for a while.'

'Shut up and take a bow,' I told him. 'The audience loved it.'

No one realised how close I'd come to blacking out, and I didn't let on. One of the shackles on the rig had broken. I replaced it and made sure all the cables were properly set up and balanced. I also double-checked the mechanism for firing the hydraulic rams.

I found the crane driver having a brew in his cubby-hole and gave him a bollocking for lowering me into the water too quickly. I'd looked up the German word for slowly in my pocket dictionary and kept repeating it to him: 'Langsam. Langsam.' It's one of the few German words I can still remember.

There was still an hour to go before the second house. Lissa (of whom more, later) came round to my trailer and we shared a pot of tea. 'You've got a great act,' she said. 'The audience loved it. Some of them didn't think you were going to get out of the coffin alive.'

'Neither did I.' That's what I thought, but I didn't say anything in case it alarmed her.

We made a date for supper after the show. After she'd gone I sat smoking my pipe, psyching myself up to get nailed back into my coffin again. But I wasn't frightened. I had rehearsed the stunt so many times that every action had become instinctive. In my head it really wasn't any more dangerous than crossing a busy main road. And Phineas T. Barnum was right. There is a sucker born every minute. Great illusions and feats of escapology are merely elaborate deceptions in which tinsel showmanship and hocus-pocus dupe a gullible public into accepting an illusion of danger or mystification. It's all moonshine. That's why I love the circus.

My underwater escape from the sarcophagus was as perilous as producing a rabbit from a hat. Just as long as things went to plan. And after that first near-disaster they did. My act was built entirely upon kidology. The ropes given to members of the audience to bind my hands and feet were purposely only long enough for them to tie one knot. These simple knots – we mostly chose women to tie them – were kid's stuff to loosen. The blindfold was a load of old madam, a theatrical gesture; underwater I wasn't able to see much anyway. The long thirty-foot rope which was then wound round my body looked intimidating. But as it was being wound I braced my elbows outwards, so that when I relaxed I would be able to wriggle free.

As soon as the lid was on the coffin and my troupe of mock-Egyptians started to nail it down, I released my hands, eased my arms on the rope round my body so it became loose, and untied my feet. By the time they began to winch the sarcophagus high over the tank I was already free from all my restraints and ready for the next stage of the escape.

The sarcophagus had holes drilled in its bottom, so as it was slowly lowered into the tank, water percolated in at a steady rate. When it was full, the pharaoh's death-mask, the fibreglass bubble Bernard Mules had built above my face, trapped a mantle of air inside which gave me enough oxygen to breathe underwater for almost five minutes.

I would wait there, listening to a countdown on the squawk box. All I had to do was stay relaxed, controlling my breathing until it was time to get out. I'd lie doggo and meditate on how much money the stunt was earning me. Any panic or undue exertion only wasted precious air. When I got the signal to get out I fired the hydraulic rams. And hey presto, I'd splash to the surface to a huge fanfare, climb out of the tank, and take my bow, removing the blindfold in one last grandiose gesture.

That night our second public performance began as usual with a triumphal parade into the arena. The blokes in our Nile finery and gold body paint looking like silly Gizas, the girls – five gorgeous girls and three gorgeous costumes – wearing next to nothing. All the while the circus band played a spectacularly lousy version of 'The Grand March' from *Aida*.

As Rameses II was prepared for his watery grave my team manipulated the audience tying me up, ensuring I wasn't too expertly bound, and supervised the operation as the coffin was lowered into the tank. While I was waiting quietly underwater the real drama was taking place outside the tank. The role of my Egyptian retinue in the fully rehearsed and entirely scripted melodrama was to lay on the suspense with a trowel. The supporting cast – particularly Johnny Crease and Alan Roberts – deserved Oscars for over-acting. You couldn't have found more ham in a mile of bratwurst.

As soon as the coffin entered the water the band started to play a medley of cod Egyptian tunes, with a heavy drum rhythm that sounded like a heartbeat. Gradually the heartbeat got louder and faster. For the first minute my retinue remained calm, but as the seconds ticked by they started to get alarmed. Johnny and Alan began to look nervously at their stop-watches. (Yes, our Ancient Egyptians possesed stop watches.)

The girls panicked and ran around the tank, trying to see what had gone wrong. A couple of them began to cry, and a third had been primed to shout in German: 'Get him out of there, or he'll drown.' Into the second minute and Johnny and Alan were losing their cool. They engaged in a shouted dispute with the ringmaster, who in elaborate pantomime refused to allow them to haul the coffin out of the water.

By now the sound of the rapid heartbeats was deafening and the audience was in hysterics. There were children weeping, ashen-faced women fainting all over the place, and men standing up in their seats shouting: 'Get him out of there.' And, 'Stop the show.' I always thought the Germans were a phlegmatic lot. But after I had been underwater for more than four minutes, the lads told me the whole audience in the Deutscheshalle was in uproar, threatening to rush the stage to lynch the ringmaster and drag me out of the water with their bare hands.

My escape from certain death was timed to coincide with that moment of total bedlam. At the second house I broke the surface of the water to a huge cheer of relief, screams of amazement and a Niagara of applause. That's show business, and they don't make acts like that any more. We were a hit. Afterwards the ringmaster, a massive man called Franz with jowls like a boxer dog, formally shook my hand and gravely informed me: 'Herr Baylis, your act was the highlight of the show.' It was a nice feeling. Now I was world famous in two places – Southall and Berlin.

Over the next few weeks I fell in love with Lissa.

She was a girl who had come to Berlin to try out for a flying act. There was a trio of South African aerial acrobats – the Azekoffs, two blokes and a girl – who were thinking of adding another female to their routine. They spent most of the day swinging around the dome, working out routines with the recruit.

The man who bossed the act was a huge catcher called Terry. He was a fitness freak – built like a Russian war memorial – who had very strong views about discipline. I spent my time with his new girl in mortal fear that the man who daily caught her in the act, would walk in one day and catch us.

I first spoke to her in the Deutscheshalle snack bar where I was having an espresso coffee and a Stulle. She said my sandwich looked tempting, so I went back to the counter and got her one. We chatted and I had the distinct impression that more than food and small talk was on the menu. There was something about our conversation – self-consciously casual and elaborately polite – that was teasingly sensual.

She'd burst out laughing at a joke, then blush as though it made her seem too familiar. We spoke easily. The way we got on you would have thought we had known each other for years. She was from Cape Town and pretended not to understand my accent. Then when I lit my pipe she ticked me off like a child. She said her name was Lissa, with two esses she insisted. We lingered after we had finished our food. At the end of half-an-hour of pleasant banter she told me she had to go and do her warm-up exercises, and I said it had been nice to meet her.

We were formally introduced later that day by the massive Terry. She gave me a tiny smile of recognition, but we didn't let on that we already knew each other. They were about to practise the new routine and I stayed on to watch them from the ringside seats.

She climbed with silky strength to the roof of the stadium. Then she stood ready on a tiny platform with the other girl while Terry swung aloft, muscling up to speed on one of the bars as the other man in the act, a young lad called Paul, worked the other. When they had got the tempo right, Lissa launched herself and grabbed Terry's wrists. There was a white puff of resin as they made contact. Then the two men threw her and the other girl back and forth as they somersaulted just under the arena roof. But I didn't really notice the others, I just looked at her swooping above our heads high in the canopy, a glittering bar of dancing light.

They stopped for a brief discussion on one of the platforms. Something wasn't going right and they adjusted a move. They went through the routine five times before they were satisfied. All the workers in the arena stopped what they were doing, faces turned up to the roof, alert to every new movement. After they finished we gave them a round of applause; even their fellow professionals were impressed.

Lissa slid back down the wire in a graceful arc. As she walked across the ring in the direction of the dressing rooms I saw her boss take her arm and kiss her on the cheek. I felt a pang of jealousy. I didn't know what had hit me. She had the most beautiful body I had ever seen, and dressed for her trapeze work, I saw most of it.

The next time we spoke was after the final dress rehearsal. All the dangerous stunts, acts of daring, bits of business, elaborate machinery, and lighting effects had worked well and everybody was on a high. I told Terry how much I had enjoyed the routine they were working on. He gave me a half-smile and grunted: 'Thanks mate.' Lissa grabbed my arm, reached up, gave me a peck on the cheek and said: 'That's very kind of you.'

That evening Terry hit the Berlin snooker halls with the other bloke in the act. They planned a few kleine helles – small glasses of pale beer with ice-cold corn schnapps chasers. Purely by chance I met up with Lissa again in the snack bar, just passing through, and things took off from there. She told me the other girl in the act had gone to the cinema. After fifteen minutes of casual chat, in which our eyes met a few times, she said she'd better be getting back to her trailer. 'You know where my rig is,' she said softly. 'The door won't be locked.'

I waited for five minutes and then followed. The door was on the latch, the bedclothes pulled back, and she was waiting in a Japanese wrap covered with red dragons. Neither of us made much conversation. A few urgent words of tenderness. Then we began, losing ourselves in the urgent rituals of unwrapping each other's secrets. Her skin was sumptuously soft, honey-coloured and smelled vaguely of embrocation.

As I caressed her someone in another trailer neaby was singing in German. The cries of the circus animals were so close, they sounded as if they were brushing past the trailer. We fell asleep almost unawares. An hour later I woke up in sudden panic thinking big Terry was bursting in, making his presence felt in the shape of a sixteen-ounce billiard cue. But he wasn't and I shut my eyes, lulled by the sounds of the circus and her rhythmic breathing beside me, and went back to sleep.

We worked every afternoon and evening, so mornings were the only time we could explore the city together. We went to the flea market, housed in a ramshackle collection of old subway trains at Nollendorfplatz, where she bought herself an evening dress for about fifty pence. She took me to see the Rembrandts at the Dahlem Museum. It took us hours to get round. We'd spend half-an-hour sitting on a bench in front of each masterpiece with her examining the Rembrandts and me examining her. One Sunday she even persuaded me to get up early to go to church in East Berlin. I must have been in love to get up early on a Sunday. We crossed at Checkpoint Charlie where the East German Volks-Polizei dragged out the passport checking for forty minutes. It was only a short walk to the Marienkirch, but we got lost a couple of times and didn't get there until half-way through the service. Neither of us could make sense of one word of the sermon. It seemed to go on for ever and the Minister sounded like he'd got out of bed on the wrong side. But the hymns were good and we enjoyed the atmosphere. Lissa was holding my hand and I gave it a squeeze.

'Do you come here often?' I whispered.

'What?' She didn't realise it was a reference to *The Goon Show*. She'd never heard of them.

I attempted to explain it to her in a stage whisper. I didn't want to disturb the congregation's devotions.

'It's a catch-phrase from a British radio comedy. When I say: "Do you come here often?" you're supposed to reply: "Only in the mating season." It's meant to be a joke.'

Even though she didn't understand what I was talking about, she gave me a wonderful smile and there was a twinkle of joy in her hazel eyes. I gave her a peck on the cheek and whispered: 'It doesn't matter. It's a silly joke anyway.'

Afterwards we went to Haus Berlin, just off Karl Marx Allee, for breakfast. It cost us five marks each for some sawdust-filled sausages, which, because I was with her, tasted delicious. Then we walked down the Unter den Linden arm-in-arm under a mother-of-pearl sky. Things were just as bad as we'd been told. Around us everything was grey and ramshackle. There were a few unlit Christmas trees. Some tatty silver decorations. The place was totally lacking in any festive cheer. The people looked pale and thoroughly miserable. Everywhere you could see the drab monotony of an unsmiling authoritarian regime. In contrast we were light-hearted, overflowing with high spirits. East Berlin didn't depress us at all, we felt there was a lively electric feel to the place. That's what being in love does to people.

At the age of thirty-three I'd not accumulated much in life. No house. No wife. No responsibilities. Not many possessions. Few achievements. Experience, a lot of that. Expenses, a lot of them. Wisdom, hardly any. But I'd had a lot of laughter in my life. I was certainly a man of substance as regards laughter. But I always worried that if I took the plunge and got married, somehow it would spoil the fun and stifle all the laughter.

My trouble is I really believe the jokes that comedians make about marriage. There's a nugget of truth in them that has made me wary of the institution. 'A good marriage lasts for ever. A bad one just seems to.' And, 'I can remember when I got married. And where I got married. What I just can't remember is why?' And, 'I've decided to end it all. I'm getting married. Thank you and goodnight. Don't clap too hard – it's a very old building.'

I suppose the closest I've ever been to asking anyone was during those Christmas weeks in Berlin. But, between all our laughter, the moment passed and I never quite got round to asking her.

On the last night of the show everybody was on a high. We were coming to the end of the run and we were about to get paid. My act went very well that night, but for one thing. Before they placed me in the sarcophagus and nailed down the lid, some joker half-filled it with fresh elephant droppings. I was blindfold and didn't know the droppings were there until the water started coming in and floated the huge turds up into my face. If you've never inhaled elephant dung, then don't bother. As an expert I can tell you that the stench dwarfs most other odours.

I suspected it was Franz, the ringmaster, because after my act he cornered me with a few heavily laboured jokes. 'Trevor, like an elephant you'll never forget your time in Berlin, eh?'

I said goodbye to Lissa an hour after the last show. She'd been asked to join the aerial act and they were driving overnight to another engagement in Italy. We held hands and our farewell kiss took place in the Deutscheshalle car park to the accompaniment of Terry revving their van, anxious to get on the road. I gave her a locket; we exchanged addresses. I promised to write, but I never did. I figured she'd always be on the road and my letters would never reach her.

CHAPTER SEVENTEEN
THE HOUSE THAT
TREV BUILT

I N 1971 I INVENTED MY OWN HOUSE.

I had always fancied the idea of living on Eel Pie Island. It's my sort of community; friendly, informal, and slightly out of kilter with the rest of organised society. It was once described as: 'Fifty drunks clinging to a mud flat.' Many of my friends work in the artists' commune here; I'd often wandered across the bridge from the mainland, or Twickenham as it's called, to visit the hotel (now burned down) where bands like The Rolling Stones used to play when they were unknown, and I liked what I saw.

The houses on the tiny spit of gravel in the Thames embrace every architectural style from beach hut to corrugated iron shanty, and I thought I'd be happy here. The nice thing about it is that once there really were eel pies on Eel Pie Island. In Henry VIII's days there was an old crone living on the island who was noted for her eel pies. Fat King Hal used to stop off at her stall to pick up a couple of pies on his river progress up to Hampton Court Palace.

A friend of mine, an estate agent called Mike Fielding, told me there was a property for sale on the island, which I could actually see from the bedroom window of my flat in Thames Eyot. I wandered across the bridge to give it the once over. He had tried to hype it. Charming character home, close to river, endless possibilities for improvement et cetera. The usual estate-agent-speak. I suppose you could best describe it as a scout hut. It was a wooden shed with a verandah out the front. Behind it was another shed and an outside toilet. It was called The Haven and was being sold by someone called Bunny Brown; it had belonged to his mother and she had just died.

In those days bank managers were much more accommodating than they are today. Now you can only borrow money as long as you can provide sufficient detailed documentary evidence to show that you don't need it. But at the start of the 1970s it was different, and I actually regarded the manager of my local Barclays, Bob Pitcher, as a mate. My balance sheet looked healthy enough to Bob and he advanced me £10,000 to buy The Haven, and £10,000 more to knock it down and build a new home.

Because I'd worked for Le Grand, Sutcliff and Gell and was trained as a structural engineer it was a fairly simple matter to sketch out my ideas and get a pal to make them into a proper blueprint. I made a slight tactical error talking to the man from the Borough Engineer's department. 'I used to earn my living working out the depth of foundations,' I told him. 'The ones I'm putting in here will be so solid you could build multi-storey flats on them.' He seemed a bit suspicious and kept coming round to inspect the site as the work progressed, to make sure, presumably, that I wasn't building a block of flats.

I had never done any bricklaying before, so I practised getting it right on the footings. They looked higgledy, with cement oozing between the bricks like a badly iced cake. When I got up to the damp course I thought I'd better call in an expert, otherwise it would end up looking as crooked as Hänsel and Gretel's cottage. But from then on I did all the labouring work, and most of the other jobs, apart from laying the bricks, myself. As it turned out it wouldn't have mattered how uneven the bricks were, because I rendered the outside of the house anyway.

I was lucky because at the same time eighteen houses were being built at the far end of the island, in a development called Aquarius. After the first six houses had been completed the project went into liquidation, leaving a surplus of builders' materials lying about unwanted, except by me. I went up there one day and told the site agent it was hardly worth the bother of humping all the stuff off the island, and he let me have as many bricks, and tiles, as I wanted for half-price.

My girlfriend at the time was Estelle Tiedre. She worked in a solicitor's office, and is now married, with two children, and lives in Spain. She was a lovely athletic girl who made a great builder's labourer. We used to have to ship materials up-river to the site by barge and it was a hell of a job unloading sand and aggregate. I'd stagger up the gangplank under a sack of sand, wobbling like an old lady with too many shopping bags; meanwhile Estelle would be carrying a similar load and making it look graceful.

She was the sexiest builder's labourer I've ever met. It was hard, blissful work. After a day toiling in the sun we'd sit together by the river, drinking beer, comparing blistered hands; with the smell of the heat-wave in the air. We'd watch the sky redden at the edges as daylight drained away with the tide.

As soon as the roof was secure I moved in, sleeping in an indoor bivouac even before the windows were glazed. It took me ages to get the house as I wanted it. For three years, anywhere you sat in the place you could always see a job that needed finishing, and some of them still aren't.

The architectural style is probably best described as post-Acacia Avenue, late twentieth-century eccentric. I thought my home should be more than a shelter or a space, I wanted it to be me in bricks and mortar, and it is; which means it's quirky, unconventional, and slightly rambling.

Open the front door and you walk straight into my workshop, an L-shaped lean-to arrangement tacked onto the main house; it's the store for all my tools and gubbins, the place where I spend hours at my bench. Inch past the chaos of spare parts, through another door, and you're confronted, on your left, by my indoor pool. So, within a few yards of each other my two great diversions are catered for: swimming and tinkering with machinery. To the right of the pool is the bathroom, and beyond that the house proper begins. There's a large kitchen-cum-dining-room-cum-living-room, opening onto a terrace which leads down to the river, and a jetty. Above the main quarters is a bedroom-cum-office, which opens onto another elevated terrace.

It's a bachelor's dream. Designed simply and selfishly as a space to fit my needs. As a machine for living it's wonderfully efficient. Devised to suit me as exquisitely and functionally as the shell of a snail. It is so undeniably Baylis, reflecting my work and pastimes on every inch of its wall space, that when the house was featured on *Through the Keyhole*, David Frost's panel guessed it was my house after a couple of token questions. Loyd Grossman's film tried to be opaque and make it a mystery, but he couldn't fool them. It was my home's shambolic untidiness that gave the game away. It's the sort of place where if vandals broke in, they'd leave it looking as though someone had dropped by to tidy up. (I told Frostie that during the filming, Loyd Grossman had got lost in my workshop for three days, and we'd had to send in dogs to find him.)

As the house on Eel Pie Island took shape, so did a new business of mine. I used the £6,300 profit from my stint with the Berlin circus to start a business building, installing and repairing swimming pools. In spite of my previous bad experience with dolphins, I used a dolphin as a logo. To echo the name of my diving display team, I called the company Shotline Pools.

The business was a new concept in pool design using heavy-gauge steel walls, zinc-coated to resist corrosion. They were lined with specially formulated blue PVC, electronically welded into a completely waterproof membrane.

Before inflicting myself on the unsuspecting public I thought I'd better have a trial run. I put up my first pool in a builder's yard at Bell Lane, Hounslow. The place was owned by the father of a friend of mine, Paul Freeman. After I'd built the pool and filled it with water I thought there ought to be some sort of official ceremony to mark the occasion, so I went up on the roof of Paul's house and dived straight off it into the water. Paul refused to follow my example. He called me a head case.

Liner pools weren't a new idea. The earliest liner pool in Britain was installed in Bath during the Roman occupation. The Romans' spa baths were lined with lead. That type of membrane is no longer used because of its toxicity, but I've built pools lined with PVC, fibreglass and butyl. There was a lot of disposable income about in the early 1970s, and having got their second car and all the electrical goods they could fit into their kitchens, lots of people were shoehorning pools into their back gardens. I've fitted pools in gardens that were so small people were able to open their French windows and dive straight into the water.

I was working flat out, often round the clock. With a level site it was possible to install a pool in less than twenty-four hours. And I was cheap too. A pool measuring 34 yards by 30 feet, plus the filtration plant, heater and ancillary equipment cost only £2,500. I was a one-man band, with my mum doing all the paperwork. Before long I was travelling all over Britain installing swimming pools for schools, colleges, universities and community centres. As the business grew I took on Chris Race and a married couple, Nick and Ollie Woodward, to share the workload with me. Another sideline was supplying large christening pools for Baptist churches. In the Baptist religion the sacrament is conducted by total immersion, so the font has to become what is in effect a small swimming pool, and my company has supplied scores of them.

Every hour when I wasn't putting in swimming pools, I was back on Eel Pie Island building my house, and when I wasn't doing that I was doing swimming and diving stunt work. I used to service pools as a sideline, using an aqualung to dive to the bottom to repair any tears in the pool membrane, so the owners didn't have to go to the bother of draining them. I was working so hard I didn't have time to be tired, and I was loving every minute of it. It was like the old joke: Work hard faithfully eight hours a day and one day you may eventually get to be your own boss and work twelve hours a day.

They used to organise an annual swimming race around the island. It would start and finish at the bridge to the mainland. The first time I took part was back in the 1970s. A big crowd of swimmers turned out for it, and most of them fancied their chances of winning. As we were all warming up I asked the starter: 'Does it matter which direction we take around the island?'

He said: 'No, as long as you swim all the way round I don't care which way you go.'

When the gun went everybody else started swimming with the tide. I decided to get half of the hard work out of the way first, and went in the opposite direction – against the tide. Then as the others were battling with the long stretch against the tide, I coasted down past them looking totally relaxed. The sight of me swanning it down stream took the heart out of most of them, and they slowed down even more. Then when I turned the corner, I just had a sharp stretch against the tide, and I was home. I won, easing up. But that's always been my attitude. Get the strenuous parts of life out of the way first, then you can lie back and enjoy the easy bits.

I love living on Eel Pie Island, and I have no plans to move. On the jetty out the back of my house is a car I have been working on for twenty-one years. It's a rust-red four-fendered heap of scrap that looks as if it belongs in *Chitty Chitty Bang Bang*. The front headlights come from a bus, it's got a Ford Cortina engine, and somewhere in the chassis there's a bit of old bedstead. I'd never consider leaving here until the car was finished. But since I'm now far too busy to work on the car, and I'd have to crane it onto a barge to take it to the nearest road anyway, it will stay where it is, a dream in progress.

For years the skippers on the pleasure boat plying the river have included me in their commentaries. They used to say: 'That house belongs to Trevor Baylis who has been building that car since 1978.' Now they say: 'That house belongs to Trevor Baylis, inventor of the clockwork radio, who has been building that car since 1978.'

CHAPTER EIGHTEEN

THE SIX-STONE WEAKLING

I COULD TELL ALL MY FRIENDS THOUGHT I WAS GOING TO DIE WHEN THEY BEGAN TO TREAT ME WITH NAUSEATING POLITENESS. It was the middle of 1972 and, in the space of six months, my weight had dropped to under eighty pounds. I was fading away in front of their eyes and they were all far too embarrassed by the apparent imminence of my death to mention what was at the forefront of their minds and say I looked a goner.

It was as though my body had developed a slow puncture. Suddenly I was the weakling in the Charles Atlas body-building advertisements. More inexorable weight loss and a few weeks later I'd shrunk to the size of a Twickenham Gandhi. Without being in the least bit funny, it was a joke; I found I could walk about inside my own trousers, no laughing matter. As I got thinner my friends became more cloying, obsequious, and Uriah Heepish. Some of them started using the royal 'we' when they spoke to me. 'And how are we today?' they'd say, as if, besides losing seven stones, I'd also suddenly ripened into Princess Margaret.

I was too weak to continue work on building my house. Most of the walls were bare plaster, the paintwork still at the undercoat stage. I was camping out surrounded by packing cases and builders' debris. My friends would enter this dislocated kingdom of the sick and proceed to be so thoroughly nice they made me feel sicker than before they had arrived, which was sick enough.

They were all convinced I had cancer. For a while I was convinced I had cancer too. But nobody ever mentioned it. For some of us the c-word has become the great unmentionable, like sex for the Victorians. I wouldn't have minded if they had talked to me about my illness.

'Is it cancer mate?'

'I bloody well hope not.'

It would have been a release and got the subject out of the way. Instead I felt they were nodding at each other across the bed, not speaking the unspeakable, mouthing the word in case actually saying its name made cancer contagious.

A year earlier I had begun to get pains in my abdomen. When the doctor asked me to describe it I said it felt like a dull toothache in my stomach. He put it down to my being a bachelor with bad eating habits. Too many cordon noir meals in greasy-spoon cafes. He prescribed some lozenges that tasted like blackboard chalk in tablet form.

My tongue soon had enough chalk deposit on it to draw the alpha-bet on a slate, but I was still in pain. Then something burst inside me and I was taken to hospital for an emergency appendectomy. My doctor said I'd be fine now. But I felt even worse than before the operation. Every time I went to his surgery he prescribed more chalk, and gave me a look that said he thought I was a galloping hypochon-driac.

Half-an-hour after each meal I would throw up. Whatever I ate it made no difference. I couldn't keep any food down. It was at this time that I met Pauline Bricker who was then working as a waitress in Peppers restaurant in Twickenham. I'd go there every lunchtime and ask her to bring me something from the menu that wouldn't make me ill. But the blandest of foods – even dry toast – had the same effect, and it all came back up again. It was a wonder they put up with me at Peppers. I was like a vomiting resident gourmet giving damning evidence about their dish of the day. I'd eat something and rush from the table to be ill. All the other customers would look edgy while

Pauline tried to reassure them with a smile. 'Don't be alarmed,' she'd tell them. 'Trevor's a regular here.'

I kept going to hospital for tests which proved inconclusive. They attached all sorts of instruments to various parts of my body and nothing much showed up on their printouts or monitor screens. I began to wonder whether a vet could come up with a better diagnosis. At least I wouldn't have to try to describe exactly how awful I felt to a vet, I could just sit there and mew pathetically.

And all the time weight was dropping off me. I'd go to hospital where they'd put me on the scales and announce: 'You've lost more weight,' as though they'd made an astonishing breakthrough on a par with the discovery of penicillin.

The thinner I got the nicer people became. There I was with the appearance of a man who by rights ought to be hanging from a charm bracelet and all they wanted to talk about was the good old days. They seemed driven by the maxim: 'Never speak ill of the dying'. As I faded away the more they tried to convince me that no kinder, cleverer, merrier pal than dear old Trev had ever trod shoe leather. As soon as I seemed fatally bound for that undisclosed country from whose Bourne no Hollingsworth returns, all my faults were forgotten. It was like reading my obituaries in advance as all my friends tried to remember the fun times we had together. What larks, Trev.

I suppose I faced up to dying. For most of the time I was in such agony all I wanted was for the pain to stop, and I suppose that's a definition of death. The closest anyone got to a philosophical discussion about my probable early departure was when somebody quoted Dylan Thomas's poem: 'Do not go gentle into that good night.' I swore at him and said: 'Speaking for myself, I want to go as gentle as possible.'

I had always expected to die of something more exciting than natural causes. Anyone who has worked as a stunt man has got used to taking calculated risks and is resigned to the possibility – however remote – of a death that's quick and showy. But I had never realised how painful natural causes could be, and found myself pondering the relative merits of a nice quick broken neck and the quiet comforts of leaving a young healthy-looking corpse.

Then the doctors started to get some vague indications from all their prodding and poking. After twelve months of making inquiries, with no prime suspects on their list of suspicious diseases, and my weight down to five stone ten pounds they suddenly concluded that I might have Crohn's disease, a chronic inflammatory disease of the gut. They attempted to improve the symptoms by giving me steroids, but the symptoms refused to improve.

I was lying in bed one day feeling lousy, dozing in and out of sleep. I woke and the sheets were soaking wet. When I looked I saw my appendix scar had burst and black liquid, the colour of octopus ink, was oozing from the wound. I rang my mother and the doctor. Mum arrived first and began to panic when she saw the big stains, black as Africa, on the sheets. She thought her boy was dying and began to cry. She was so upset that when the doctor arrived the first thing he did was to make her a cup of tea.

At West Middlesex Hospital I had a barium meal and the x-rays showed a blockage in my intestines. More than a foot of my gut had adhered, like the inner tube of bike tyre that's got stuck together with rubber solution. It had probably been like that since my appendix operation, and was the cause of all my problems. Why no one had spotted it before was one of those mysteries of medical science that no one ever got round to enlightening me about.

They operated on me a few days later to remove the infected gut. I remember being wheeled along the corridor to where an anaesthetist gave me a couple of injections and asked me to count to five. I got muzzily as far as five, there was blackness, and I woke up again.

'When am I going to have my operation?' I asked the first nurse I saw.

She laughed and replied: 'You had your operation two days ago Trevor.'

I was in hospital for seven weeks. My mother spent the time telling all her friends: 'Our Trevor's had his insides cut away.' Each time the consultant surgeon brought his students on their ward rounds I was treated like a prize exhibit. I got used to being spoken about in the third person as if I was an inanimate object, a slab of meat lying naked on the sheets, while everybody examined how well my flesh had been carved.

Once he even wheeled me off to a lecture room and gave everybody a blow-by-blow account of my operation. At the end of his little talk he asked me how I was. 'How are we feeling now?' was how he put it. I got a laugh from the students by replying: 'Both of us are doing very well thank you.'

As I got stronger I managed to shuffle around the ward to talk to the other patients. There was a lovely old bloke in the bed opposite me who'd had an operation to remove a tumour from his stomach. When they saw the state of him they quietly sewed him up. There was no hope, and he'd asked them to discharge him so he could go home to his own bed.

'They've said I can go home to die,' he told me brightly. 'But they want to build me up a bit first.'

He was slightly deaf and you could hear his voice all over the ward. One morning a young doctor came to examine him and closed the curtains round the bed.

'I've been thinking about this euthanasia business, doctor,' he was almost shouting. 'Couldn't you just give me an injection and put me to sleep like a pet?'

'I'm sorry,' the doctor replied. 'It's against the law. Euthanasia isn't available on the National Health.'

'What if I went private?' he said.

At first I was fed intravenously, but after a while they began to let me take first liquids, then solids. The big test for whether everything in my gut had healed properly would be my first bowel movement. It became a topic of speculation for the whole ward. One of the patients even ran a sweepstake to predict the time and the day.

One of our favourite nurses was a smashing girl from Hong Kong called Rose. Every morning she would ask me the same question.

'Trevor, do you want to do your business?'

I would say: 'No, Rose. Not yet.'

And one of the patients who'd predicted that this would be the big day would shout: 'Give him an enema, Rose.'

It went on like that for five days until I felt as bloated as Buddha.

On the fifth morning Rose asked me the same question, I gave her the same answer, and to ragged cheers and shouts of 'It's a fix', she said: 'We've waited long enough, Trevor. I'll give you a laxative.'

She gave me a large dose of medicine and asked me to position myself in a chair close to the toilets. The excitement in the ward was like that for Grand National Day, with people who still had valid tickets in the sweepstake urging me to hurry up and get under orders. At about half-past ten I broke wind noisily. There were outbreaks of cheering. This was followed by an SBD (Silent But Deadly), and the tension reached fever pitch. I rushed into the cubicle at exactly 11.34 and did the business. It was the first time in my life I'd ever answered the call of nature to wild applause, ribald cheering and someone shouting: 'I've won.' A weasel of an insurance man (varicose veins) in the end bed by the window won £3 in the sweepstake – his estimate was only half-an-hour out.

When they let me go home I was still weak and underweight. My father had died of a heart attack on 22 October 1973. He was sixty-five and just about to retire when his life-long dedication to the delights of a good fried breakfast caught up with him. I managed to get to Ealing Hospital just in time to hold his hand as he drifted into his final sleep. We both looked as ill as each other. You wouldn't have taken a bet about which of us was going to go first. The beautiful thing about our relationship was that we were more like friends than father and son. He was a good gentle man who taught me so much. I sat there thanking him, for the first time ever, when he couldn't hear me.

His death and my illness made palpable how little time any of us has got here, how precious each moment of life is, and I made a resolution not to waste any of it. There's a line in one of Johnny Carson's routines on the NBC's *Tonight Show*. 'For three days after death, hair and finger-nails continue to grow but phone calls taper off.' My slow return to health was like arriving at one of those clear-as-glass mornings that signal the coming of spring. I made up my mind to value each day ahead and enjoy life before the calls tapered off.

I got back into the diving routine quicker than I'd bargained for. I was out in my speedboat on the river with a friend of mine, Polly Burn. The boat is a Revenger driven by a 5.8 V8 Chrysler engine that develops 250 horsepower. I call it 'Puffadust'. There is nothing better on a sunny morning than to putter along the empty river listening to its engine idling, not calling up its power, just delighting in the infinite delicacy of the throaty noise it makes.

I was three months out of hospital, scars nicely healed, but still convalescing. Back supervising the swimming pool business, but taking it easy. I hadn't taken on any stunt work for almost a year. We were going up-river, just out to take the air, when we noticed a commotion on the bank by Ham Common. There were a couple of fire engines and some police cars drawn up on Ham riverside.

A crowd of people stood on the towpath looking down into the fast-flowing water. As our speedboat got to where they were peering, you could just make out the outline of a car, bonnet down in the Thames.

'What's happened?' I shouted to the bank.

One of the policemen told us a young boy out walking his dog had spotted the car and called the police. 'We don't know whether anyone's in it,' he said. 'A team of police divers are on the way.'

I explained I was a trained diver and I'd take a look if they wanted. He warned me not to take any risks and said I might as well leave it to the experts with their breathing apparatus.

'I'm used to bare-knuckle diving,' I told him. 'I'll just take a look to see if anyone's in there. If there is, they might still be alive.'

I took off my shoes, and stripped down to my underpants. Before he could raise any more objections I was in the water. The flow was running rapidly down-river from Teddington weir and it took me a couple of dives to locate the driver's door. It was a Mini, deep in the mud. From the amount of silt collecting around the bodywork I could see it had been in the river some time. I went down five times to make sure, but I made no gruesome discoveries.

I surfaced to give my final negative report to the policeman, and he radioed through to the diving team not to bother coming. The water was bracing, and I was enjoying it. I had a good long swim. Before clambering back into the speedboat, I attached a hawser from one of the fire engines to the Mini. As Polly turned the speedboat downstream to take me home for a shower, the firemen were pulling the car from the water. It must have been a slow news week, because it all got written up in the *Twickenham Times*.

I felt so good the next day I booked the first stunt since my illness for the following week. It was a film for the Ministry of Transport advising motorists how to escape from a car underwater. It involved me driving an old banger into the Thames at Laleham.

It was a complicated set-up, and to get it right I had to escape from the car three times. It took us a couple of days to get it all on film, and by the time the job was finished I was back into the swing of stunt work. The dangerous edge of things still gave me a buzz. I was only thirty-seven, and I felt stronger and fitter every day. I was almost the familiar gung-ho Baylis again, the same old chancer eager for the next challenge, but deep inside I think I conceded that my licence to dare anything now carried one endorsement.

It took me months to get my weight back to what it had been. I swam at home every day and slowly my body muscled out and returned to shape. Within six months I was back in the old routine doing my diving act, underwater swimming, in between selling my pools.

One of my specialities through the 1970s was barefoot water-skiing. I joined a display team run by a West Countryman, Reg Prytherch, who put on water spectaculars at boat shows and regattas across the country. One of our regular venues was the Boat Afloat Show at London's Little Venice, which we did until around 1975. Reg's grand finale involved skiing down the canal after dark carrying a flaming torch. He would ski through a wall of fire, and then cut across, close to an island, where he'd pick up a bottle of beer. As he put the bottle to his lips it cued the start of a spectacular fireworks display.

Every day I badgered Reg to let me do the finale. He got so fed up with my constant chivvying that eventually, in our last year at the show, he agreed. Everything that could go wrong in my first, and only, performance did. As I sat on the side of the canal holding the flaming torch the arena lights suddenly went out. In the inky darkness the assistant whose job it was to light the wall of fire anticipated his cue and set it alight too early. Meanwhile George Gould who was driving the speedboat pulled away from the canal bank too fast, and the ski-rope snapped.

I was dumped into the canal and the water put out my flaming torch. George managed to fix the tow rope in seconds, but the wall of fire had already begun to die down, and when I skied through it, the spray I was putting up doused all the flames. By now the timing had gone completely to pot and the firework display started prematurely. We missed out the bottle of beer trick because rockets, big maroons, and a volcano of sparks had put a molten curtain right across our path in the canal.

George took his speedboat through the inferno as fast as he could, with me twenty yards behind him, eyes tight shut, but still smiling and waving to the crowd trying to pass it off as though everything was going according to plan. George took refuge in a side arm of the canal, and I sank down into the water to take the sting out of hundreds of spark burns.

I swam up to the boat and watched the rest of the firework display with George. 'What would you like to do for an encore?' he said.

'Go back in the boat with you,' I replied.

There's not a big leaving ceremony, a day when you actually retire as a stunt man and collect your gold watch. It just creeps up on you as your bones get more brittle and *Anno Domini* slows you down. One day Reg Prytherch rang me to discuss some upcoming water shows. During the course of our conversation he happened to say: 'What about the question of retirement?'

'That's ridiculous Reg,' I replied. 'You're still a young man.'

But I knew what he was getting at. Soon after I decided to give up the stunt game before it gave up me.

In my workshop with my prototype clockwork radio.

Pictured with my mum in 1986.

Dad's shed, where it all began.

Estelle Tiedre, the girlfriend who helped me build my house on Eel Pie Island.

At the wheel of Johnny Pugh's Rolls-Royce.

Pipe Smoker of the Year 1999, with Pauline Bricker (left) and Countess Falenska. (*Bill MacKenzie*)

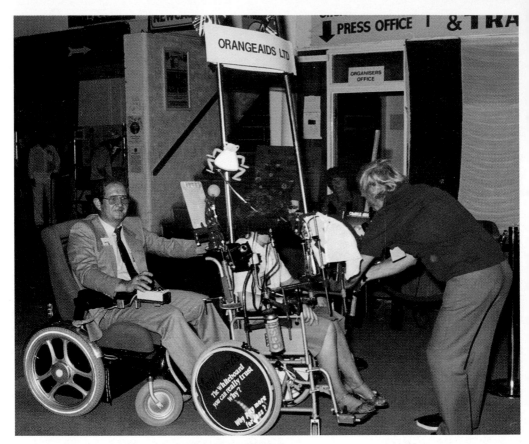

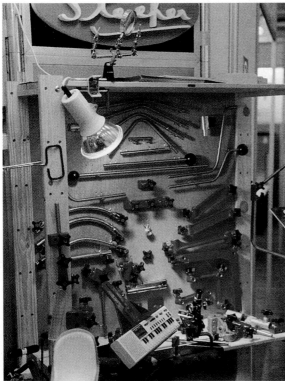

Orange Aids: a whole range of products designed to enable people to lead more fulfilling lives.

With Nelson Mandela at the Tuynhuis in Pretoria and, below, meeting some of the workers at the factory in Cape Town.

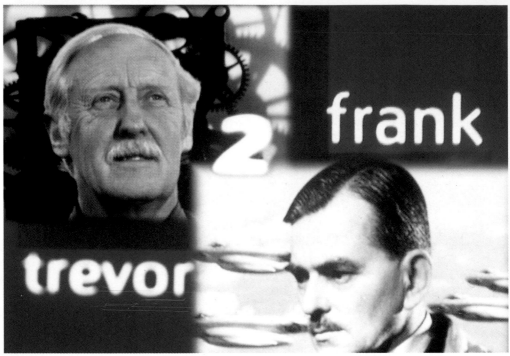

My One-2-One with Frank Whittle, my greatest hero. (*Bartle Bogle Hegarty*)

With *Big Breakfast* colleagues, Johnny Vaughan and 'WPC' Kelly Brook.
(*Peter Aitchison*)

'From Me Shed, Son'. (*Peter Aitchison*)

After receiving my OBE from the Princess Royal, I found *This Is Your Life*'s Michael Aspel lying in wait outside the gates of Buckingham Palace. (*Thames Television*)

With the famous red book and friends: (left to right) Tony Hutchings, Bob Flowerdew, Austin Mitchell, Mike Dodds (hidden), John Glazier, the Earl of Strafford and Johnny Pugh. (*Thames Television*)

CHAPTER NINETEEN

I DID IT FOR A BET

I T'S ODD HOW TRIVIAL EVENTS CAN ALTER THE COURSE OF OUR
LIVES. A squall of rain, which stopped me taking a boatload of my
friends out on the river for a Sunday jaunt in 1982, changed the
direction of my career at the age of forty-five.

Instead of going out on my speedboat, we stayed indoors at my
house, eating a picnic lunch, drinking wine, and playing silly games. As
a direct result of a bet with the late Vivian Smith I found a new voca-
tion (see Prologue). He said I couldn't invent a new gadget in under
half-an-hour. To prove him wrong I went straight to my workshop and
knocked up the prototype for a one-handed can opener. I lost the bet
– I was five minutes over the limit – but I had discovered something I
wanted to do with the rest of my life. The rain was providential interference. If it had been sunny instead we'd all have been out enjoying
ourselves on the Thames, I would have continued to earn a good living
making swimming pools, and the clockwork radio might never have
been invented.

After dad's death I cleared out his shed. Clear out is the wrong
word, but that's the one mum and I used. It didn't need clearing or
sorting, because everything was just so, symmetrically arranged, exactly
as he had left it. Shining ranks of tools and implements. Cutting edges
on blades and chisels burnished to silver. To move anything amounted

almost to desecrating an altar. But mum wanted me to have and use the tools dad had used. The thought of leaving his things to rust away out the back, she said, would only remind her all the more that he was no longer there to cherish them.

His ethic and his passion was virtuosity; he took pride in being able to do, with immense skill, not only the job which earned him his living as a quality inspector at the Britannia Rubber Company, but any job that arose around the house. He could turn a new leg for a broken chair, weld a new handle to a saucepan, or fashion a spare part for his car. He did everything himself, not DIY in the pejorative sense it has recently acquired of botched work and incompetence; he did things for himself because he was far better at doing them than anybody else.

I took his tools and used them because it seemed a way of being close to him. I took pride in getting things as right as he did, in keeping his saws sharp and gleaming because he had, trying to find new techniques for doing things because that had been one of the games he played.

As the decade of the 1970s went on, I was busy earning a living, but I was also spending hours in my workshop playing around with gadgets; trying to go a step beyond this, or simplify that, taking things apart and putting them back together again and, above all, trying to be original. I didn't come up with anything mysterious or earth shattering in the 1970s. There were no fantastic breakthroughs. It was more like a hobby I had, making odds and ends for my own amusement, playing around with possibilities.

Although I had invented components for filtration plants, swimming-pool fittings and accessories for my own company, Shotline Displays, and earlier for Purley Pools, I had never regarded myself as a fully fledged inventor. I thought the work I did fell into the category of clever improvisation. I was a skilful machinist, no more. An artisan engineer who could cobble together something that did a job, and provided an answer. Real inventors were geniuses like Frank Whittle or Sir Robert Watson-Watt, colossi like Daimler, Diesel, and the Wright Brothers; all of them way out of my league. Using my engineering skills to improvise gadgets and gubbins was just something I did as a hobby, a sideline to my main job, which was making pools, and selling them. But that rainy Sunday afternoon in 1982 changed all that and the beating drum of my imagination began to march me down a pathway I never dreamed I'd take.

All my other activities were put on the back burner. By this time my swimming-pool business was virtually running itself; it could chug along nicely with me keeping an eye on it part-time. As for stunt work, at the age of forty-five my buckle had long swashed, so I had ample time to throw myself into my new, all-consuming interest – creating inventions.

Ideas for gadgets for the disabled were coming into my head so fast they seemed to be arriving from somewhere outside of me, beamed down by an unremitting force. I had little control over them, or their flow. I would wake up in the middle of the night. A blinding flash of an idea would rouse me from my bed and I'd rush down to my workshop to have a go at it before the inspiration dimmed.

A mate of mine, Nick Wincott, used to help me out with the swimming-pool business. If he'd been working late he would sometimes sleep over on my couch and I'd drive him mad with my early morning brainwaves. Every time I ran through to my workbench I'd wake him up shouting: 'Mate! mate! Come and have a look at this.' Nick would be sleepy-eyed and complaining: 'Why can't you have your ideas during working hours like everybody else?'

Anyone who has ever earned a living as a stunt man knows he is only one mistake away from being disabled himself. A mistimed jump, a broken shackle, just allow your mind to wander for a second, and any dangerous exploit can become the last feat you attempt as an able-bodied man.

Even before I began inventing gadgets for the disabled, the way society treats that group had become one of my preoccupations. It seemed to me to be one of life's great injustices. If you slip on a banana skin and wind up paralysed, you will be treated like an inferior being, counting for very little, for the rest of your existence. And yet the difference between you and a man lucky enough to retain his health and strength is just one banana skin. The language we use when speaking of the disabled may be more circumspect: we don't speak of cripples any more, for instance. But not much else has changed. Fit people still don't regard the disabled as the same in every respect but one.

I was on automatic pilot; ideas for gadgets kept coming, fed by a force of energy flowing through me and around me. I wasn't really conscious of pausing to eat or sleep, I was caught up in a flurry of activity. I must have been experiencing the same sort of rapture of creation I imagine composers or poets get carried away by when they lose themselves in their work. I forgot about everything else to concentrate on what I was doing. I'd work eighteen-hour stretches and fall asleep in my clothes. Then I'd wake up in the middle of the night, brew a pot of tea, and start work again. I was tired, but work had become pure enjoyment.

The BBC gardening expert Bob Flowerdew used to drop by with plates of food he'd prepared for me. Not only does he grow marvellous produce, he's very good at cooking it too. He still pulls my leg about the stock phrase I used to berate him with then. I'd keep telling him: 'Bob, even instant mashed potato isn't quick enough for me!'

I was impatient to get on. I wanted all my ideas to be realised and I wanted them to happen quickly. It was the first time I had ever been carried away by such a buzz of inspiration, I worried that if I slowed down the light would go off and not come on again. The days and nights all blurred together as I stayed in my workshop, fiddling with bits and pieces of metal at my lathe, building up my own sophisticated construction kit.

By the time I had reached the end of my phantasmagoric spurt of energy three months later, I was exhausted, the shadows under my eyes were dark bruises, but I was well on the way to producing more than 200 different products to help the disabled. I called them Orange Aids.

The gadgets I made were designed to enable people with a range of handicaps to achieve the simple tasks able-bodied people take for granted. I devised tools that could be operated with one hand to open bottles, tins and jars. There were foot-operated gadgets like scissors, and a leather punch. A range of special kitchen appliances, including whisks, graters and sieves. And accessories that would enable partially paralysed people to sketch at an easel, embroider a tapestry frame, or spot wildlife through binoculars. There was even a gismo to assist smokers who had difficulties co-ordinating their hands to enjoy a cigarette.

They were ingenious tools, but making them came easy. Once I had the outline of an idea firmly in my head, achieving it was a straight-forward metalwork job, using processes I'd been familiar with since I was twelve.

There are so many different types of disability and disorder, the system had to be versatile enough to cover a whole range of needs. The concept of the design was to use sets of standard interlocking clamps, and a variety of interchangeable metal poles and adaptors to enable anything to be mounted anywhere. The system helped users to place and hold firm a variety of everyday objects and special aids in any position where they needed them. The aim was to increase indepen-dence for handicapped people, allowing reading lecterns, cameras, headswitches, glass holders, and numerous other appliances to be attached to wheelchairs, armchairs, tables, beds or even walls.

It was as well integrated and easy to fix as Meccano. Indeed, Meccano was one of my inspirations for it. I figured that if I could develop a system as flexible and fully harmonised as a child's construc-tion kit then it wouldn't be too complicated for hospital staff, relatives, or the disabled themselves to set up.

I used to take my early prototypes out to hospitals and centres for the disabled to gauge how well they worked. It justified all the late nights I'd spent devising the system to see a patient with minimal movement of his arms use my camera grip, focus the camera, and take a photograph independently for the very first time. A picture, they say, is worth more than a thousand words, and that one certainly was.

In a community centre kitchen the whisk, sieve and grater enabled some people to join in group activities, like baking, for the first time in their lives. They could contribute by sieving flour, whisking eggs, grating lemons. The pain of watching them struggle to complete simple tasks was sometimes difficult to bear, but the surge of joy that washed over them when they realised the kit was helping them to improve their performance and achieve the slow sifting of flour, moved me in a way like nothing had before. When the lemon cakes came out of the oven, hot and golden, the moment of triumph was like an Olympic win for them, and I'd helped them to the victory.

There were all sorts of heartwarming occasions: a one-handed patient able to attempt embroidery and so have a hobby for the first time since her accident. My simple tray which was appreciated by a wheelchair user because it wasn't as confining as a standard tray, which was like a baby's high chair. Even the smoker with cerebral palsy (would he be allowed his fags in these politically correct days?) who was able, for the first time, to enjoy a cigarette without holding it continually in his mouth.

People with disabilities are no different from the rest of us. The fit person's problem is that all he can see is the infirmity and not the real human personality underneath. Working with handicapped people opened my eyes to how sharply humorous they can be about their own disabilities. A young man in a wheelchair once asked me what brand name I'd given my equipment. When I told him he said: 'That's a good name. Orange Aids for the Raspberry Ripples.' I had a discussion with him later about the names of diseases. He thought it unjust that syndromes were named after the doctors who discovered them and not the first person to be found suffering from the disease. 'It's the only chance of immortality some of us have got,' he complained.

The DHSS funded a nine-month study aimed at discovering the potential of the system and purchased eight sets of Orange Aids equipment to test them in occupational therapy departments at eight hospitals across Britain – among them Chailey Heritage Hospital, in Lewes, and the Aids Demonstration Centre, Belfast.

The sixty-eight patients who used the system had a total of twenty-three different diagnoses, ranging through spinal injuries, and multiple sclerosis, to amputations. The people taking part in the survey attempted ninety-seven different activities, with a success rate of 76% and a failure rate of 24%. The DHSS findings, eventually published in *Health Equipment Information*, an NHS publication, were very encouraging.

The report's conclusions read: 'Generally it was found that the Orange Aids System was of definite value in helping to improve the quality of life and the degree of personal attainment, with its flexibility making it suitable for departmental or home use. Certain items were considered aesthetically to dominate in a confined space, although in a workshop environment they were found to be acceptable.'

It added: 'The Orange Aids System was found to provide an immediate solution to many problems where previous attempts had proved unsuccessful . . . The system is considered to have the potential to meet the requirements of a wide range of people with special needs, wherever those needs occur.'

Things seemed to be turning out well. But not for long.

CHAPTER TWENTY

A PAINFUL
APPRENTICESHIP

THAT RINGING ENDORSEMENT IN THE DHSS REPORT
SHOULD HAVE ENSURED THE ORANGE AIDS SYSTEM WAS
TAKEN UP EVERYWHERE, AND SO PROVE ITSELF OF THERA-
PEUTIC BENEFIT TO THE HANDICAPPED, AS WELL AS A COM-
MERCIAL SUCCESS FOR ITS MANUFACTURERS. The fact that it wasn't,
and that I walked away from the project having lost more than
£20,000, taught me my first bitter lesson about the perils of trying to
earn a living as an inventor.

The first complication was that I could not safeguard the equipment
I had devised with a patent. There were more than 200 ways in which
it could be used, and to patent every possible application would have
cost far more than I could afford. When I looked in detail at the possibility of patenting the various Orange Aids components I further
discovered that, while taken as a whole the system was original, its
individual parts were not so unique that they could be patented.

I decided to plunge ahead anyway, hoping that if I got enough
publicity about being the originator of the system it would protect
me if there was ever any dispute about who first created it. I got in
touch with a company called Hugh Steeper, which manufactured
artificial limbs. My contact there was a delightful fellow called

Johnny Mirams with whom I had a very good working relationship.

The firm could see the commercial possibilities of my designs, but to manufacture all the components and make a reliable and aesthetically pleasing system involved tooling up a factory, and the launch costs were astronomical. To aim Orange Aids at a worldwide market would be an even more expensive proposition, requiring much more heavy funding.

So I turned to the City and sought help from corporate bankers. It was a fateful error. Within eighteen months they had relieved me of my inventions and changed the name of my products, all without any financial reward. They had done me up like the proverbial kipper, eaten me for breakfast and spat me out, bones and all. My experience at their hands was a painful apprenticeship. I learned that a corporate banker is simply a pawnbroker or a bookmaker with a manicure, and far less dependable than either of them. I've always tried to live by Nelson Algren's advice. 'Never eat at a place called Mom's. Never play cards with a man named Doc.' If only he had added: 'Never trust anyone who has a double-barrelled name,' I might not have made a fool of myself.

But there is only one person I blame for getting shafted, and that's myself. I went into the deal which I thought would secure the future of Orange Aids with culpable impetuosity. I had been used to doing business on a handshake and my word of honour, and I made the error of actually believing what the men in the pin-striped suits told me. I was a text-book example for trainee inventors on how to do everything wrong. I took no legal advice, I assumed people would keep verbal promises, and even when things were written down, I didn't bother to read the small print. In short, I was greener than little green apples.

My only excuse is that I was a raw beginner and I had been so carried away by the excitement of creating a new product that I was in a state of almost drunken elation. I was so fired up by the drama of attending board meetings to discuss subjects I'd only ever read about, and barely understood in the *Financial Times*, that I committed the cardinal sin of stupidity.

I should have realised I was out of my depth when I arrived for the initial meeting and the girl at reception gave me her I-dare-you-to-smile-at-me look. She told me to wait and I sat in the foyer while braying young executives walked past me to the lifts. After ten minutes I went back and reminded her who I was. She switched to her I-think-you're-something-disgusting-that-should-be-in-a-black-bag-waiting-round-the-back-for-the-binmen look, and said she'd call me as soon as they buzzed down. They buzzed down eventually and I buzzed up to the seventh floor full of bravado, in a daze of breezy confidence.

The men at the meeting were very nice to me. On reflection too nice. Half-way up a tall building they explained the panorama of good fortune that lay ahead if we worked together. No one actually took me over to the window and said: 'One day my son all this will be yours,' but that was the general tenor of our discussions.

We agreed a deal and I came out thinking I owned 20% of the new company which was to manufacture Orange Aids. What I had, it turned out, was 20% of the B shares, which gave me virtually no say in the running of things. In the months to come these shares were diluted by more and more share issues until they were worth next to nothing. Then, without consulting me, they changed the name of the product, then they stopped taking my calls, and eventually, utterly depressed, I stopped making them. I had worked full-time on the project for more than a year and received nothing back from the venture. I reckon that wasted year cost me at least £20,000.

It was a salutary lesson. In the pop business they say you have to make two fortunes because sharks always rip you off and relieve you of your first million. It's not much different when you're an inventor. Anyone in possession of a good idea is at the mercy of jackals wanting a piece of the action. They're money men. They know how to move the decimal points around, they can work the profit system like a highly tuned instrument so it becomes highly unprofitable for every-one but them. If an inventor doesn't have a rock-solid watertight contract that secures all the rights to his intellectual property, as soon as the money rolls in, he's in danger of being rolled out.

The whole rotten experience put me on my guard. It made me

suspicious of people's motives. I am now a much less trusting person, and it's not a trait I particularly admire in myself. I'd hate to become the kind of person who consults his lawyer before signing a birthday card. But I suppose that's the way you have to be. In business basic decency has no cash value.

For months I licked my wounds, alone, a bear hiding in his den. I turned back to the swimming-pool business and gave it all my energy. Through my life I've had a succession of dogs, either named Monty or Rommel. The dog I had at that time was a lovely cross-bred black and white border collie called Rommel, who was one of the cleverest and most personable dogs I've ever met. I suspect he had a better IQ than I've got. Rommel used to come with me on site whenever I built one of my swimming pools. He was a barking master of works who used to shepherd me and the labour force to where he thought we needed to be. A foreman who was paid in Pal and Rolos.

On one occasion we were putting in a pool in North London about thirty miles across the city from Twickenham. We worked a long day and it was getting dark when I loaded up the van, assuming that Rommel was lying down in his normal place, just behind the driver's seat. I drove a couple of miles down the road, thinking the van was unusually quiet, and when I looked behind me for Rommel, he wasn't in his place. I turned the van round and went back to the site, but there was no sign of him.

The following couple of days I experienced a rising feeling of despair as we looked everywhere for Rommel, with no result. Work was abandoned as we went back to all the other places in North London where we'd installed pools, hoping that the dog might have wandered back there. I reconciled myself to the fact that he'd gone for ever; consoling myself with the thought that Rommel was so lovable and intelligent, anyone who found him would be bound to take him in.

Eight days later I was sitting at home in Twickenham on a Sunday morning when there was loud barking at the front door. When I opened it, there was Rommel looking very thin, very tired, very wet, but wagging his tail. My work mates and I had long discussions about how he found his way home. The pads on his paws were very worn, so he must have walked for miles. He was also very wet. Rommel loved splashing around Eel Pie Island and Nick Wincott had a theory that somehow he'd made his way to the Thames and swum up-river back to the island. But knowing Rommel, I suspect he probably came home on a bus.

Even with Rommel as my constant companion on site, I soon found installing swimming pools was no longer enough to satisfy me.

I suppose a less determined (less pig-headed?) man would have given up on inventions for good; after all, why bother? I had a good business, and my own home in a perfect spot on the river. I had never wanted to be a millionaire, I get enough taste and colour out of life the way I am. By now, though, I'd been seduced by the pure joy of discovery; not even by the actual moment of breakthrough, just the act of trying to get there, the learning, probing, tentative kite-flying, going up alleys to see if they are blind, have given me the best moments in an already happy life.

I couldn't stay away from my workshop for long. Soon I was back there every evening after I'd got home from work, waiting for intuition, like lightning, to strike again. I'd often wondered about the rising incidence of respiratory ailments and allergies caused by carpet mites and dust particles. I'd read somewhere that using a vacuum cleaner can make these problems worse because the exhaust from the back end of the machine agitates all the harmful particles in the air.

I thought if you put an ionising filter up the back of a vacuum cleaner it might solve the problem. I experimented with a couple of old cleaners, worked out a prototype, and sent the outline to Hoover. Their patents engineer, A.C.R. Harvey, sent me back a friendly note saying the subject had already received attention in their laboratories and had been put on the back burner. (Later he was kind enough to send me a fax after the success of the clockwork radio. 'Please accept my congratulations on an invention brought to fruition – and a particularly philanthropic one.' It was good of him to remember a struggling inventor whose efforts had succeeded.)

The other device I started working on in 1990 was an automatic electric trowel for gardeners who had weak hands or some form of manual impairment. It was like the sander on an electric drill, adapted for digging out window-boxes and herbaceous borders. It reciprocated the trowel backwards and forwards in a kind of digging motion. Well in theory it did. I could never quite get the digging action right. My field trials with the contraption in a neighbour's garden resulted in my digging up a few prized blooms and sending fine gobbets of earth all over Bob Flowerdew.

I was back in my workshop, nevertheless, happy to be working on new ideas. If I kept on asking myself lots of questions, all my 'Why nots?' might one day come up with a right answer.

CHAPTER TWENTY-ONE

1% INSPIRATION

ALL INVENTORS, THEY SAY, ARE A LITTLE MAD. I reckon that only completely sane people are willing to admit they are slightly crazy. Visionaries and dreamers have always been dusted with a little oddity. Sir George Sitwell, father of Edith, Osbert and Sacheverell, spent his time at Eton inventing a toothbrush which played 'Annie Laurie' while you were cleaning your teeth, and a revolver for shooting wasps. He then went on to create an elaborate desk you could lie down in, a car with a bed in it, and a rectangular synthetic egg for sportsmen, travellers, and big-game hunters. (It had a yolk of smoked meat, a white of compressed rice, and a shell of synthetic lime. He proudly showed a prototype of his egg to Sir George Selfridge, founder of the famous Oxford Street store, who quietly showed him the door.)

The notion that inventors are anorak-wearing crackpots with glasses held together with Sellotape is beguiling but wrong. Some inventors are, without a doubt, geniuses. Others, and there is no denying this either, are as mad as hatters. At one end of the scale stands Leonardo da Vinci – artist, architect, musician, geologist, physicist, designer, mechanic and inventor – one of the greatest men in western civilisation. At the other are ranged a legion of cranks convinced that their marvellous idea is going to change the world. Diana Cooper is one of my favourites. Her capacity for abstract thought has been described as 'roughly that of a strawberry mousse'. She had her moment of blinding insight when the blitz began in 1940. She contacted the War Office suggesting that large magnets should be placed in the London parks to attract German bombs.

Ranged between these extremes, though, are those like me: ordinary people who have a bright idea that actually works, and are blessed with the extra luck and the determination needed to turn that idea into a marketable product.

Everyone who writes about the process of invention invariably drags out the famous remark of Thomas Alva Edison, the man who invented the phonograph and the electric light-bulb, and who, thanks to the flood of ideas that spilled from his factory at Menlo Park, New Jersey, owned more than 1,200 patents. He was the bloke who said: 'Invention is 1% inspiration and 99% perspiration,' and he wasn't wrong.

The key to success is to risk thinking unconventional thoughts. Convention is the enemy of progress. If you go down just one corridor of thought you never get to see what's in the rooms leading off it. But having had your bright, fresh, original idea, the really hard part is turning it into a successful product. That's what takes all the sweat.

As long as you've got slightly more perception than the average wrapped loaf, you are capable of inventing something. If you think about it long enough, and hard enough, you can invent a more efficient corkscrew, or a better way of catching mice. When trying to find the answer to a tricky puzzle Sir Barnes Wallis, the man who invented the bouncing bomb, made the question: 'Why not?' his criterion. It's a good touchstone for would-be inventors setting out to solve a problem and coming up with what they suspect is a hare-brained solution. It might not work, but it could succeed, so why not try it?

You don't need vast research facilities and the might of Sony or ICI behind you either. I made the first prototype of my clockwork radio in a small workshop with the kind of basic tools and equipment you need to service a vacuum cleaner.

The world is complicated and the products of innovation constantly serve as a reminder of our ignorance. I am in awe of Bill Gates and his chums, amazed that lap-top computers can perform so many complicated tasks. Noel Coward once admitted that he had tried to grasp the rudiments of such inventions as the telephone, the camera and wireless telegraphy, but without success. Television, radar, and atomic energy, he confessed, were also far beyond his comprehension. 'My brain shudders at the thought of them,' he said, 'and scurries for cover like a primitive tribesman confronted with a Dunhill cigarette lighter.'

I know exactly how he felt. What I don't know wouldn't fit into the Bodleian Library. But ignorance doesn't stop the imagination taking flight. Most of the world's greatest inventions are achieved by someone either being clever enough to know it can be done, or too naive to realise that it can't.

Ideas strike at the most unlikely moments. George de Mestral walked through an unmown meadow where some prickly burdock seeds stuck to his trousers. He looked at the burdock seeds through his microscope and came up with the idea for Velcro (which comes from the French words *velour* for velvet and *crochet* for hook). Felix Wankel claimed he got the idea for his rotary engine (a rotor in a bulbous triangle in a chamber shaped like a figure-of-eight) after eating too much Christmas pudding. Dietrich, the man who invented Pritt-Stick, an unmessy way of applying glue, came up with his idea after watching a woman applying her lipstick.

Archimedes had his most famous idea in the bath. I had mine for the clockwork radio when I was watching television. These days there are not as many thought-provoking programmes as there ought to be. Maybe it has something to do with my age, and a yearning for the halcyon days of Hugh Carlton-Greene, but for me the thought television most often provokes is: 'Why am I watching this rubbish?'

It was the autumn of 1991, on the kind of wild September evening that drives even that thought out of your head. Wind and rain were lashing the Thames beyond the jetty at the end of my house. On a rough night it feels as though the river is determined to claim back the tiny spit of land that makes up Eel Pie Island and sweep us all downriver to the sea.

While the weather turned nasty outside, I ate a stodgy supper. For company I had my furry friend Rommel, and the remains of a bottle of red wine, whose pedigree was more exalted. I had read all my library books, and with nothing better to do, I turned on the television. The following hour passed like a dream. I switched on the set absently, without consulting a programme guide. The screen came to life and I dumbly watched what was offered. I just sat there, your standard couch potato. But I soon became absorbed. The programme sent my mind racing, stretched like a spinnaker on a fair wind.

That period of no more than ninety minutes was like an enchanted time, an out-of-body experience shot through with a strange and haunting clarity. It completely changed my life. Call it luck, serendipity, or the devil looking after his own, but my life has followed a golden thread of happy and unexpected accidents. For years people wait for Dame Fortune to come knocking, only to find when they open the door that Dame Fortune's youngest daughter, Miss Fortune, is staring them in the face. But I've always had a Micawberish optimism.

The programme was about the spread of AIDS in Africa. The Black Death, the great plague of the fourteenth century, killed twenty million people, a quarter of Europe's population, in four years. The Spanish influenza that swept a debilitated Europe after World War One, in 1918–1919, killed twenty million in a year. But now, this programme reported, AIDS was ravaging Africa and other Third World areas far more fiercely than either, and the outlook was cataclysmic.

The programme lowered my spirits. I had the zapper in my hand and could easily have switched to less harrowing fare. But I stayed with it. The narrator was telling me that the biggest problem was getting the health education message across to the population. A campaign to broadcast propaganda counselling safe sex was being hampered by lack of cheap receivers. In remote villages there was no electricity, and the cost of batteries was prohibitive – as much as one-month's income for one set alone. Solar power wasn't the answer, the narrator intoned dismally, because most people did their listening after dark, when they came home after spending a day working in the fields.

I was sitting there, taking in this sombre picture, when all at once my mind began to take flight. Maybe the red wine helped, but I was suddenly aware of a blindingly obvious way in which the problem could be solved.

Watching television frequently introduces me to that best friend of the discerning viewer, sleep. I sometimes wake up to a scene where Jeremy Paxman is being beastly to William Hague and wonder what on earth they're doing in the Clint Eastwood spaghetti Western I started watching a couple of hours earlier.

Now, however, I was absorbing all the information coming from the screen, but at the same time I had been transported to the edge of the desert somewhere in the Sudan. In overpowering heat, sandflies high-diving into my gin and tonic, my faithful bearer Hassan attending to my every whim, I was suddenly some sort of colonial wallah in tropical uniform, plotting gun-boat diplomacy on the outer edge of The Empire. As the civil servant sipped his drink, he listened, wrapped in the magic of Enrico Caruso, his ear close to the horn of an old-fashioned gramophone.

I thought about that gramophone. Enrico's mighty top Cs shimmer in the heat because a needle followed the inscribed pattern of the aria on a piece of Bakelite. The vibrations of the needle in the groove of the disc made a noise which was amplified by the horn, and the whole glorious noise was driven by a simple spring that operated a gear that drove the turntable that dragged the disc past the needle. Instantly I had this glaring flash of something so obvious a child of six could have thought of it. If a clockwork gramophone can produce that volume of sound, then why not apply the principle to building a spring-driven radio.

That was the Alka-Seltzer moment, the moment when the tablet hits the water and begins to fizz. I left the television set on, with the narrator still submerging viewers in a tidal wave of dismal statistics and, late as it was, went to my workshop. A good idea turns every cog in your mind, making you scared of bed in case the whole machine grinds to a halt.

I lit my pipe and had a think. Smoking a pipe is my main hobby. It has contributed to every one of my 200 or so inventions simply because, during my waking hours, it is nearly always fired up. My pipe gives me something to do with my hands that is marginally more macho than knitting. For forty-five years I've pickled myself in so much pipe smoke my moustache has turned from dirty silver into deep ochre. If my upper lip is anything to go by, my insides should be the same rich dulse brown as a Manx kipper. But I like it. I once tried some of those Nicorette patches, but they didn't draw very well and tasted like a hayrick on fire.

As I smoked I sorted through some odds and ends on my workbench. To say that my workbench is untidy is an understatement. (My father was an immaculately tidy man. I am not.) The room, a sort of vestibule to the main house, has the same sense of symmetry and order as a car-boot sale that's just been unravelled by Hurricane Bertha. Finding anything is a prolonged torture, an assault course requiring Olympic training. Before me lay 1,000 dead components from a defeated army of mechanical carcasses, waiting to be bodged back into life. Eventually I found an old transistor radio, a primitive two-inch by four-inch Pine HQ set I'd picked up at a car-boot sale for five pence. I removed its batteries. Then I cannibalised a small electric motor from a device for automatically tuning a guitar that a mate of mine had left for me to look at.

Then, in a growing fever of excitement, I linked the radio and the electric motor with a couple of wires. The aroma of my Condor blended with the solder fumes. The result was more sulphur mine than Soir de Paris, but it's a perfume I've grown to like. I could hear the concerned voice on the television still talking to an empty room, and the echo of the tideway outside. Rommel padded out to see what was happening. He growled once, as if to register his disapproval of all this late-night agitation, then walked back inside to his favourite sofa next to the jumbo cheeseplant.

I fixed a hand drill to the electric motor. Basically, an electric motor is a machine that changes electrical energy into rotary motion that can perform useful work. If you reverse the process and rotate a DC motor the other way it becomes a dynamo and you produce electrical energy. I turned the hand drill briskly at the rate Delia Smith would use to whisk eggs into a souffle. But would the souffle rise?

There was a tiny bark of sound from the loudspeaker that cut through the clutter of other household noises. It died immediately I stopped turning. But when I cranked the handle faster, there it was again, that precious little voice. Someone, somewhere, was discussing the strength of the pound against the deutschmark. I listened, transfixed. The words were sweeter than Shakespeare's. Never has the arcane jargon of the money market sounded so gloriously poetic. I kept whisking it on and off, like a kid playing with a toy, feeling an orgasmic sense of triumph.

Now I had to work out a system of gears driven by spring power which would produce the same energy as my hand-driven crank. Solving that problem called for another pipe and a lot more brainstorming, but as I puffed away I was more than ever convinced that my idea would work.

After some cursing and a few blind alleys I rigged up a logarithmic spring to a simple planet gearbox. The spring was the common type you'd find in any time piece or clockwork toy. The one I used was from an old alarm clock. The power from the spring going through the gears, rotating like planets around the sun of the central shaft, made my tiny electrical generator rotate vigorously. After an hour of tinkering I discovered that, on a full wind of the spring, I could make enough electrical energy to produce about a minute of sound from the radio. I was ecstatic.

The trouble with inventing something that works is that you can't boast to anyone about it. Telling means disclosure, and disclosure spells the ultimate stupidity. The natural human reaction of the inventor who has had a good idea is to leap out of the bath and run naked down the street yelling: 'Eureka!' This is the most foolish thing you can do, because in the ideas-stealing business it's known as 'disclosure'. Good ideas are worth money, they are 'intellectual property'. If you talk to just one person about your brand new idea, your intellectual property becomes common knowledge. Once a secret becomes an open secret it has no value, and if your brilliant idea becomes an open secret it's as much use to you as a hairnet in a thunderstorm.

I walked back into the living room and filled myself one last pipe of the day. Thinking about it again, my idea seemed so obvious I couldn't understand why it hadn't been done before. I poured the lees of the red wine, raising a half glass to Rommel. He was asleep, gargling through a twitchy kind of dream, as I filled him in on the details of my discovery.

Behind every successful inventor there stands, if not an amazed wife, then very often a faithful dog. That is another reason why inventors are frequently regarded as crackpots. We spend a lot of time holding one-sided conversations with dumb animals.

I went to bed at about two in the morning and dreamed about the endless possibilities of clockwork energy. It was the last good kip I had for weeks. Lots of problems, and the odd recurring nightmare, lay ahead.

CHAPTER TWENTY-TWO

99% PERSPIRATION

MORNING, PERFECT AS A CLEAN SHEET OF PAPER. It was time to start thinking again. The clock said seven. I'd only had four hours' rest. It's hard to sleep the sleep of the just when you're being tormented by a mystery yapping around your brain and refusing to come to heel like a good dog.

When you're an inventor, snagged and floundering, snuffling and puzzling, it's as infuriating as those games you play as a child when, blindfold, you stumble around a room in search of a reward.

'Am I warm?'

'No, you're stone cold.'

'Am I warmer?'

'Yes, boiling.'

'Warmer still?'

'No, you're freezing again.'

The day and night following my first breakthrough had been unproductive, and on the second day I stayed up late dredging my wits for ideas to make the spring on my clockwork radio give me more than four minutes of the *Nine O'Clock News*, Wogan's blether, or anything. On a full wind, Radio One was just about rewarding me with one record before the spring ran down and Mick Jagger's 'Not Fade Away' did exactly that.

The drawback with a logarithmic spring is that, although when fully wound it has pent up energy in superabundance, as the spring gradually unwinds that vitality inexorably wastes away. Any child who has played with a clockwork mouse has experienced the effect. When you put him down on the floor, his spring tightly wound, the mouse whizzes about at high velocity. Then, as he squanders his energy, he slows to an arthritic skitter before finally coming to rest (usually somewhere inaccessible).

For forty-eight hours, almost without sleep, I had experimented with a range of spring sizes and numerous configurations of gears. The big enemy of any device which has moving parts is friction. One of my prime objectives was to eliminate friction as far as I could through the careful selection and assembly of components. My aim was to get the optimum amount of energy from each wind, through the gears, into the dynamo, and so work the radio. But my logarithmic springs persisted in losing power as they uncoiled and my radio faded to a disappointing silence after about four minutes.

On day three I woke an hour after dawn and made myself some builder's tea. Rommel was gazing out over the misty Thames, snuffling and licking at the windows. I stood with him, drinking from my mug, taking in the river and the trees on the far bank being whittled by the wind. Looking out across the tideway I had half an idea, but dismissed it as a silly conceit that was too absurd to run with.

Another mug of tea later I was in a frame of mind to try anything. I seemed to be at an impasse anyway. The idea, however impractical it was, would at least get me out of the house, and after two days cooped up getting nowhere I felt as though I could do with a breath of fresh air.

I waited until after the postman had made his delivery, so that the hour was not quite so indecently early, and then presented myself on the front doorstep of The Sycamores, the house of my neighbour Gladys Heath. She was then in her late eighties, fit and spry and as straight as a pound of candles. She looked at me sideways through a crack in the door.

'I was wondering Gladys,' I said, tentatively.

'Yes Trevor?'

'I was wondering whether I could borrow your big tree?'

She put one hand on the doorjamb and gave me her withering Joyce Grenfell look. 'What on earth do you want it for?'

'I'd like to see if I can use it to power my radio.'

She laughed. Nervous hilarity. Gladys has experience of my size seven-and-a-halfs rushing in and treading all over the place. 'You're not going to chop it down are you?'

'Oh no, Gladys. Your tree won't come to any harm.'

She knows that sometimes my actions defy logic. Gladys is a wonderful friend, but she skirts around my activities warily like the natives in *Tarzan* movies confronted with their first camera. Over the years I have tried out several of my inventions on her, in fact she was one of my guinea pigs when I was perfecting my foot-operated nail clippers.

I explained to her what I wanted to do, and she said: 'Oh all right then, just as long as you don't trample my flowers into the ground.'

The biggest sycamore in Gladys's garden is far taller than any tree in mine, and its height was vital to my experiment. I climbed up to a stout branch about thirty-five feet above the ground and fixed a pulley there. Then I threaded eighty feet of rope through the pulley and tied a bucket filled with sand to one end. The idea was to haul the bucket of sand up until it was thirty-five feet from the ground and then release it to use the energy generated by its descent to operate a windlass, which would turn a gearbox, to activate the dynamo, which would then power the radio.

It was a perfect example of energy conversion. In hauling up the bucket my body was converting the chemical energy gained through food, first into movement or kinetic energy, and then into potential energy stored in the heavy bucket suspended at the top of the tree, waiting for gravity to return it to earth. Then as the bucket came back down to earth the kinetic energy was applied to the windlass.

I worked out a wonderfully complicated gearbox, and made sure all the elements in the experiment were in place and properly wired-up. Then I heaved the bucket to the top of the tree, which was much easier work than I imagined it would be. But I was out of condition.

Breathing like a cart-horse, I tied off the rope while I made a few minor adjustments.

I unhitched the knot, made sure the bucket wasn't caught on a branch, and after a token countdown from five, let go of the rope. Mrs Heath's back garden was hardly Cape Canaveral, but I was dry-mouthed and strangely nervous. I looked up with trepidation through a curtain of leaves and took the precaution of stepping out of the way just in case the bucket flattened me.

I needn't have worried. Governed by the forces of gravity, my bucket of sand made an imposingly slow descent to earth, turning the windlass and activating a curious assortment of wheels and cogs to give me sixty minutes of music and chat on my tinny transistor. The power obtained from the descending bucket depended on the height of the tree multiplied by the weight of the bucket, giving a certain number of foot pounds of energy. By looking at my conversion tables I could work out how many watt hours I produced each time I hoisted the bucket to the top of the tree.

The system wasn't very efficient. As much as 40% of the energy I expended hauling up my bucket of sand was getting lost en route to the radio. But I'd proved the idea worked. The taller your tree, the longer your rope, the heavier your bucket, the more minutes' worth of radio you got out of it for each haul to the top of the tree.

But it was an absurdly crazy arrangement, a dotty contraption Heath Robinson would have been proud to have rigged up. It was totally impractical as a commercial proposition, hardly a product you could market, let alone write the operating instructions for. They'd have to begin with: 'First climb your tree.'

But I played with it for three or four days, trying to improve its efficiency. It was like a holiday from the problems I was having with the logarithmic springs, and besides I enjoyed the view along the river from the top of Mrs Heath's tree as much as I liked experimenting with my bucket of sand.

My combination of rope, pulley and heavy bucket is not the kind of sophisticated generating system that would have much appeal for the mollycoddled West, but I still think it has potential in Third World countries where low-tech resources are urgently needed. As long as you've got a tall tree, or even a deep well, it's a very simple answer to energy needs. In developing countries there is no shortage of willing hands to provide the muscle power to haul the bucket that produces the electricity, and I still think it could be an idea whose time will come.

More hours of grumbling over the puzzle of the fickle logarithmic springs, then suddenly, in mid-October, the seedling of a new idea broke through stony ground. I'd walked, deep in thought, across the bridge to the mainland, over the goosemess on the river-bank to where my old Range Rover was parked.

I was on my way to the shops, still fed up and preoccupied with getting my radio to run for more than four minutes. I sat in the driver's seat for a few moments puffing on my pipe, miles away, before pulling the seat belt across my chest. As the metal clasp clicked into place, so did a brand-new thought. The mechanism that makes a seat belt work is a spring. But, compared to a logarithmic spring, it operates on a completely different principle. Maybe that was where my solution lay?

I decided to strike while the iron was hot, undid my seat belt and stepped out of the vehicle. I took the plastic cover off the seat belt housing and had a look inside. Coiled in on itself was what is called a constant force spring. I pulled on the webbing of the seat belt a couple of times and watched how the spring rapidly recoiled each time I relaxed my grip on it. There seemed to be a lot of energy there that might be harnessed via a dynamo to my radio. (The same principle also works self-retracting builder's rulers.)

All thoughts of my shopping trip were immediately abandoned. I locked my vehicle and walked back over the bridge to find out more about constant force springs. A few phone calls and a couple of skimmed reference books later I'd done enough homework.

My refresher course reminded me that these springs use a tight coil of flat steel spring stock that has been bent in a particular direction. Then the textured carbon steel spring is rotated in the opposite direction around another spool. When you deform steel to a certain confirmation, even if later you alter its shape, it always wants to revert to its old familiar form. Set into the spring is a sort of memory which says: 'I want to get myself back to the way I was.' And that movement gives you a constant rotational force. You simply wind the spring from one spool to another. As the spring returns to its original position, it releases its energy and applies a rotational torque to a transmission.

I experimented with a couple of constant force springs and began to get a steady signal from my radio giving me fourteen minutes of sound for every two minutes of winding. I got that down to fourteen minutes on a thirty-second wind simply by replacing the wind-up key with a handle. But as soon as that snag had been dealt with, another one cropped up.

I noticed that whenever there was a pause in a conversation in a radio programme, or a moment of quiet between records, the silence was invaded by a loud electronic yowl. The cause was simple. During the brief silences the radio needed less electricity to power it, but as the same amount of power was being generated constantly, the radio would get excited, run away with itself and produce a resonant shriek of protest.

I thought if I put in a resistance it would control the flow of electricity into the radio, thus solving the problem. The first one I tried cured the yowling, but it also burned away a lot of vital power. More days of searching for an answer. In the end I solved the problem during a coffee-break. Thumbing through an electronics catalogue I spotted a small Zener diode costing two pence that I thought would do the trick. A quick trip to their warehouse and I had what I was looking for. The diode eliminated the noise and didn't eat up too much of the clockwork-generated energy. QED.

By early November I was confident I had cured the radio's teething problems. There comes a time when, like an artist putting his brushes away, you have to stop tinkering with the mechanism. The search for 'defects' you want to correct, and 'improvements' that can be incorporated into the design, can become an obsession if you're not careful.

In the eighteenth century John Harrison, a self-taught Yorkshire clockmaker and the mechanical genius of his age, built five revolutionary clocks and spent forty years in his single-minded pursuit of an answer to the greatest scientific problem of his time – how to accurately calculate longitude. But I am not that patient. I worked out that if I devoted my life to a similar quest for perfection I would be ninety-four before my radio went on sale.

I decided it was time to apply for a patent for my device, so that on payment of about £400 I could protect my invention for a period of one year, and keep the sole rights to make and sell it. I got in touch with a patent attorney, Jacqueline Needle, and took my prototype radio to her office at W.H. Beck, Greener in Lincoln's Inn. She was impressed with the idea, played with the radio as though it was a new toy, and agreed to write up my patent application.

The clockwork radio, at that stage, was clearly not the sleek and sculpted, transparent plastic designer model you can buy in the shops today. The original set was uglier, much heavier, less efficient and the gears made a grating noise. But it worked. The office agreed that it was an innovation, that I was the first inventor to have produced a clock-work radio and my patent application – number 9124506.8 – was allocated on 19 November 1991.

Jacqueline's searches through the Patent Office archives revealed some tantalising information. In 1902 Guglielmo Marconi, the Italian engineer who was the first man to use radio for communications, had made a clockwork radio of sorts. It was a wind-up Morse transmitting device called the Magnetic Detector.

Marconi's wireless was used on ships to receive messages in Morse code from spark transmitters. In it a clockwork mechanism drove a band of soft iron wires past the poles of two horseshoe magnets. The magnetised wires, then passed through a wire coil with an earth and an aerial, and headphones were attached. An incoming radio signal received by the aerial partially demagnetised the wires, producing a click in the headphones. It was a precursor to my device, since it was also driven by clockwork. But it was not otherwise comparable as it was designed merely to receive pulses before broadcasting existed.

In the 1950s someone else in Britain had tried to power a huge old-fashioned valve radio by using a logarithmic spring. But this was long before the invention of transistors and printed circuits. The big valves in his radio ate up far more power than his puny clockwork motor could generate, and his invention did not get onto the market.

But that is part of the lottery of being a successful inventor. Some ventures are nipped in the bud by fate and easy mistimings. You have to be lucky enough to be working on your prototype at a time when other scientific advances have eased the way. Alan Blumlein, a pioneer of radar during World War Two, had patented an idea for recording in stereo on gramophone records while working for EMI in 1931. His patent included the key notion that twin sound channels can be imposed on the same groove of a record. But his idea only became practical with the arrival of light plastics in the 1950s. Without the transistor, my radio wouldn't have happened either. It's all a question of catching the right tide. As Milton Berle used to say: 'We owe a lot to Thomas Edison – if it wasn't for him we'd be watching television by candlelight.'

CHAPTER TWENTY-THREE

DESPERATION STAKES

OBTAINING A PATENT GIVES AN INVENTOR BREATHING SPACE, A YEAR'S GRACE IN WHICH TO LAUNCH HIS OR HER INVENTION. When Alexander Moulton, an expert in suspension systems, designed his revolutionary bike with fourteen-inch wheels, no manufacturer would look at it. So he founded his own company, acquired a factory, and built the minibike himself. It became one of the successes of the 1960s, as much a part of the swinging scene as the Mini and the miniskirt.

But not everybody has the financial resources to do what Moulton did. For those without the big bucks needed to make their own products it means approaching big multinational firms, cap-in-hand, hoping they will take you and your handiwork under their wing. Finding the right vein for these entreaties is a subtle art. Unsolicited mail rarely makes it to the desk of someone important whose opinion counts. Most ends up with an underling who places it in the filing cabinet of last resort where unprompted correspondence is customarily processed: the shredder.

That initial letter has to pitch justified confidence in your achievement somewhere between overblown pride and false modesty. Its tone needs the breezy confidence of Richard Branson, the hard-nosed flair of Rupert Murdoch, and the selling technique of a salesman who could sell an underarm deodorant to the Venus de Milo. It has to sound competent enough to have been dictated by the chief analyst at Kleinwort Benson, checked for style by the poet laureate, and had a few topical *bon mots* added by Ben Elton. Whatever you do, you should never write such letters in green ink, or add more than one postscript, otherwise people think you've got a screw loose.

I drew up a list of companies I thought would be interested in my idea – firms like Marconi, Philips, BP, and National Power. I drafted my letter several times and politely communicated to industry at large the message that a marriage of my invention with their expertise could make us all a lot of money.

Nothing happened. My ongoing two-year mailshot provoked an overwhelming wave of indifference. A deafening outburst of apathy. The replies, from those who bothered to reply, were frostily polite, full of calculated euphemisms, and so dismissive I could imagine the ice forming on computer printers as the letters were run off.

A common attitude among large companies, when an outsider suggests a new product to them, is that if it hasn't come from their research and development programme then they're not interested. It's an outlook that can be summed up as: 'If we didn't think about it mate, then your idea can't be any good.' New ideas are awkward blighters. They upset the status quo, they bring with them the threat of more work for busy departments, upheaval, reorganisation and a lot of extra paperwork. It's far easier to shuffle them off your desk with the excuse that they don't fit into your company's grand strategic plan.

What made the rejections even harder to take was the condescending manner in which some of them gave me two cheers for trying and then implied that I would be far better off leaving such complex matters to the big boys. There was a peevish unanimous consensus: 'We're not interested. Don't bother us again.' I was disappointed, deflated, and angry in equal measure. I think I would have been marginally less affronted if they had returned all my letters unopened.

A typical reply was the five-line fax I received from Boele de Bie, Product Manager Portable Audio, with Philips in Holland. 'Although we agree that there might be an opportunity for your idea, it is a smart way of addressing the communication problem, we are not interested as a company.'

The letter from National Power, dated 30 March 1993, cut straight to the bad tidings: 'I regret that this letter arrives to bring you some unwelcome news.' After the formulaic praise: 'We were all impressed with your approach and the novelty of your idea,' came the 'however'. 'However we also questioned how the device would fit in with our corporate strategy and business. It is for this reason that I have to inform you that we shall not be proceeding further with your idea.'

John Hargrove, Business Manager of the BP Innovation Centre at Sunbury-on-Thames, Middlesex, writing on 11 June 1993, wished me well in my attempts to exploit my fuel-free generators, but said: 'Having now reviewed the information supplied by you, I am sorry to inform you that BP Solar have concluded that this is not a topic they would wish to progress.'

I had written to The Design Council hoping to attract attention from manufacturers by being given a slot on the Council's Innovation NoticeBoard. The reply I received from Susan Cottam, Manager of the NoticeBoard, in March 1992 was very friendly. The Council even went so far as to congratulate me: 'The general consensus was that the clockwork radio was a well thought-out product which would certainly benefit its target market. The panel agreed that its low-tech design would be ideally suited to meeting particular communication needs in the Third World.'

But then came a very big but. 'The issue is not so much the quality of the innovation, but the mechanics of launching it as a commercially viable product.' Later Susan politely applied the *coup de grâce*: 'It is very unlikely that UK industries could enter profitably into a licensing agreement with this product. The major customers are Third World countries which, with severe debts, would not be in a position to pay for this device. The extent to which component parts could be manufactured in the UK was also felt to be limited.'

The letter ended with the usual sincere wishes for 'every success with this project', but contained the, by now familiar, brush-off: 'In the light of these issues, it was felt that NoticeBoard would not be the best medium through which to progress this idea.'

The British have always had a talent for invention. British industry has also developed an unenviable tradition for ignoring that talent. The Japanese Ministry of International Trade and Industry has stated that more than half the successful inventions since World War Two began life in the UK. Only one-fifth came from the USA, and a meagre twentieth from Japan.

Where the UK goes wrong is the way it singularly fails to exploit new ideas, leaving them to other countries to develop. My radio is just one example of this long and depressing drift. It is manufactured not here where it was conceived, but in South Africa.

All through 1992, 1993, and into 1994 British industry offered me the most glacial of cold shoulders. I couldn't understand why they weren't as excited as I was by the clockwork radio. I got very depressed: depressed for me that is. Once I was reduced to melancholy silence for almost five minutes. I began to wonder whether their doubts about the clockwork radio were justified after all, and that I was the only person resolutely out of step in the matter. I consoled myself by questioning their competence. If they were florists, I argued, they would probably close on Mother's Day.

Among the blizzard of rejection letters was one that puzzled me for days. At first I thought it was from somebody having me on because it read like a piece of vintage deadpan whimsy. I scrutinised the signature to see if I could recognise the handwriting of one of my leg-pulling mates. But then I realised it must be genuine because I remembered I'd phoned a man in Manchester called Ormiston-Chant to discuss some practical aspects of the clockwork radio.

Although I'd told him my radio was up and working, the letter he sent me was a treatise explaining exactly why my clockwork radio couldn't possibly work.

'Further to our telephone coversation I have discussed the matter with Mr George Eyres of Levenshulme, a master clockmaker, having much experience of spring engine design and development,' he began.

'We lack specific details of the workload upon an engine, viz, shaft, speed of dynamo and power output required, but if we assumed a few tens of milliwatts at say 200 rpm then a spring engine weighing around forty pounds might give an endurance of five to ten minutes at the most. If the shaft speed is to be a decade or so above then he feels that a spring engine could be devised but would weigh one hundredweight and again have an endurance of no more than ten minutes or so at the very best. In any case the cost of developing and producing such an engine would be very high.'

Here was dear old Robert Ormiston-Chant, AFPWI, with all the pretension those letters after his name gave him, projecting the image of a radio weighing one hundredweight. A clockwork monster that would have had to carry a government health warning and a truss with every set. His theoretical Goliath had a ten-minute endurance, while I had already built and patented a model that weighed just four-and-a-half pounds and, on a thirty-second wind, had a playing duration of fourteen minutes, and growing.

Ormiston-Chant's final ringing paragraph was the clincher. 'Mr Eyres wonders if you have considered biological electro-chemical means, as of local plant life: cf Clive Sinclair's lemon-powered transistor radio.

'But best of all he feels that the energy used in winding up a spring engine or in turning a dynamo by hand etc. etc. might today be more efficiently and compactly converted direct from the body heat of the radio user. Something on the lines of a Thermocouple held under an armpit or between the thighs at the groin; areas offering maximum body temperatures. Yours sincerely . . .'

Was Robert Ormiston-Chant sending me up? Or was it just his polite way of saying stick your radio up your arse? Frankly, my dears, I didn't give a damn. I framed his wonderfully barmy letter and hung it on the wall of my lavatory. Every time I received another rebuff over the next twenty-four months I compared it for absurdity and hauteur on the Ormiston-Chant scale of pedantry. His letter ensured that cheerfulness had a way of breaking through even in a barren run of disappointments.

One of the many people I wrote to was Richard Branson at Virgin.

Since he'd taken on the might of British Airways I had admired his energy and his track record for taking chances and giving new ideas a go. I've always reckoned that if you could somehow harness his hairy-dog enthusiasm you'd probably light up half of Birmingham. So I was very disappointed when I got the stock reply from Virgin: 'Thank you, but no thank you.'

I recently met Richard and reminded him how the clockwork radio might have been a Virgin enterprise. He smiled and said something about getting together over my next invention. The fact that every new idea has its version of the man at Decca Records who turned down The Beatles wasn't much consolation, he agreed, especially when every post contains letters declining your idea with thanks. Then he reminded me of a quote from the British novelist Rosamond Lehmann. 'One can present people with opportunities. One cannot make them equal to them.'

In November 1992 I had extended my patent for another year, but to renew it yet again and secure my rights to the clockwork radio around the world would have cost me a lot of money which I did not have. So if nothing happened before the end of 1993 I'd more or less had it.

Nearly every delivery was bringing me more letters of rejection. I was longing for a little ordinary human enthusiasm. I opened every reply with a fragile display of optimism, hoping it would be the one where my luck would turn. Then, when it was unfavourable ('Turned down again, like an old bedspread,' was how Pauline Bricker put it) I felt awful. Another rebuff meant I'd have to write more letters and have my nose rubbed in it yet again.

The whole process was making me feel frustrated, humiliated even. I am a very resilient sort of bloke, but I was beginning to think that perhaps I ought to quit while I still had an ounce or two of self-respect left. If at first you don't succeed, try again, and if that fails give up. There's no point in making a complete ass of yourself.

But I was encouraged to keep going by the support of some good people at the BBC's World Service. I thought that as industry wasn't taking any notice of me then contact with the people who broadcast to the Third World might help launch what was, essentially, an invention for the Third World. They were a delightful, civilised bunch of people – among them the late Dorothy Grenfell Williams, head of the African section, her then deputy, Mick Delap, and a BBC engineer, Kevin Cawood. Kevin took apart the prototype of my radio to prove to himself that it worked, and gave it his seal of approval. Dorothy and Mick helped me to put together a presentation for the Overseas Development Agency, which months later led to a grant which helped set up our factory in South Africa. The enthusiasm for my radio at the BBC World Service gave me the morale boost I needed. As every other approach had failed, they advised me to go public with my ideas. It was a risk. Inventors, paranoid as we are about the piracy of our innovations, are wary about too much early publicity.

But after more than two years of utter failure I decided I had absolutely nothing to lose. This was desperation stakes. I rang the telephone number Mick Delap had given me for the BBC Television Centre. By that time I didn't even care whether somebody stole my idea. Having an ego as big as a truck, I thought I deserved a bit of attention after months of being totally ignored. If I did my little TV spot, even if it came to nothing, I'd be able to put the tape into a continuous loop and bore the socks off anyone who came to my house. It would be my swan song. My Andy Warhol fifteen minutes of fame.

Once again, a television programme was to play a crucial role in the development of the clockwork radio. This time it was the BBC's showcase for scientific invention *Tomorrow's World*. I'd been a regular viewer of the programme since Raymond Baxter started the show in 1964. For me watching it was like a blood sport. I used to tune in waiting for the demonstrations of new gadgets to go wrong. My abiding memory of the show was when a lady demonstrated a new portable bath. In the best BBC tradition, she was suitably concealed with bubbles – until the heat from the studio lights began to melt the foam . . .

My appearance on 15 April 1994 involved a bit of undressing as well. They got me to swim a couple of lengths to show off the pool at home. But most of the item was taken up with the presenter, Carmen Pryce, interviewing me about the clockwork radio. She took me back to film at the World Service headquarters at Bush House where Mick Delap was very complimentary. He recounted stories of people in Somalian refugee camps saving their rice ration and bartering it for batteries for their radios, ending with a timely recommendation for my invention: 'I think there's a tremendous market if it can work, but also if it is marketed at an affordable price.'

As soon as the programme finished the two telephones at home began ringing and didn't stop until three the next morning. People from all over the country, people I'd never even met, had got my number from directory enquiries and were calling to offer their congratulations and say: 'Bully for you.' I had some friends round to watch the programme and celebrate with a few drinks. Between us we fielded those calls until the early hours. Knowing all those strangers were on my side gave me a huge lift. They gave me more encouragement in six hours than the big shots had given me in two wretched years. It was a lovely confidence restorer.

If it had all ended there I would have been content. At least I would be able to say I had gone out with a bit of a bang and not a pathetic whimper. But while all those calls had been blocking my telephone lines a businessman was desperately trying to get in touch with me. In the end he found my fax number from somewhere and sent me a business plan. In the excitement of manning the phones, I didn't get to read it until the next morning. But it was the breakthrough I had been waiting for, and when I'd read it and reread it I gave the fax a big wet kiss.

I had never heard of the man before, but in an amiable message written on BDO Stoy Hayward headed notepaper, the firm of chartered accountants in Baker Street, he represented himself as an accountant dealing with acquisitions and mergers with considerable experience of what can make or break a company. His name was Christopher Staines.

I rang him and he said he'd come home from work and happened to switch on *Tomorrow's World* by chance. He'd seen me beat the drum on behalf of my clockwork radio and had been impressed. Half-way through my interview he'd suddenly thought: 'I can help this person.' He seemed young, enthusiastic, and a man who would make a good ally. The things he said and the way he said them added up to the kind of guy I could like. And might be able to trust.

He'd fallen instantly in love with my radio. 'It seems to me to be such a simple idea, with such an obvious application with no recognisable flaws,' he said. 'I can't see a reason why it should fail.' His words were like music to my ears. He wanted to see me as soon as possible and we arranged a meeting at my house for the following Sunday.

CHAPTER TWENTY-FOUR

LET'S DO IT

NOT SURPRISINGLY, MY SOUR EXPERIENCE OVER MY ORANGE AIDS INVENTIONS HAD MADE ME INSTINC- TIVELY WARY OF ACCOUNTANTS. An adherent of the Monty Python view of the profession, I'd come to regard them as an extremely dull, irrepressibly drab, tedious, and probably felonious crew. But Christopher Staines proved to be completely the opposite. He was bright, funny and personable, and we had a lovely first meeting.

After my first mauling by venture capitalists I was understandably cautious about men in suits making me promises about financial backing. But Christopher's approach was very measured and decent. He didn't exhibit any signs of being a chiseller or a spiv in sheep's clothing who would rip me off.

It was a perfect spring day. Christopher had brought along his wife, Emma, and children, Sebastian and Isabella, to scrutinise the mad inventor in his lair. I had a few friends round and we sat out by the river in the sun eating a few nibbles and drinking wine. It was very relaxed, low-key and friendly. Christopher was still buzzing about my appearance on *Tomorrow's World*. As he saw the story unfold, with me having a hard time trying to get my product noticed, he realised he was in a position to help. He was convinced his experience in product development would make the radio a winner. He told me: 'I saw all the elements coming together before me as the programme unfolded.'

My terrace by the river was an odd venue for such important discussions. Christopher's son Seb was excited by all the traffic on the Thames. Every time something interesting ploughed past the end of the jetty he'd say: 'Look at that ginormous boat,' and the meeting would have to adjourn while we all went and waved at whatever vessel was sailing by. But we did conclude our business satisfactorily. Christopher had already discussed the clockwork radio with his South African business partner Rory Stear, and before he left Christopher had made me an offer that led to the deal which set up the BayGen Power Company. I was to own the technology and trademarks in a holding company which granted a licence in perpetuity to BayGen Power to make and distribute the radios.

Next stop Africa. Christopher Staines flew to Johannesburg for a meeting with Rory Stear. Christopher was given an easy ride. Rory didn't take much convincing that the radio was worth backing. 'It was immediately apparent,' Chris said. 'He didn't even question what I said. His reaction was: "This is fantastic. This is for Africa".'

At the time Rory Stear was doing a lot of work on mergers and acquisitions in Tanzania. One deal he was working on had taken him to Mwanza, on the shores of Lake Victoria, which was where the United Nations were flying in the bulk of their aid for Rwanda. Rory told me: 'What I'd seen there absolutely convinced me that anything that obviated the need for electricity or batteries on a continent of 600 million people was most certainly going to be beneficial.'

Then another happy accident occurred. The long arm of coincidence has seemed to rest happily on my shoulder for most of my life. News of my invention was spreading. I gave an interview to a radio station in Johannesburg. By chance someone heard it on his car radio and made contact with Rory Stear.

He was Hylton Appelbaum, Executive Trustee of the Liberty Life Foundation, the philanthropic arm of the Liberty Life group. The foundation gives £5 million of its profits each year to invest in worthwhile causes. He was to say later: 'You were on the radio talking about a radio that used no batteries, solar power or any other source and I was enormously struck by the relevance that this had to South Africa. We have a country where the vast majority of the people are rural, most people are poor, and most people don't have access to electricity.'

One month after seeing my appearance on *Tomorrow's World*, my mother died. She was eighty-four, her heart was worn out, and she died in Ealing Hospital in May 1994. During all the years of rejection I sometimes felt that she was the only person who believed, as much as I did, that the clockwork radio was a good idea. She had always been my most faithful supporter. My optimism began in her warm lap as a boy when I picked up her jaunty attitude to the world. I'm glad she lived long enough to see my best idea start to succeed. During her final months she was ailing and became progressively weaker, but not once did her faith in me desert her. I'd visit her in hospital and, pale from lack of sleep, she'd be the one doing the cheering up. I still miss her and her happy gift of looking on the bright side of everything.

Liberty Life seemed to be an ideal investor in our project so Rory went to see Hylton Appelbaum. Everything was coming together like a smoothly oiled machine. After more than two years of no progress, we were now making headway with jaunty speed. Rory was impressed by Hylton's attitude to the radio. 'I knew that Hylton was becoming very interested in companies that would make a social difference and where the profits generated could be returned to the community at large. Therefore Hylton wouldn't be a rapist as so many other investors would be. He saw the project for what it was.' The meeting in August went so well that Hylton immediately decided to fly to Britain to meet me and see the radio for himself.

The head of Liberty Life was slightly taken aback by the doggy, untidy state of my house. I'd tried to straighten it up for his arrival. I even did a spot of dusting, but it still looked like the Augean stables after a rough night when he and Christopher Staines stepped into my living room.

I showed him the bench where I carried out my first experiments on the radio and gave him a blow-by-blow account of its origins. We both got on comfortably, like old friends, and I remember we all became very animated as we sketched out our plans for manufacturing the radio. At that meeting we started to explore the question of whether or not disabled people could assemble the radio components. 'Do you think there could be jobs on the production line for disabled people?' he asked. 'They weave baskets. With the same skill they could assemble radios which would have a high value both economically and in self-esteem.'

'Why not. Marvellous idea,' I said. 'Let's do it.'

When Hylton Appelbaum got back to South Africa after his visit to my workshop he got in touch with a friend of his, Dr William Rowland, an internationally respected leader in the disability movement. He told him about me and the radio, and Chris and Rory's plans to open a factory in South Africa using disabled people as a major part of the workforce. The more he was told about the project, the more excited William became. Hylton's enthusiastic and breathless résumé of our plans earned him a measured two-word response. William Rowland, who is blind, immediately said: 'I see.' Our plans had his immediate seal of approval.

'I just thought what an amazing idea, and how obvious,' said William. 'I immediately felt that this was something that was going to work. We had had many suggestions, many approaches to involve us in all kinds of things, this one just made immediate sense to me.'

Baroness Chalker of the Overseas Development Agency gave us a cheque for £145,000 to kick-start the project. Our enterprise was well and truly on its way. Encouraged by that gesture, Hylton Appelbaum offered to fund a group of organisations for the disabled if they became business partners in the venture. They did. In November, eight months after my appearance on *Tomorrow's World*, Liberty Life Foundation, South Africa's biggest life insurer, and an arm of Kagiso Trust, a not-for-profit urban and rural development financing organisation, put up a total of £200,000. They subsequently invested another £300,000.

I'll always thank providential interference, or whatever stars were shining on me, that Christopher Staines chose to switch on his television the night of my appearance on *Tomorrow's World*. I couldn't have wished for better partners in my enterprise than Chris Staines and Rory Stear.

Chris once admitted that he could never have done what I did, invent the clockwork radio and then have the tenacity to keep faith in it through a barrage of scorn and rejection. When he came into my life I was at the end of my tether. I couldn't have kept up my struggle for recognition much longer. After more than two years I still hadn't found anyone to take me seriously and I was ready to pack it in, light the blue touch-paper and retire immediately.

But, by the same measure, I could never have achieved what Chris and Rory did either. They brought my invention to the attention of investors who agreed that it was a revolutionary idea. They had an entrée to the kind of people who probably would have shown me the door. What they gave the project was credibility. They had the right contacts with influential investors whose faith and money set us on our way. Both of my partners are talented business dynamos, and they are the best thing that ever happened to me.

The next stage of the setting-up of our business was a big market research campaign in Africa to find out exactly what consumers wanted from the clockwork radio. With my prototypes I had endeavoured to make the radio as small as possible, arguing that in this transistorised, miniaturised age, small was beautiful. I had evidently been wasting my time.

Our researches found that whilst there was a big demand for a clockwork-driven set, Africans didn't want a miniaturised radio. They weren't much bothered about ease of handling, or how much it weighed; what they required was a radio that was big, heavy, very robust, and able to deliver a lot of noise. They appreciated the advantages of a radio that didn't need batteries or electricity, but their fortissimo demand was for blasting volume, the louder the better.

We certainly couldn't deliver that with my first model. Clearly it wasn't yet a marketable product. The radio only produced fourteen minutes of sound on a thirty-second wind, and our potential customers had just told us that almost certainly it wasn't going to be loud enough. We still had a lot of work to do. Our progress from my first rough prototype to a mass-produced manufacturable product was to prove a long and incredibly stressful odyssey.

Before we could go into production every component in my prototype would have to be examined, evaluated and improved. My invention clearly worked, but it wasn't yet an item we could sell in the shops. It was a case of back to the drawing board. It was to take more than a year before we got things right and the first clockwork radio rolled off the production line.

In pursuit of technical enlightenment the prototype was sent west to the Electronic Engineering Department at Bristol University, where Dr Duncan Grant and his team took it to pieces. Every component was tested and checked for its effectiveness. The findings were unequivocal. Most components were found wanting. Dr Grant's conclusions were pandemically gloomy and my new-found optimism congealed inside me like a rat in a tar barrel.

The biggest item of bad news was that our spring would never deliver us the sound volume we wanted. Dr Grant's monitoring equipment showed that even a slight increase in volume demanded a surge of power. The needle on his apparatus peaked alarmingly as the volume switch was turned up, and it was clear that we were never going to store the requisite amount of energy in our existing spring. 'You aren't going to do it,' he said. 'With the radio you've given us you cannot have more loudness. It's impossible.'

Chris Staines was in the laboratory when this depressing verdict was delivered, and he passed it on to Rory Stear in Johannesburg. 'The thought: "You'll never work in this town again," was going through my mind,' he says. 'You don't bring a group like the Liberty Life organisation to a project, selling them on the fact of its potential and the fact that it does exist, and then phone them up a bit later and say: "Look we've already spent a huge amount of the money you've invested, but there is really no product at all." So the next few days were a very bleak time.'

By this time David Butlion had joined our team, working with me on the technical development of the radio. We realised that the gloomy Bristol University's findings were correct. It was impossible to make the prototype radio any louder. The criteria the scientists had been given were far too strict. Every time the radio was turned up, the sound distorted into a mushy squall. There simply wasn't enough power coming out of the clockwork generator to drive the electronics properly.

The solution to the problem was easy. We simply moved the goal posts. The original constant force spring was replaced with a constant force spring twice its size, giving double the amount of energy, and increasing our volume.

To make sure that most of this power got to our generator we knew we had to improve the efficiency of our gearbox. At the still points of the turning world there is always our old enemy friction. Bristol University had built us a Rolls Royce of a gearbox. It was a very superior piece of work that, like all good examples of engineering, was a thing of beauty in itself, the essence of elegance and unruffled movement. But it was made of metal and would have been far too expensive to mass produce. We decided to cut costs and made an exact replica of the Bristol gearbox in plastic. It didn't look as good as the metal version, and we soon discovered it wasn't quite up to the job either.

David Butlion sat up until three o'clock one morning wrestling with a solution. Since friction occurs in the bearings at the end of the axles, his idea was to reduce the friction by simply cutting down on the number of bearings and axles. The following day we tested the new gearbox layout for efficiency with Process Analysis and Automation in Farnborough, the firm of development engineers we had been working with to evaluate our ideas. They tried out the new design by running it through their computers, and it worked like a dream.

The radio we eventually put into production had a ten-metre long, fifty-millimetre wide and 0.2-millimetre thick, heavy carbon steel spring, preformed and wound around a storage spool. This 'B motor configuration' – more commonly known as the constant force spring – is wound against its curvature onto another spool, called the 'Talk' spool. Once fully wound and released the spring then returns itself to its original position, thereby producing a constant force on the torque spool as it unwinds. The spring has an 'end stop' for overwind protection.

This torque is transmitted by a ratchet system into a transmission speeding up from one to 1,000 in a three-stage gear arrangement. The transmission drive is a small DC motor (in reverse) providing about 100 megawatts to the FM, MW and SW radio. For sixty winds, the spring was generating twenty-five to thirty minutes of air-time.

The spring within the radio was guaranteed to deliver a consistent performance for 10,000 'spring cycles', which equates to approximately three hours' play every day, for nearly five years, or 5,000 hours' playing time. After that the spring gradually decays giving diminished power output to the radio, which can still remain usable for some time.

It had taken almost four years from the moment of my brainwave until we were satisfied that the radio was ready to go on sale. It had been a hard slog. But as it took the ancient Egyptians 1,000 years to develop the scythe from the sickle, we hadn't done too badly.

The months of testing and retesting, trial and error, were vital to smooth out all the design modifications and ensure that when we went into production we would be making a radio that worked efficiently and was also pleasing to the eye. The industrial designer Andy Davy was brought in to give the radio's appearance customer appeal. He sculpted my utilitarian box into the sleek, startling, streamlined shape that went on sale.

The radio's design is constantly being improved. Our tough plastic model has proved its durability in the scorching heat of Africa and the cold of Arctic Canada. Now there is also a transparent pastel-coloured designer version of the radio that's become a fashion statement for those looking for something less rugged.

Without all these moneymen, scientists, engineers, and designers adding their two penn'orth to my original idea, the clockwork radio – as a desirable object you buy in the shops – would not have happened. The experts helped transform my basic concept into a marketable product, and my partners were there to orchestrate everything and keep the momentum going.

By the time our factory in South Africa went into production the design of my prototype had altered considerably. For some inventors this could have caused more friction – of the angry 'I'm leaving in a huff' variety. But I was quite happy for other people to run with the ball once I had kicked off the idea.

Sometimes the inventor causes problems when his project is taken up, because he has this terrible thing called ego, and it can get in the way of launching a successful invention. An inventor who tries to run the whole show on his own can cause chaos. His talent doesn't necessarily run to organising complex industrial operations. An inventor's skill equips him to be a versatile one-man-band, not the conductor of the Royal Philharmonic. Inventors should stick to inventing, and the entrepreneurs who help them should keep to what they do best – the commercialisation of good ideas. There should be a decent bond between the inventor and the people who make things possible for him, making sure that when the money starts rolling in, it's shared. Inventors should always bear in mind that consultants and accountants are men who are smart enough to tell you how to make the most of your invention, but not necessarily smart enough to invent anything themselves.

When our factory in Cape Town opened in 1995, I was stupidly proud. I had been too busy to fly out there. Like a father awaiting the arrival of his first child I didn't quite know what my role was, apart from standing around beaming, and ringing up to find out how the birth was going. The four years between getting my big idea and the first radios rolling off the production line had been a helter-skelter ride of mixed emotions – hope, despair, elation, tears, laughter, doubt, fatigue, and joy.

Christopher Staines rang me to say that day one of trial production had gone smoothly. 'Your first radios will be on sale in the shops any day now,' he said. 'You've got something to be really proud of.' I put down the phone and walked out to my workshop. I remember tinkering with a few bits and pieces on the bench, shedding a few tears and thinking: 'I love creating things. And I don't want to stop. This is what I'm here for.'

CHAPTER TWENTY-FIVE

A FANTASTIC
ACHIEVEMENT

THERE USED TO BE A FILE OF ARCHITECT'S DRAWINGS IN MY OFFICE SHOWING ROUGH SKETCHES OF THE BAYGEN FAC-TORY IN CAPE TOWN. Through the winter of 1994–1995 I'd take them out and enjoy imagining how the completed building would look. But all those hours of poring over the plans were no preparation for the impact the place had on me when I saw it for the first time.

On a perfect African day in June 1995, Christopher Staines, Rory Stear and I took a car out to the factory lot. We talked excitedly as Rory, at the wheel, did his impersonation of the get-away driver after a bank robbery.

Table Mountain overwhelmed the view as we sped from the Vineyards Hotel out into the suburbs. The factory was a one-storey steel, glass and brick building located in the middle of a new industrial complex called Montague Gardens. The estate was lush with exotic trees, sprinklered lawns and gaudy tropical flowers. Our route there was a confusion of scrubby roundabouts and we careered around them in a Snowcem fog of dust. But for the sun shining down and the brilliancy of the sky, it could have been Milton Keynes.

From the factory's security gates I caught my first glimpse of the company logo. The words BayGen Power Manufacturing blared out from a white board in bright-blue lettering three feet high. BayGen is short for Baylis Generators and it was the first time I'd had my name – or even part of it – emblazoned on anything. For my circus stint in Berlin I'd been billed as Rameses II, and poor old Trevor Baylis hadn't even got a tiny mention in brackets. Now my name wasn't exactly up in lights, but it shone out brightly nonetheless, picked out by a midday sun against a cloudless sky.

Seeing the first syllable of my surname on a board outside our Cape Town factory was as stirring as landfall after a hard voyage. It moved me more powerfully than any sentimental song, and my eyes began to prickle. It was an overwhelming moment for me, the culmination and vindication of four years of struggle and frustration, and I burst into tears. There was a film crew recording it all for the BBC's *QED* programme, and my mind was going back over all the rejection and all the shit I'd had to take, and it was too much for me.

It was just an ordinary sign, but I was prouder of it than anything I'd achieved in my life. I looked at it through a smear of weeping and wished that my dear old mum and dad could have lived to see that all their guileless faith in me had been justified.

What made it even more emotional was that Rory and Chris were there to share the moment with me. Without their skill, enthusiasm and expertise the radio would never have gone into production. They had come on the scene and rescued the project at a moment of crisis and despair when I'd just about resigned myself to the inevitability of giving up. I hugged them and said I'd always be indebted to them for their belief in me and their immense support. If I had provided the 1% inspiration required to invent the radio, they had sweated most of the 99% of the perspiration that was needed to make it into a commercial reality.

David Butlion was waiting in the foyer to greet me. I locked him in a tearful bear-hug, complimenting him on the factory. 'Oh it's a blinder mate. It's terrific,' I blubbered, moistening his lapels. He gave me a reassuring: 'What's the matter?' look. 'Tears of joy,' I explained. 'It may not look like it, Dave, but this is just about the happiest day of my life.'

There was a notice in the foyer which announced: 'BayGen welcomes Trevor Baylis.' As soon as I spotted it I went again, choked with tears and trying to hide them. I got out my handkerchief to wipe my eyes. 'I'm sorry about this,' I told my guides. 'You must think I'm a big girl's blouse. Just give me a few moments and I'll be OK.'

I haven't got any children; never will have, probably, so my first glimpse of the factory was like seeing my first-born. I blew my nose, took a deep breath, then Rory and Chris led me through a set of swing doors out onto the factory floor where the production line was operating. There was a faint electric hum of machinery, the whirr of power drills. A few heads turned to see what was going on, but the ordered efficiency of the production line rolled on as ranks of clockwork radios slid by on the conveyor.

It was one of the most moving sights I have ever seen. I had been party to all the plans and knew we were setting up a multi-racial factory employing people of differing abilities. But none of our discussions had prepared me for the emotion of seeing our grand plan in action. On the same production line were people of all colours and talents. It was a totally integrated workforce – black, white, brown, male, female, English, Afrikaans, Xhosa. The limbless working next to the blind, deaf people in partnership with the able-bodied, wheelchairs and crutches among the benches, the feeble co-operating with the strong.

It was very humbling. The girl smiling at me there is blind. The bloke sitting at the bench, deaf. Those two guys pushing the heavy trolley have only got two legs between them. That fair-haired woman is schizophrenic, and her neighbour's an epileptic.

All of them worked with rhythmic precision. Chatting and laughing. A few singing along to a Freeplay radio (the name we gave the clockwork radio). Some of them could only work four hours a day, so there was a shift system. Every one of them had travelled to work under their own steam. As part of their training programme a staff member had found the easiest and most cost-effective travel route for the new employee, then taken them backwards and forwards until they got used to it. 'Most of them hadn't travelled alone since their trauma,' I was told. 'We give them that confidence.'

The factory is partly owned by Disability Employment Concerns, an agency sponsored by the Liberty Life Foundation. They are responsible for training the 35% of the workforce who have handicaps. All the workers – able-bodied and disabled – earn the same and their rates compare well with other factories – like Panasonic and Plessey.

In microcosm it is Nelson Mandela's declaration for South Africa come true. Throughout his twenty-seven years in jail, the world's most famous political prisoner had carried the ideal of a democratic and free society in which all persons could live together in harmony and with equal opportunity. Here in the world's first clockwork radio factory it had become a reality. I had helped bring that about, and the realisation put all my struggles in perspective, and made me feel miraculously happy and fulfilled.

As I walked along the line and chatted to the people making the radios I was overwhelmed by their warmth towards me. 'This is the first job I've had since I lost my arm,' said one young man clasping my hand in his. 'I can go one better,' said the blind girl sitting next to him. 'This is the first time anyone has ever employed me.'

Everyone was in place at their workbench efficiently performing their allotted task. I had a sudden skewed thought. It was the first time in my life I'd ever had anything to do with setting up a factory. I thought of Charlie Chaplin, *Modern Times*, and his send-up of the perils of automation. 'Are they going to change jobs now and again?' I asked of nobody in particular. 'I'd hate these guys and girls to get bored to tears doing the work I've given them. I'm not a hard-faced tycoon you know.'

Somebody laughed and said: 'You could always sit down and join us.' And I did for a while, but I was nowhere near as efficient as the blind man who showed me what to do. (And by the way, the jobs are rotated.)

Walking round the plant was like a tonic. People in Africa have a wonderful capacity for laughter and enjoyment, whatever they are doing. In Britain we may be better off, but our lives seem harsher and more embittered by comparison. There was more undistilled delight there that morning than I'd met in a long time, and for me it was a reawakening.

I found the best way to stop myself getting tearful again was to crack a few jokes and guffaw at everything. One of the blokes wiring up components asked me if I was having trouble with the volume control on my laugh. The spontaneous friendship and humour of my BayGen colleagues stayed with me throughout my journey round the plant, and by the time I left it was like saying a long farewell to old friends.

They all gathered round me in their blue company uniforms to shake my hand. They kept thanking me and I told them: 'No, it's me who should be thanking you, because you lot have made all my dreams come true.' I walked slowly round the sun-dappled factory one final time, taking it all in, enjoying the moment, fired up by the emotion. Then I said my goodbyes all over again.

The link between the clockwork radio and the disabled was to lead to a meeting I will never forget. Two days later I flew to Pretoria to present one of the first radios to come off our production line to President Nelson Mandela.

I remember sitting at home watching television as the cameras captured the moment he walked free from Victor Verster Prison at 4.17 pm on 11 February five years earlier. For most of us waiting for that historic moment it was our first sight of a man whose name was a household word, but whose face and voice were unknown. Now he was the most famous man in the world and I had an appointment with him at the presidential residence, the Tuynhuis, in Pretoria.

My friend Dr William Rowland came along with me, and so did Christopher Staines and Rory Stear. As we waited, William told us of a conversation he'd once had with Walter Sisulu, the Secretary of the African National Congress. He said that when Sisulu and the President were in prison on Robben Island they used to read in the newspapers how disabled people outside were challenging the government on all kinds of issues, even demonstrating and marching.

'It was such an encouragement to know that even disabled people were resisting,' he said. 'I think perhaps that's where Mr Mandela's interest stems from, and that's why he has a very good feeling for the needs of disadvantaged people.'

We took our radio with us into his private rooms, where I was expecting lots of protocol and stifling etiquette. As it turned out there was no bowing and scraping at all. When he appeared, in a blue casual shirt worn, as usual, outside his trousers, Mr Mandela was taller than I had imagined him, one of the most dignified, yet relaxed people I have ever met. There was a genuine warmth to his courtesy and he seemed so sure of his authority he did not need to assert it at all.

He had two pens stuck in the breast-pocket of his shirt. They were the closest thing to a badge of office he wore. There was nothing of the grand statesman about his demeanour; he was more like a friendly headmaster who'd interrupted his work for a while to come out and have a chat with some visitors.

As soon as the door to his sitting room opened he was welcoming us inside. 'Let them come and sit here. Just bring the chairs will you?'

William gave him a demonstration of the radio, and I carried the set nearer so that he could fiddle with the tuner. He seemed surprised that its only source of power was a spring, and wanted that confirmed. 'No electricity? No batteries?'

'Nothing else at all. Absolutely nothing,' I told him.

He sat listening for a while, switching to several different stations. Then he gave the radio his personal accolade with the most prestigious endorsement it's ever had. 'I find it very interesting. It's a fantastic achievement.'

The President had just made the kind of remark advertising men, raised in the mysterious arts of publicity, would have given their eye-teeth for. What could I say? I simply mumbled: 'You're so kind.'

Mr Mandela went on to thank us for the employment policy at our new factory. 'I'm very happy that this new and fantastic invention is associated with people who have been despised by society,' he told us. 'One of the things that is impressive today is the emergence of men and women who are thinking in terms of the disadvantaged, the poorest of the poor.'

Later William Rowland said that he thought President Mandela was proud of the fact that South Africa was the manufacturer of the clock-work radio, and that South Africa's technology would be harnessed for the benefit of all Africa.

The President's dazzling good will radiated around the room. Here were four white visitors, not very different, outwardly, from the kind of people who had kept him in jail for twenty-seven years for his opposition to apartheid. Yet here he was promoting good will between black and white, a will to forgive, to forget and rebuild. People who have met him talk about his pervasive charisma, but there is a decency and goodness about him that goes beyond that. Anyway, in an age of sound bites and focus groups, charisma has now become a downgraded, prefabricated commodity. If you have Mr Mandela's basic integrity you don't need to have anything else.

Mindful of his words, we've set up a programme with the United Nations, the Red Cross, UNESCO, and some fifty other agencies, to distribute clockwork radios to those parts of the world where they are most needed. There is a growing list of low-tech applications of clock-work technology that will be of value to emerging countries. The aim is to harness them all for the benefit of Africa and the whole of the Third World.

CHAPTER TWENTY-SIX

A CLOCKWORK UNIVERSE

THE ENORMITY OF THE CLOCKWORK RADIO'S IMPACT OVER-WHELMED ME. The best part of its success was having so many people around, the friends who had encouraged me during the bad times, who were happy for me. But even in my most fanciful dreams I never imagined so many people would get so much pleasure from the emotional tale of one man and his screwdriver.

The public mood was nicely caught by a leader column in *The Times* on 10 August 1995. 'In this corporate world of research and development and international patent conferences, the lone inventor is an anachronistic figure,' it said. 'Big business has little time for the man who had a brainwave in his garden shed. The likelihood of a former underwater escape artist inventing and successfully developing a device of use to millions would seem extremely small. Yet Trevor Baylis has, against all odds, come up with something so simple and so practical that no one could believe it had not already been invented: the clockwork radio.'

The leader went on: 'The radio will probably do more to bring information, education and social progress to dark areas of the developing world than any other device for a generation . . . The lessons to emerge from this uplifting tale are as simple as the clockwork radio itself. The first is the supreme importance still of the individual human imagination. Visionary ideas, lateral thinking and sheer ingenuity can tease out of the inventor's brain solutions that others are blind to see.

'The second lesson, however, is the danger that too often inventions that could change the world languish unrecognised because of corporate envy or indifference, or because they lack financial and organisational midwives.

'The third lesson is the importance of not discarding old and tested principles just because they seem old-fashioned. Clockwork is a mechanism that has powered machines since the Middle Ages. Refined to an art form, it has produced some of the most exquisite watches that still rival any powered by quartz crystal. Now the old mechanism can be adapted to more modern products; a new world of possibilities opens up.'

By the time the *QED* programme on my trip to Africa was broadcast on 8 August 1995, I had become an object of curiosity. I could hardly cross a street in London without a total stranger shouting at me: 'Hello Trev, it's a wind-up.' For someone who, just a few months before, was just another anonymous person it came as a very agreeable surprise.

The story of the clockwork radio had been given wide coverage in India and early in 1996 I received a long airmail letter from M.R. Nagpurkar of Matunga. He'd addressed his envelope to: Trevor Baylis, Scientist Inventor of Radio Working on Key, Whitehall. Somehow the Post Office managed to deliver it to me at Twickenham.

The fact that the radio was driven by clockwork struck a romantic chord with many people. That it had also been invented in a lean-to only added to the feel-good factor. Writing about my invention, Matthew Bond of *The Times* said: 'On paper that [a radio driven by clockwork] sounded akin to the everlasting light-bulb and the water-powered internal combustion engine. But in practice it actually works. I felt good about that.'

The clockwork radio became so widely known it began to feature in newspaper cartoons. The *Financial Times* artist, Ferguson, depicted the Russian leader Boris Yeltsin angered by a NATO broadcast he was listening to on his clockwork set. It was captioned 'Wind-up radio'. A caricature of me appeared in a *Guardian* comic strip, where the comments of one character contained a barbed truth: 'If it wasn't for our mail-order catalogues, invention would be a thing of the past!'

With his tongue firmly in his cheek Auberon Waugh in his column in the *Daily Telegraph* suggested a new use for the invention. British teenagers, most of whom spend all day asleep pretending to listen to radios, should all be supplied with wind-up radios. 'If British teenagers were equipped with clockwork radios,' he wrote, 'they would have to wake up every forty minutes to wind it up and continue the noise. This would be good training for when they have to think about a job. The winding operation will also teach them a new skill, which might do wonders for their self-respect.'

But my favourite joke was a cartoon in the *Spectator*. It was a scene in the Patent Office where a hopeful-looking man is sitting at a desk with a large clockwork key protruding through his ribcage. The Patent Office clerk is saying to him: 'The clockwork radio I loved, the clock-work pacemaker I'm not so sure about.'

On Tuesday 9 July 1996, for the first time in my life, I dressed up in white tie and tails to attend the state banquet given by the Queen for President Mandela of South Africa at Buckingham Palace. Most of the places I eat at have sauce bottles on formica tables, and even there I've never been too sure about what knife to use for what; so I had misgivings about committing some dreadful gaffe in front of royalty.

I could see the shock-horror headline in Nigel Dempster's column: 'Inventor toasts head of state with finger bowl.' There was a flicker of tension in my knife and fork work, straining not to spill hollandaise on my chin because I didn't exactly know the polite way of wiping it off with my serviette. And anyway wasn't it politer to say napkin?

But in the end I just went with the flow, behaved like I do at home, and it was a wonderful evening. The Queen does a very good meal. Everyone went out of their way to make me feel I belonged in the Palace, even if only for one night.

Before the banquet there were drinks in one of the state rooms.

Everybody mingled self-consciously, waiting for the royals to mingle also. A month before I'd sent Her Majesty one of my radios. When she spoke to me she'd obviously enjoyed using it and was enthusiastic about the benefits it could bring to developing countries. I nodded, smiled, called her 'Ma'am', and couldn't think of anything sensible to say back. I suppose that's one of the great burdens of being the monarch. As soon as you start speaking to people their brains turn to sago pudding.

I hadn't realised it until I saw it all set out, but at these grand state occasions they bring out the gold plate, and for everybody, not just the VIPs on the top table. So I ate my filet de sole Newburg from a gold platter, which had a touch more style than my usual routine: haddock and chips eaten straight from the wrapping paper. I was seated next to a lovely woman called Kate, Lady Guthrie, the wife of General Sir Charles Guthrie, Chief of the General Staff. I asked her what indiscretion she'd committed at a previous banquet to deserve being placed next to a former lance corporal. But she was a dear lady, guiding me though the maze of cutlery and reminding me to save a drop of the Chateau Figeac for the toasts.

Having got the dress code utterly correct for the Palace, I lapsed later that month. The radio was on the short-list for the BBC's Design Awards, the high-profile prizes for the best of British design. I arrived at the presentation ceremony in Glasgow with the designer, Andy Davy, looking like a refugee from an Oxfam jumble sale.

I thought we didn't stand a chance against the other short-listed designs, which included the snout of the Eurostar train and Richard Rogers's spectacular rust-red headquarters for Channel 4. And so because I wasn't expecting to go up and collect anything I turned out in a scruffy red shirt and a pair of baggy old jeans. When Janet Street-Porter announced my name and then Andy's, we had to go up and collect our prizes from BBC boss Alan Yentob, with me in scruff order. We collected the trophy in the best product category, and also the overall award for the project that received most votes from the public.

With Savile Row to the left and Armani to the right of me, I looked like a dosser who had just walked in off the streets. I managed to mumble: 'This is really wonderful,' before retreating to hide my creases among the crowd of designer suits.

At the state banquet I had told Prince Charles I would send him a radio. On 29 July he sent me a charming letter from Highgrove. He said the radio would be extraordinarily useful all over the world when he had to travel, adding: 'I do congratulate you for such a simple and brilliant idea.'

On 9 October 1997, I took Pauline Bricker, Rosalind Addison, and my assistant Jill Hemmerle to Buckingham Palace where I received the Order of the British Empire. It was given to me by the Princess Royal. Ever since then I've kept meeting the Princess at various dinners and award ceremonies. The last time we spoke she'd heard I'd been an international swimmer and said: 'When you were in training wasn't it boring just swimming up and down the pool?' I replied: 'It was ma'am, but no more tiresome than constantly falling off a horse.' She was gracious enough to laugh.

The investiture was a very British event, with amiable pukka-types gently telling you what to do, while a military band played musical selections from the shows. You can't escape the ubiquitous sounds of Andrew Lloyd Webber, not even in Buckingham Palace. As you wait to go up to collect your honour all the various ranks of orders are lined up on different strips of carpet, all the knights on one strip, all the OBEs massed together, and the MBEs with a section of carpet to themselves. It's odd what thoughts go through your head at such moments, but I got to wondering whether, in this hierarchical society of ours, the weave of the various carpets was of a quality that befitted the rank standing on it. I even had a glance across at the knights' strip of Axminster to verify my theory, but the quality of their carpet looked exactly the same as ours. With my lack of refinement I was lucky not to be standing on coconut matting.

When we all strolled out through the gates of Buckingham Palace I was asked to go direct to the Canada Gate for a television interview. But the interview was merely an invention of Thames Television. While I was talking happily into the microphone about my big day, Michael Aspel surprised me with the big red book of *This Is Your Life*. I'd often watched the show and wondered what it would be like to have the small potatoes of your life's story served up for the entertainment of millions. Being all mouth and trousers, I enjoyed every minute of it. The show's researcher, Clare Thompson, had done a marvellous job tracking down all my old friends and bringing them together from around the world. Johnny Pugh was flown in from his circus in Florida and we met for the first time in ten years.

The show could be an embarrassment, but Michael Aspel treads a deft path between laughter and tears, and his tribute to me is a half-hour tape I'll always treasure. One of the bonuses of the programme is that you get to be taken prisoner, in the nicest possible way, by the producer Sue Green. She holds you incommunicado for three hours, plying you with refreshments and pleasant conversation, keeping you away from your friends who are rehearsing their parts in the show. She's a delightful woman to spend three hours locked away with, and any time she wants to do it again, I'm her man.

The radio was launched in Britain in May 1996 – a year after its African debut – going on sale in Harrods and Conrans, and high street retailers like Comet and Currys. By this time BayGen was employing 200 people to make the radios in Africa, with forty more employed in three operating divisions in Africa, Europe and North America.

Since the company's foundation the radios have been playing well to international audiences, but commercially there have been a few precarious moments as the company took off. Liberty were persuaded to put in more money and extra help arrived in the shape of Gordon and Anita Roddick, the founders of the Body Shop. They invested personally, and helped secure extra bank loans. In fact I've always been grateful to Gordon and Anita for the support they gave our fledgling company at a crucial time.

Then, when more capital was required to boost the development of a range of devices based on my wind-up mechanism, Rory Stear and Chris Staines sought investment from the American giant General Electric. In the spring of 1997 they bought a one-third share in the business, valuing it at $40 million (£24.7 million).

Low-tech human energy technology was the big attraction for

General Electric, which routed the purchase through its pensions trust because it regarded it as an investment – a corporate venturing exercise rather than a strategic acquisition. As David Wiederecht, Vice-President of alternative investments at General Electric Investment Management, said at the time: 'This is an investment in personal power, which will have a broad range of other applications.'

That July, at a Commonwealth Conference for Education Ministers in Botswana, I was able to demonstate exactly how exciting those applications could be. I had flown out to the conference to help fly the flag for Britain. I got bored with listening to speakers saying exactly the same thing in different accents, so I spent most of my time there playing hookey from the main hall.

I had a little stall exhibiting clockwork radios in the conference exhibition centre. Right opposite me was the Apple computer stand and I got friendly with the bloke manning it. One afternoon I wandered over for a chat and noticed a low-powered computer in his display. Something slotted into place. I suddenly wondered whether the clockwork generator on my stand could power this bit of gear.

The man in charge of the Apple stall looked as bored as I had been during the interminable speeches. I asked him if I could muck about with his computer.

'You might be about to see something very interesting,' I told him. 'On the other hand I might be about to make myself look like a big idiot.'

I connected my clockwork generator with a jack lead to a low-powered lap-top, an Apple E-mate 300. I wound the clockwork. When I turned the lap-top on it booted up. By this time a crowd of curious delegates had gathered round the stand and they burst into applause. I was in a state of slight surprise that what I had hoped for had worked so easily. The computer ran for sixteen minutes before crashing.

It was a euphoric moment. I'd proved there was nothing to stop us putting computers among the family's assegais and Masai shields in the mud huts of Africa. Later when I addressed the conference on invention I repeated my party trick with the computer and got a standing ovation. Everybody was excited because we all realised the lap-top could now go anywhere around the world and not be mains dependent.

The second generation Freeplay radio was launched in September 1997. It had an additional 'energy saver' circuit that slowed the unwinding of the spring to conserve energy when the radio was operating at low volumes or during quiet passages. This enhancement meant that the radio could now run for up to an hour from a single winding.

Two months later the first spin-off product – using the same clock-work power source as the radio – went into production. It was the Freeplay Self-powered Lantern. But a torch requires far more power than a radio, and at a constant level. Despite the use of a low-energy bulb and a lens designed to focus the beam tightly and make as much use of the bulb's light as possible, the running time from the clockwork power source was reduced to five minutes.

This was enough for many applications. Research shows that torches are generally used for three-and-a-half minutes at a time. But a five-minute cut-off would clearly deter some potential buyers. To get around this problem the flashlight has a facility to dump the mechanical energy stored in the spring through the generator into a patented electrical energy store, which is capable of holding up to two hours' worth of power. This was one of the benefits of the BayGen links with General Electric – we could make use of the massed brainpower of their vast American research and development laboratories.

To store enough energy to use the torch for fifteen minutes – to produce enough light to do a simple repair on a car on a remote road at night, for instance – you wind the torch up fully and dump the energy into the store three times. This ingenious way of extending the scope of clockwork energy opens up a whole new range of applications for personal power. Soon you'll be able to store enough energy, for example, to use your lap-top computer, CD player, tape deck, talking book, yachtsman's global positioning system, or mobile phone.

I am lucky to have made the opening strike in a new technological revolution fuelled by human energy. But it is only a beginning. We need to build ourselves a whole universe of clockwork devices. As the earth's resources – oil, coal, timber, minerals – diminish, as global warming irrevocably changes the world's climate, I'm convinced inventors need to look for even more low-tech ways of sustaining life as we currently enjoy it.

In the West the colourful, see-through version of the clockwork radio is marketed almost as a luxury item, a toy for the well-to-do. In Africa the tough, workhorse model is sold because it works in remote places where conventional radios are inadequate. It is useful, practical and above all sustainable, the only resource it needs is human energy.

Increasingly we in the West are going to have to put aside our toys, the multitude of appliances and accessories that devour electricity and suck dry our earth's resources. Or else we must find new ways to power them. I looked in a shopping catalogue recently and wondered what 'Personal Electrics' were. I discovered there were pages of them – items like deep-heat massagers and electric hair crimpers – frivolous articles, but gadgets that all use electricity and waste the earth's precious assets.

I'm not going to devote a lot of my time trying to make the break-through that will result in the clockwork muscle toner. There is, though, a lesson we need to learn and act upon, sooner rather than later. Unless we devise alternative low-tech methods of running the gadgets we use in our daily lives, eventually none of them will work. One day all the wonderful machines will show us how powerful they are, how much they control our lives, when they finally lose their power source and refuse to work. If we could all take a glimpse into the future, I'm sure we'd see that a lot of it will have to run on clock-work, or other forms of personal power.

As people step into the next millennium they will be going into uncharted, probably hostile, territory. Many of the things we've grown up with and taken for granted cannot be guaranteed to continue infinitely. When will the last oil well run dry? How soon will all the lights go out in Piccadilly? Will we have to fuel our jets with duty-free alcohol after all the aviation fuel is finally exhausted? I doubt whether I'll be around to ponder any of these problems. (Though I might well be, in a different form. Ever since I was a young gerbil in the Sudan I've firmly believed in reincarnation.)

I've travelled all over Africa in the past five years and I've discovered that sometimes even a spanner is too high tech. The dead tractor is a feature of the African landscape. So is the wounded generator. These things may be useful to an African farmer, but only while they're working. If there are no tools, parts, or skills to repair machines when they break down, or fuel to power them when they're working, then they're just rusty piles of junk.

Once a headman showed me his splendid television set. He was very proud of his status symbol. It was a perfect example of Sattinger's Law: it works better if you plug it in. He couldn't switch on his television because electricity had not yet arrived in his village.

If we really want to help people in the Third World we must give them ways to help themselves that are sustainable. They need simple devices they can easily operate and maintain with resources from within their village. They need sources of power – like a mini-hydro, clockwork, or my rope-and-pulley-heavy-bucket-up-a-tree generator – that will give them alternative energy.

If we provide low-tech answers for the problems of Africa, Asia and South America, we'll be helping ourselves as well, because in the long run our part of the world will have to start using simple practical solutions as well. Before dead tractors become a feature of our landscape too, we'll have to find something more high tech than the hoe, less high tech than the tractor, that's more useful than either.

A friend of mine, Professor John Knapton, from the civil engineering department of Newcastle University is a great believer in simple solutions for Africa. Many aid efforts founder on the misconception that the best answer to a problem is automatically the most sophisticated and technically advanced one. He's developed his own 'bottom up' style of aid in the Ghanaian village of Ekumufi-Atakwa where nothing is done without full consultation with the villagers. He doesn't have grand plans to change the whole world, he just wants to improve part of it. It obviously works for the villagers because they've made him a Tribal Chief.

He got hold of seventy-two of my radios and distributed them among villagers to tackle the problems of literacy, health education, and to enable them to learn English while providing them with a more global picture through the BBC World Service.

My two latest projects are both inventions designed to help the developing world. On my last visit to Africa I was horrified to discover the spread of AIDS is accelerating and millions of mothers are infecting newborn babies through their breast milk. Even where powdered baby food is available many mothers refuse to use it because water sources are often contaminated.

Early in 1998 a telephone call from an academic at the University of Northumbria in Newcastle was like a time-warp conversation, reminding me of when I used to zap the bugs in swimming pool water with cocktails of chemicals. My phone chat with Professor Rob Reed took me in the space-time continuum back to my days at Purley Pools where I had spent hours tinkering with swimming pool systems. We both became so excited about Rob's experiments on the production of sodium hypochlorite by means of electrolysis that we arranged for him to come down to my workshop at Haven Studio and take the idea further.

The process has been used for many years in major chemical plants, and it's the kind of simple experiment most people have done at school. You put two carbon probes – one positive, one negative – into water and run a low DC current through them. Oxygen is released from one of the probes and hydrogen from the other. If you then add sodium chloride – common household salt – to the water the process of electrolysis turns it into sodium hypochlorite – bleach to you and me – the oxidising agent which burns the life out of any bacteria when used to clean swimming pools.

Rob demonstrated that one of my radios could easily provide enough DC current to purify small quantities of brackish water for mixing with dried milk. We rigged up a simple sealed container, incorporating carbon probes powered by a clockwork generator, and it worked like a dream. It was one of those moments when I actually slapped my forehead for not thinking of the idea first. It was the perfect low-tech task clockwork power could perform: simple, ingenious and, when you thought about it, blindingly obvious. Soon, thanks to Rob, women in remote parts of the world should be able to sterilise water and mix baby food with this cheap and simple device. I'm not a chemist, but obviously further work is being done to check out the process thoroughly to ensure there is no danger of it spoiling the milk or harming the babies.

The other idea is one I'm working on with Professor Reg King of the Royal Military College at Shrivenham. He invented the talking book – where a wand activates a word or sound effect when you touch the correct contact with it – and sold the rights to the Tomy Corporation of Japan. I've adapted one of his books to run on clock-work power instead of batteries, and the implications for poor and remote parts of the world are immense.

Clockwork versions of the talking books could be used to teach literacy, or to create simple talking manuals giving instructions about hygiene and health. There is no end to the possibilities. They could instruct people how to de-activate land-mines in Angola, disseminate information about agricultural methods to farmers in the Nile Valley or boat building techniques to people in southern India, or teach any simple skills to distant communities.

While governments are often most enthusiastic about spending development money on large-scale and lavish projects like new airports and motorways, I think it is the more affordable educational projects and the simpler technologies that make the biggest difference to people's lives. I am certain small-scale self-sustaining ideas will solve the problems of the developing world. And ours too, eventually.

CHAPTER TWENTY-SEVEN

ANYONE CAN HAVE A GO

FOR SOMEONE USED TO WORKING LONG HOURS IN SOLITUDE, IT IS GOOD TO HAVE AN ESCAPE INTO THE WORLD OF COL-LEAGUES, THE EXCHANGE OF GOSSIP OVER COFFEE, AND THE SWEET INSOLENCE OF WHIPPERSNAPPERS YOUNG ENOUGH TO BE MY GRANDCHILDREN.

My appearances on Channel 4's *The Big Breakfast* mean getting out of bed every Wednesday at the very small hour of four in the morning when the only people entitled to be on the streets are burglars, all-night chemists, and toffs in white ties wending home from *Hello!* parties. Obscenely early they may be, but I enjoy the chauffeur-driven dashes across deserted London taking me to the East End and the bedlam of Lock Keepers' Cottages where I become Johnny Vaughan's resident in-house old fart for the morning.

All vanity of course. Who could resist the chance to ritz about on the box? Sonsy make-up ladies on hand to powder-puff my cratered face. Kelly Brook pretending she is wildly in love with me. Plus, of course, the question of money. I pay them £500 a week just to let me be there.

Young Master Vaughan treats me as though I was older than Methuselah. One of his recurring themes is how many pipe-tobacco scorch marks there are on my shirts. In fact there are so many burn marks on one green shirt that I regularly wear on the show, that if you joined them all together with ink they'd probably make a pin-up of Denise Van Outen; or an outline of the double helix, take your pick.

Of all the motor-mouth presenters doing so-called zoo television, Johnny Vaughan is undoubtedly the sharpest, funniest, and most widely read. The item we do together, 'From Me Shed, Son', has its full ration of jokes, but it does have a serious and worthy objective: to provide unknown inventors with an opportunity to showcase their innovations on television. I've been doing the spot for more than a year and in that time a cluster of intriguing ideas have been sprung on the world from out of the wooden shed where Johnny and I present the item.

Just to mention three of the inventors: there was the toilet-training chamber pot, designed by an Essex housewife, Irene White. It's a normal looking potty with an in-built mini-recorder into which a mother can tape her own message. There's a chip built into the device which activates the tape each time the chip senses the child has left a message in his potty. So young James will hear his mum tell him: 'Well done James,' and hear a burst of: 'We are the Champions' each time he does what he's there to do.

David Penn from Stowmarket in Suffolk was only ten when he demonstrated his idea. His dad, who is often away from home on business, had told him he had difficulty tracing the way from hotel reception desks to his room. So David invented a hotel room swipe card that not only opens your door, but also displays the quickest route to your room and shows you exactly where you are in a hotel.

Andy Warren from Wolverhampton talked me through an ingenious device called the Slide Safe, that's now been selected to be one of the products in the innovations section of the Millennium Dome exhibition. It's a small safety wheel that prevents children from trapping their fingers in the sliding sections of double glazing.

Over the year I've highlighted many amazing brainwaves that have occurred to ordinary people. They include a digital spirit level; a revolutionary type of slotted swivelling fencing made from recycled plastic; a motor-cycle helmet incorporating a rear lamp that shines even brighter when the rider touches his brakes; and the clever Pram

Wellies: cuff-like shower caps that fix on to pram wheels during bad weather. When you return you can remove them and wheel the pram indoors without muddying the carpets.

Valuable though it is as a platform for first-time inventors, 'From Me Shed, Son' is primarily television entertainment. The project closest to my heart is a blueprint for a much more formal and impressive clearing-house for new ideas: an Academy of Invention. It's an idea I have been pressing the government to put their weight behind for the past two years in a campaign that has involved writing hundreds of letters, numerous visits to Parliament and Ministries, and giving evidence to the House of Commons Science and Technology Committee.

The Academy will be a place where inventors can safely take their ideas to establish their merit and have them developed until they are marketable products. Initial funding would come from industry and the government, via the lottery fund, but in the long term the Academy would generate its own income through a share of the profits from inventions which it helps to launch.

As I said in a letter to *The Times* (8 February 1997) in which I set out my proposals for the Academy: 'If lone inventors . . . are to receive fair treatment for their ideas then an academy must be established where they can take them to be vetted for economic potential. This would overcome the primary fear of all inventors, that their proposals might be stolen.

'They should be asked only to pay a small fee in return for confidential advice on the viability and likely pitfalls in going ahead with any project. In return they should be expected, if it proves successful, to give some of the royalties to the Academy to finance its activities.'

My letter was prompted by the tragic case of the unfortunate, then forty-seven-year-old lone inventor, Paul Barker, who, in January 1997, was sentenced to nine months in Bullingham Prison for strapping a bomb to his body and threatening to blow himself up. He did this outside the headquarters of Halma plc, the company which had purchased his big idea – but had been unable to use it.

In 1994, Barker, a freelance security consultant from Anglesea, invented three devices to protect supermarket cash registers from thieves. Halma, a security company from Amersham in Buckingham-shire, had purchased the intellectual rights to Mr Barker's idea for £10,000. After a year they said they couldn't find a market for the prototypes and returned the rights to the inventor. The British patents were still valid, but Halma did not renew the worldwide patents. Barker blamed them for putting him in a situation where anyone outside Britain could rip off the idea without him getting a penny. Peter Tett, a director of Halma, said: 'We had a right to renew the world rights, but not an obligation. It would have cost us up to £20,000. We did not think it was worth it.' Barker's frustrations at the lone inventor's lot had driven him to threaten to blow himself up, and this earned him a prison sentence.

I feel deeply for Paul Barker. Sometimes the lone inventor does believe, however misguidedly, that the whole world is ranged against him. In the years I was struggling to get people to take notice of my clockwork radio, I often felt like resorting to high explosives (to give other people a rocket maybe, never myself).

The patent system, even though it has been simplified, is still a Byzantine maze that can confuse the first-time inventor. Too often patent agents who advertise an easy route through the patents labyrinth on payment of a £2,000 fee, or more, are on the lookout for rich pickings, more interested in putting the money received into their own pockets than securing their client's rights.

In addition a patentee needs a healthy wallet if he or she is to secure rights around the world. The costs of legal and translation fees can make the process ruinously expensive for the struggling lone inventor. Even successes like James Dyson, the man behind the Dual Cyclone vacuum cleaner, was once £1 million in debt while trying to maintain his international patent payments. Some of the smallest countries in Europe charge the highest patent fees; and, more ominously for an inventor's potential earning power, many nations in Asia and the former Soviet bloc do not recognise patents.

James Dyson has spent nineteen years inventing, but only achieved any success in the last five. Would he have been successful earlier if there had been an Academy of Invention to promote his ideas and help him through the tangle of international patent legislation? Probably.

Inventors like James Dyson have the inner resources and determination to keep going in spite of rebuffs and blighted hopes, but many more simply give up. How many cunning prototypes lie discarded on workbenches? What number of blueprints rot in bottom drawers because their makers lost heart? We shall never know. But I'd wager there are scores.

Once you've got your patent, there's still no guarantee that your brainchild will make it to the market place. The Institute of Patentees and Inventors estimates that of the 4,000 patents taken out by individual British inventors every year, only eighty – that's 2% – make it to the market place.

Initially the Academy would be a clearing-house. Some of the inventions brought to it wouldn't be patentable. Some would already have been invented. Not all of them would work, and do what they were supposed to do; and not all of the things they were supposed to do would be worth doing.

The Academy would have to cherry-pick the best ideas. Even academicians wouldn't always make the correct decisions. Hindsight makes sages of us all. In 1933 the J.B. Morton fictional comic creation Dr Strabismus (Whom God Preserve) of Utrecht patented a new invention. An illuminated trouser-clip for bicyclists who were using main roads at night. It was meant to be a silly joke. But what do we find selling very well today? Ha, ha! Luminous trouser-clips for bicyclists who use main roads at night.

Throughout history British inventors have got the dirty end of the stick. I sometimes give a slide lecture in which I list all the heroes of British invention who have been disillusioned by our system. Pioneers of the textile industry were given a particularly hard time. John Kay, inventor of the flying shuttle in 1733, had his house wrecked by angry workers who considered his revolutionary machine was a threat to their livelihoods. After two of his homes had been smashed and the government had refused to uphold his patent claim, he fled to France where he died in poverty and obscurity. James Hargreaves who, in 1768, built the multi-spindled spinning machine (the spinning jenny) was also forced to flee from his home. He patented his invention in 1770, but like Kay's, it was later declared invalid, and he received scant financial reward.

There is a distressingly familiar pattern to it: lack of belief, even derision from the world; endless struggles to avoid ideas being stolen; monumental financial difficulties; despair and poverty. Isambard Kingdom Brunel, 1806–1859, railway architect and pioneer of the broad-gauge railway, made no money and died early from overwork, stress and 'profound pessimism'.

The gloomy picture gets no better. In 1953 Ronald Hamilton, who invented the floating roadway used on the D-Day beaches, died aged fifty-four, described as an 'unfulfilled genius' after a life of constant financial troubles.

My own hero, Sir Frank Whittle, filed the first patent for his turbo jet engine on 16 January 1930 while still a flying officer in the RAF. His gas turbine took air into a compressor, burned it with fuel and used the force of the burning gas to create jet thrust by directing it through a narrow nozzle. Although nobody was able to disprove his calculations, he lacked the money to build his engine and was unable to arouse any interest in the RAF, the Air Ministry or the aircraft industry. He dutifully went back to routine work in the RAF, and it wasn't until 1936 that he managed to organise a private company, Power Jets Limited, for the development of his engines. It was only the impending war that spurred government interest, and the first flight powered by Whittle's engine took place during May 1941, in an experimental fighter plane, the Gloster E28/39. It took the genius eleven years of perseverance and argument to get his idea from patent to reality; yet his was the prototype of the jet engines that now fly us all around the world. Meanwhile, in Germany, Pabst von Obain met with a very different reaction. He did not begin turbo jet study until 1935, but had the good fortune to interest Ernst Heinkel, who was able to both finance an engine and fly it in an aircraft, the HE 178 (first flight 27 August 1939) long before the dilatory English.

In 1997 I was able to pay my own awestruck tribute to Sir Frank when an advertising agency working on behalf of Mercury asked me who I'd like to have a One-2-One with. I made the obvious and coarse suggestions the poor agency man probably hears every time he asks that question, but went on to say there was no question about it; the one man I would have loved to meet face to face was Sir Frank Whittle. I've read everything I could find about the quiet, dogged gentleman who, to my mind, has never received the praise he deserved as an aviation pioneer. It still amazes me that in May 1948, when the Royal Commission on Awards to Inventors recommended that he get a financial reward for inventing the jet engine, the government awarded him a measly £100,000.

The director making the Mercury commercial flew me out to Africa to film some moody shots in the veldt. With a touch of cinematic trickery they somehow managed to get me in the same workshop as Sir Frank, serving tea to the great man. I used to stand for ages staring at the prototype of his jet engine in the Science Museum. It was the closest I ever got to him. If only that trick scene in the One-2-One commercial had been for real.

The late Sir Christopher Cockerell was yet another British inventor who I believe was shabbily treated. In 1955 he created the phenomenally successful Hovercraft, the air-cushioned vehicle that operates above the surface of water or land, and has commercial and military applications all over the world, yet he made very little money from his invention. 'When you look at what I made out of the Hovercraft it is negligible,' he said. 'Inventors are always at the bottom of the pile.'

The aim of the Academy would be to improve this sorry picture; to turn the pile upside down, and enhance the status of inventors; to ensure that the economic benefits flowing from their discoveries enrich, not only the innovators, but also Britain. A grant of £3 million a year for three years would get the Academy up and running. (That's less than the price of three operas at the going rate.) A selection panel of successful inventors, specialist patent lawyers, and businessmen would vet the prototypes put forward by inventors for Academy support. If the panel was passably effective in selecting and launching successful products, the organisation should be self-financing after the initial three years. It is vital that the Academy is run on a strictly commercial basis. It mustn't become a place where extinct volcanoes sit around waiting for their knighthoods.

Inventors are often not very good business people. It comes with the territory. I don't suppose many classical composers or lyric poets, people who work at a similar pitch of intuitive creativity, would be very good at working out detailed business plans and patent applications either. So the prime purpose of the Academy would be to ensure that when people come to sell their products they don't get ripped off. But part of the Academy's role would also be to act as nursemaid to inventors who came up with unworkable ideas, gently dissuading them from mortgaging their houses to launch products that had no commercial appeal.

Another aim would be to ensure that ideas conceived in Britain are developed here, to generate jobs and exports that would benefit our economy. Too many inventors have to take their ideas or projects abroad to earn a living. Tim Berner-Lee, inventor of the worldwide web, had to go to the United States to further his career. My radios are manufactured in Cape Town because it's cheaper to produce them there. But, by rights, they could just as easily be built in Croydon or Coventry. The most extraordinary statistic is that 56% of all Japanese exports since World War Two are based on British innovation. We invented the television set. We pioneered the high-performance motor cycle. But we don't make either of them any more.

I see the Academy as an advisory body influencing government on the shape of laws concerning intellectual property. Inventors should have the same automatic rights to copyright – the same wealth potential – that songwriters and authors enjoy. It's grossly unfair that someone like Sir Tim Rice, nice man though he is, can collect royalties from his lyrics for the whole of his lifetime and beyond, while an inventor has to expend vast sums around the world on patents to keep the entitlement to his creations. There should also be tax breaks for inventors, to give innovation a cash incentive.

An Academy would also make its voice heard about the syllabus in our schools which, I believe, needs to give students a stronger grounding in practical skills. The standard of craft, design and technology teaching in our schools has improved considerably in recent years. It's no longer regarded as the preferred subject for the dim and the slow. But even more progress needs to be made. If there is room in the syllabus for 'media studies', 'leisure studies', and 'sports studies', why not courses on 'invention studies'?

Such a course would examine the rise of Britain as a great trading and manufacturing power. It would teach students basic woodwork, metalwork, engineering and design skills; look at the theory of such historically important devices as the clock, the steam engine, the internal combustion engine, and require students to try their hands at making them. It would also outline the basics of taking a good idea, and proceeding with it to prototype, patent, and manufacture.

Behind the expansion of higher education lies the belief that economic success depends upon a very well-educated population; but most of the time we are not educating young people in the skills of making things for export that would help attain that target of economic success. We prefer to base our economy largely upon the manufacture of hamburgers, in which dispirited teenagers are paid a pittance to sell American-style food that saps the nation's health, sags its waistline, and clogs its arteries.

In my secondary modern school, but mostly in my shed at home taught by my dad, I learned skills that enabled me to start 'thinking with the hands' which is an essential part of invention. As my friend, the economic historian Michael Denny, says: 'The study of invention might have advantages for the embattled (as it seems to the outsider) world of education. In school, it might serve to engage the imaginations of some of the bored and alienated young.

'A Course of Invention in which theory was related to practice and past to present, which involved the idea of turning a bright idea into a thing-that-worked, and possibly a saleable product, might give more point to education than it presently seems to have for many children.'

So my hope for the Millennium and beyond is that the government will fertilise the nation's innovative talents with funds for an Academy of Invention. Lord Puttnam has been given an annual budget of £10 million as seed money for science and the arts through his National

Endowment for Science, Technology and Arts. But his organisation straddles so many different interests I don't think his money will stretch as far as it should to promote new inventions. Of course I wouldn't turn down Nesta help, but to set up an Academy of Invention on a proper footing would certainly take more resources than Lord Puttnam is likely to have available.

As we go into the twenty-first century our future will depend on how successfully we can generate, protect and exploit new ideas. Now most discoveries take place in large research organisations supported by universities, government agencies, private industries, or privately endowed foundations. But the lone inventor still has an important role, and I hope in the next century there will be a British Academy of Invention in place as patron and inspiration, to help the creative sparks to fly.

My life turned a corner after I watched a television programme that inspired a bright idea. That happy fluke has brought me honorary degrees, visiting professorships, the Presidential Gold Medal from the Institution of Mechanical Engineers, and, my dottle runneth over, the 1999 award for Pipe Smoker of the Year.

I've been to the ends of the world on behalf of the British Council. I have given lectures, made speeches, and judged competitions for aspiring inventors. I was even asked back to present the prizes at the annual speech day of my old alma mater, Dormer's Wells Secondary Modern, which I am pleased to say is now a much more vibrant place than when I was there.

But busy as I have become, I still try to spend some hours of every day thinking about inventions, dabbling at the bench in my workshop. I am currently testing the potential of rubber bands to see whether they could be a simple source of energy; a more sophisticated version of the old wind-up rubber bands that sent my childhood model planes soaring into the air. There are lots of problems to overcome: rubber bands snap, they perish, and as I've found in my trials, they can overheat and make nasty smells. But I am still playing around with rubber bands.

I am also looking again at Hooke's Law. Robert Hooke in *De*

Potentia Restitutiva (1678) showed that a force may be applied to an elastic material, such as steel, in such a way as to stretch or compress it without causing a permanent dimensional change. (That is, a change in length.) It is this elasticity of materials that makes springs work.

Hooke showed that for an elastic material the amount of deformation (the strain) is proportional to the applied distorting force (the stress). The greater the deformation, the greater the restoring force. So, for example, you can stretch a piece of steel, or compress a chunk of rubber, and when the force is removed they return to their old shape.

The law obviously applies only within strict limits. The value of the stress at which materials cease to obey Hooke's Law is known as the limit of proportionality; a critical point above which they experience plastic flow, ie, they are irreversibly extended. You can see this demonstrated when you put too much weight on a spring and it goes wobbly and will not revert to its unloaded shape.

My experiments with Hooke's Law, however, aren't with springs. I want to see if I can harness the energy that, say a length of wire, or a chunk of rubber creates as it reverts to its old shape after being stretched or compressed. It's early days, and I'm still fiddling about with bits of wire and lumps of rubber. Could this be the next breakthrough to another cheap and sustainable form of energy? I have no idea; but I am enjoying myself enormously trying to find out.

And that is what I intend to go on doing: enjoying myself. So far I've had sixty-two wonderful years. The clockwork radio now sells at the rate of 120,000 a month. Their value was graphically demonstrated in the summer of 1999 when 47,000 of them were distributed to Kosovar refugees in Macedonia and Albania to help them trace family members and follow developments in the war. The radios – sent by the Department for International Development (DfID) and the International Committee of the Red Cross (ICRC) – enabled people living in refugee camps, where there was limited mains power or batteries, to keep up to date with news and find friends and family in other camps. The project was my proudest achievement. I was thrilled beyond belief to have my invention used for something so worthwhile.

Every day I am sustained by a sense of gratitude that I've had at least one good idea in my life, and an enduring hope that I live long enough to have a few more.

If I can become an inventor (Dormer's Wells Secondary Modern: Failed) then anyone can. Michael Faraday didn't know mathematics yet he was a pioneer in establishing the principles of electromagnetism on which all electric motors and generators are based. The steam engine was largely invented by rule-of-thumb craftsmen – the equivalent of today's skilled factory hands. John Harrison, the Yorkshire clockmaker who solved the epic riddle of measuring longtitude, had no formal education or apprenticeship to any watchmaker.

Anyone can have a good idea and turn it into something that works. So why not try it? The answer to all our tomorrows could lie in the shed at the bottom of your garden. Invention isn't some impenetrable branch of magic: anyone can have a go.

May all your dreams be patentable.

INDEX

Note: Subheadings are in approximate chronological order where appropriate. TB stands for Trevor Baylis.

If you are interested in purchasing any of the Freeplay products mentioned in this book, or would like to receive a catalogue listing the complete range including accessories, please contact (quoting reference CLOCK THIS):

FREEPLAY ENERGY EUROPE LTD
Cirencester Business Park
Love Lane
Cirencester
Gloucestershire
GL7 1XD
UK

tel: 01285 659559
fax: 01285 659550
email: freeplay@lineone.net